on women and anger

Pissed
Off

finding forgiveness on the

other side of the finger

spike gillespie

seal press

Pissed Off
On Women and Anger

Published by
Seal Press
An Imprint of Avalon Publishing Group, Incorporated
1400 65th Street, Suite 250

AVALON
publishing group incorporated

Emeryville, CA 94608

ISBN-10 1-58005-162-6
ISBN-13 978-1-58005-162-0

9 8 7 6 5 4 3 2 1

Library of Congress Cataloging-in-Publication Data

Gillespie, Spike.
  Pissed off : on women and anger / Spike Gillespie.
    p. cm.
  ISBN-13: 978-1-58005-162-0
  ISBN-10: 1-58005-162-6
  1. Women—Psychology. 2. Anger. 3. Interpersonal relations. I. Title.
HQ1206.G575 2006
 152.4'7082—dc22

2005033892

Cover and interior design by Domini Dragoone
Printed in the United States of America by Malloy
Distributed by Publishers Group West

This book is dedicated to

Diane Fleming for always listening

Blossom Bennett for kicking so much ass

and, as always, to my greatest love,

Henry Mowgli Gillespie

Contents

part three
The Upside of Anger

appendix
What I Think About When
I Think About Forgiveness

Introduction

I have written three novels in my life, none of which was ever published traditionally (although I did publish one online). In each, we follow the protagonist, Alice, as she drinks and smokes her way through one anger-laced scene after another. The writing improved with each new installment, but I never found an agent interested in any of them. With the last episode of the trilogy—"Sole Mate"—I heard again and again from agents who applauded the writing but felt that Alice was just *too angry* and not sympathetic enough. No one wanted to represent the book because, I was informed, no one would want to buy a book about a woman who was so pissed off.

Seeing as Alice is more than a little autobiographical, I would read these rejection notes, take them as personal stabs at my own character, and scream, out loud (often to no one) and always with more than a hint of anger, *"Of course she's angry, you idiots! Because people keep rejecting her!"* That was my little inside joke to myself, sown with more than a small kernel of truth.

All of the Alice books ended with Alice not getting the guy. She always found her freedom and joy in getting *away* from the guy. My goal in continually liberating her from bad relationships was twofold.

First, I wanted to break the tradition of sappiness that saturates so many novels, particularly the so-called chick lit variety. Second, in my own real-life experience—given my incredible track record for picking wrong men—being single was always much more peaceful. For Alice to work through her anger and get to the other side, she needed fewer men and more time alone. So I gave her these things.

I also, accidentally at first and then with purpose, gave a similar break to myself. In early 1998, I broke up with my last bad boyfriend, George the Second (G2). And though I allowed myself (or, more aptly, was unable to fend off) a series of crushes in the ensuing six-plus years, no other romance materialized. If you believe in the power of the subconscious over the conscious mind, you might say I chose the crushes with great care because, looking back, there's no way in hell any of them would've turned into anything substantial.

This lack of romantic success felt frustrating at the time, as unrequited love is wont to do, but it kept me from getting involved in yet another painfully dramatic relationship in which I might lose myself. And I did lose myself when I was with G2. And I lost myself with the one before him—Joe, the guy I married hastily and filed for divorce from inside of ten months.

One thing Joe and G2 had in common is that both accused me of being angry. They wielded the accusation like a butcher's knife pointed at my heart, implying that if only I weren't angry, the relationship would be perfect, and implying further that their own behavior was flawless. Being accused of being angry only made me angrier. "You idiot!" I wanted to scream at each of them (and I probably did). "Of course I'm angry—because you *make* me angry!"

And they did make me angry. *Really* angry. In each case, you could argue that mine was a justified anger. Joe had a habit of waking me up in the middle of the night to "work through" problems. This is a torturer's technique—to break someone while that person is exhausted and incoherent. Joe also physically restrained me, lied about his addictions to prescription drugs and booze, and played Sheryl Crow albums even when I politely asked him to choose something else from his vast CD collection. G2 cheated on me, told me all about the other woman and how superior she was (and how much tinier), and withheld sex if I beat him at Scrabble. Yes, these infractions, large and small, made me angry, because at the root of each was one thing: manipulation. And manipulation is a wicked thing.

On the other hand . . . and certainly not to let these guys off the hook, but . . .

Let me rewind for a moment, and then fast-forward, and then return to the idea of justified anger. To rewind: Once upon a time, I was visiting my friend Jonathan in Manhattan. Jonathan and I met when we were teenagers working at the Jersey Shore. We bonded quickly and were inseparable during our summers together, and best friends despite the miles that separated us most of the year.

One night when I was visiting him in New York, Jonathan introduced me to his friend Diane, assigning me quite a dubious distinction. Describing the early days of our friendship, he said, "Spike was the angriest person I'd ever met."

I was? This totally surprised me. I had no idea. Really. I mean, certainly, I had a knack for getting pissed off. And I wouldn't hesitate, particularly under the influence of booze, to sound off with my opinions (to put it mildly). But the angriest person he'd ever met? The comment stung and has stayed with me all these years.

Fast-forward. Last week, I had a wonderful opportunity. I spent the week at one of the top spas in the country, teaching a workshop series dealing with healing and meditation. There I was, staying in an incredible room, sleeping on an incredible bed, having incredible gourmet meals served to me that somehow were filling but only had about two calories per five-course meal. When I wasn't teaching my grueling two-to-three-hour-per-day work schedule, I was either swimming laps, working on my tan, having a Swedish massage or seventy-dollar pedicure, or wandering around with a totally blissed-out look on my face. Spa face. I couldn't help myself. I grinned so much my cheeks hurt.

My first night there, I plopped down in the hot tub and let the turbo jets do their thing, and I thought how very absurd it was that I would be sitting here, alone, in a bazillion-dollar compound, the poor South Jersey waitress of yesteryear—now a spa lecturer, feeling simultaneously totally out of place and perfectly serene. I was also thinking about writing this book, which I'd hoped to start during my stay. And the thought came to me: *I have no idea how I will be able to write about being pissed off while I'm here.* For possibly the first time in my life, not a trace of pissed-offness was in my bloodstream. Not a hint.

Then in walked Catherine. I smiled my spa smile at her and waved. She joined me in the hot tub. And then, with little fanfare, Catherine proceeded to tell me about her pending divorce, how she'd been in the courts for over a year, how she was in mediation and how awful that was, and how she loved her husband still, but how he was really sticking it to her.

That wasn't the last time Catherine told me her story. And she told it to a lot of others while we were there. She was in that painful, angry place where she had to tell her story again and again to try to make sense of it and move past it. From the way she was talking, it didn't seem like she was making much progress. I actually began avoiding her, despite the fact that I empathized with her need to bitch incessantly.

I'd been in Catherine's situation before, more than once, spitting out the ugly details of one life drama or another over and over again to anyone who would listen. I remembered what a total mess I was during those times. But I was approaching the seventh anniversary of the breakup of my last bad relationship, and was on the cusp of the eighth anniversary of my divorce. I had moved on past the worst in my life (hopefully the worst) and could only do so much revisiting of my own distant pain through Catherine's stories.

A lot has transpired over these years of being alone. I still don't like the way those men treated me, and I still want to roll my eyes at their insinuations that my anger was the root of all our relationship problems. What I think really happened is that I quickly intuited that each of those guys was very bad news. And I chose, in spite of this, to stay with each one for much longer than I should have. Let's call it my personal chaos theory: If I'm having a calm, peaceful lull in my life, sometimes I just need to go out and find me some chaos. And what better, faster way to do that than by hooking up with some asshole, right?

So while my anger at some of the things those guys did might have been justified on the one hand, on the other hand, to lapse into a little therapy-speak here, I did invite them in in the first place. And I allowed them to stick around and repeatedly provoke me. That wasn't anything I could see or believe at the time. I created intensely complex narratives to justify remaining with those bad partners. Only seven years of distance gave me true clarity.

Now, I listened to Catherine and observed her pained expressions as she talked about how she'd given over twenty years of her life to her husband, how they had so much joint property, how she was entitled to some of it. And she was—that I couldn't argue. But I told her how much better she would feel once the ties were finally cut, and said that no amount of property could equal peace of mind. She didn't hear a word I said, and I can't blame her. I never heard a word my friends told me when I was mad, at least not as they were being spoken. Some of the words, thankfully, did slip through, sink in, and revisit me later, during calmer moments.

I wished I could wave my hands in the air around Catherine and move her forward to a place where she could just let go and move on. Of course, this was impossible. Catherine needed to get through her own anger in her own time.

Sometimes, looking back, I've played the *If only* game to try and imagine how I might've done better, sooner in my life. *If only I hadn't gone on that job interview and met George the Second. If only I hadn't responded to that fan email Joe sent.* But more likely, the real *If only* that would've helped me the most is this: *If only I had been able to see the anger Jonathan had seen in me, way back when he saw it. If only I had understood it, the root of it, what fanned the flames, and why I always went after things that would only exacerbate my angry feelings.*

Maybe if I had recognized the source, worked to comprehend it, striven to overcome the anger sooner, I would have saved myself a good deal of grief. But I didn't and couldn't understand the source at that time, or the complexity of my anger. Only now, after over four decades of living with myself, after having stumbled into some amazing teachers along the way, and after accidentally having been hit in the head—as if by a falling anvil in a kid's cartoon—by what I can only refer to now as *grace,* have I come to a place where I can better see why I was as angry as I was. And for the first time in my life, I am beginning to understand what forgiveness is, and how exercising forgiveness enhances the effects of grace.

I worry that a lot of people will stop reading at the first mention of the words *grace* and *forgiveness,* or anything else remotely religious or New Age. But stick with me. Because this book isn't about any particular religion—although several (particularly Catholicism, which fed my anger, and Buddhism, which soothed it) do come into play. This book is a series of portraits of me, in a rage, often due to circumstances that have pissed off countless women over the ages: involving our men, our kids, our families, our in-laws. And it is also a reflection on how I've gone from being very angry to being not exactly Miss Benevolent Forgiver but much, much less pissed off than I used to be.

Because there is strength and hope in numbers, I've also asked some of my friends to contribute their own tales of anger and forgiveness. Some of these stories made me smile as I recognized my own anger. Some made me bawl my eyes out. All of them were (and are) a great reminder that, despite the sense of isolation anger can instill, we are hardly alone when we are pissed off, and we are hardly alone in our struggle to understand forgiveness and apply it to those who've hurt us deepest.

part one

Anger Starts

chapter 1

The Root of It

When I think of anger—my own anger—and the earliest sources of it, I immediately flash back to my Uncle Jake. Jake was my godfather and as such, technically speaking, was supposed to provide me spiritual guidance. I remember being at the Jersey Shore one summer, on the beach with him. I spill a bucket of ocean water on our beach blanket. Jake yells at me. Maybe it's a small admonishment, but to my little ears he is screaming at me, and I shrink in terror. I feel very bad, like I've done something terribly wrong.

Here's another childhood memory. I'm about four years old, and it's nighttime. I'm coloring in my coloring book and my mother tells me it's time for bed. I tell her I'm not done yet. My father intervenes, and shreds the book. Again, revisiting a memory that is nearly forty years old makes details a little sketchy. (Did he rip it into many pieces, or simply in half?) But it doesn't matter. Because the sense that I'm left with, which will stay with me for another thirty-odd years, is that this man is a terrifying, unpredictable brute who can rule me by force, and that I have no choice but to obey.

Here are the thoughts that did not occur to me as Uncle Jake yelled and my father tore up my project:

It is never okay to treat a child like this.
Of course your blanket got wet—we're at the beach!
Acting out in rage is always wrong.
Naturally, a kid wants to finish coloring a picture!
I deserve an apology.

My only conscious thoughts were these: *These are scary men. I must obey them or I am in big, big, big trouble.*

A couple more snapshots of my father. I'm in college, going to the state school down the road because we couldn't afford the prestigious private school that accepted me, and this shitty college is our compromise. I drive a hundred-dollar beater that's nearly twenty years old and hardly roadworthy. It's a vehicle my father has tracked down for me, and he takes pride in finding a bargain, never mind at what cost. I'm at my bowling class, and afterward when I go out to start my car, I discover it's dead. It's around ten in the morning and I need to get to my mall job.

Instead of calmly assessing the situation, I panic. I go over certain details: *My father just worked the night shift at the rail yard over in Philly. He's tired. He's going to be pissed off if I call him. I am fucked.*

In the fourteen years between the ripped-up coloring book and the bowling alley parking lot, there have been countless other moments of rage—him hitting me in the face when I came home drunk, him telling me how worthless I am, him flipping out over something as minor as a can of soda exploding when opened. I have learned—from watching my father's response when things do not go the way he wants them to—to respond to any crisis, large or small, with anxiety, hysteria, and drama. Calm isn't part of my repertoire. Problem solving eludes me.

I call my father and tell him the car has died. He's furious. The truth is that this car simply isn't a very reliable vehicle, but he reacts as if I personally have broken the car in order to ruin his day. By the time he arrives, the owner of the bowling alley has joined me outside to try to help. My father yells at him. I'm beyond mortified. I want to put myself under the wheels and will the car to roll over me.

Flashing back further: I'm about twelve, and my brother is ten. We have a shore house my folks built in the mid-'60s. Nothing fancy—a sheetrock box a mile from the ocean on a tiny island, a blue-collar paradise. Whenever we are at the house, my father thinks up improvement plans. This particular summer, he decides to build a back deck.

My father thinks building inspectors are full of shit, just looking to get their palms greased. Therefore, he undertakes his various home improvement projects sans the benefit of proper paperwork. Then he gets caught, and threatened with fines. Then he blows his stack. It's like the old Rice Krispies commercial: *Snap, crackle, POP!*

My brother and I are swinging our hammers when a man drives up. He is the building inspector, and also the police chief. He and my father exchange words. The man tells my brother and me that we have to put down the hammers and stop now, or my father is in big trouble. My father—a man I know much better, a man who has clearly demonstrated over and over his version of cause and effect—tells us we better not dare put down our hammers.

I am sick to my stomach. Later, in the house, my father is furious, yelling that he is going to kill the guy, flat out murder him. I have no reason to think this is a hollow threat. My father, I believe, is perfectly capable of murder. With no other way to intervene, I retreat to my bedroom and pray, begging God to please let my dad not do it.

You see the pattern here. I have written about my dad so often in my life that the process is almost as normal as breathing for me. Some readers have said, "But he loved you. He bought you cars. He gave you a beach house." It's true: My father provided for us. But he was not a pleasantly grumpy, lovable curmudgeon. Presumably, those readers who find my father sympathetic don't understand what it's like to live an entire life built on a foundation of constant anxiety, brought on by the close proximity of a human time bomb. You never know when he might explode next. There's just that *tick, tick, tick, tick—Whatever you do, don't piss off Daddy!*

But if you have lived this life, then you know it, and you know there's nothing ambiguous or funny about it. Anger is a very scary thing.

My dad was hardly unique in his anger. Maybe there was a huge, unspoken movement of dads across the country in the '70s, all of them angry, a collective bundle of rage. When I think of the angry-man archetype, I always conjure an image of those native to where I grew up—South Jersey and, by extension of my parents' roots, South Philly, both parts of the country perpetually prone to what a friend of mine (who is also from the area) described as "that northeastern sarcasm."

It took me about twenty years of living away from New Jersey to finally see this sarcasm with any clarity. Prior to that, I'd been so fully baptized and raised in it that I didn't even recognize smart-ass as it was pouring out of my own mouth. As I understood it, any opportunity to shoot a wise remark back at someone, no matter how serious that person was being, was an opportunity not to be missed. Likewise, if you could squeeze in an implied *No duh, you fucking idiot,* then you were holding your own on my childhood stomping grounds.

So this is what I came from, a land of angry men and pervasive sarcasm. I raised my son, Henry, who is now fifteen, to have deft sarcastic skills of his own. I didn't set out to do this. He just learned by watching me.

My habit became problematic when, as I approached forty and started contemplating the tenets of Buddhism as a possible form of life guidance, I decided to try to lay off the sarcasm a little. Even though I was trying to spew fewer cocky remarks, they still filled my head at every turn. Like a sardonic *New Yorker* cartoonist wandering the streets of my town, I would observe a situation and think of some fantastic caption, mildly mean at best, wicked at worst. Biting my tongue was painful when the chance to evoke laughter at someone else's expense was mine for the picking.

The temptation to blurt out these things remained with me not because I wanted to be cruel—I was very clear on the fact that I wanted to move away from cruelty. The temptation remained

because my lifetime of sarcasm had brought me heaps of reinforce-
ment and mountains of laughter from anyone within earshot of my
commentary. My sarcasm wasn't only mean, it was also funny. Very,
very funny.

I'm not bragging, here, I'm explaining. We all love peer approval,
and, growing up, I had a greater need for it than some. I certainly
wasn't getting approval at home. I also wasn't garnering attention
for being society's version of a stunning beauty or natural athlete—I
was neither. No, what really got me noticed was that, in the land of
sarcasm, I had grown up to be the most sarcastic of all. And now, if I
gave up my sarcasm, would I become unfunny and, as a result, lose
one of my (perceived) greatest sources of appeal?

The dilemma became worse when I thought about my son. My
awareness and suppression of my own sarcasm heightened my awareness—and the lack of suppression—of his. I'd get on his case about
being a smart-ass, but how could I undo in him what I'd ingrained
for so many years? Not to mention the fact that he's a teenager, and
they're sarcastic anyway.

With this legacy confronting me, I didn't need any further
reminder of the anger and sarcasm I came from. Nevertheless, I
scheduled a trip to New Jersey in the summer of 2004. I hadn't seen
my family in years—we're different (very different), and no matter
how hard we try (or pretend to try) it doesn't take any time at all
before we get pissed off at each other and the critical remarks start
flying. Still, I like to see my mother sometimes; plus, regardless of
my opinions, I figured these people are Henry's family, too, and he's
entitled to know them and make his own choices about whether or not
he wants to be around them.

And so off we went, planning to spend the majority of our visit
down the shore, on that very beach where Uncle Jake yelled at me
long ago. Two of my older sisters, Mare and Kit, each have houses
in Wildwood, New Jersey, Wildwood being to exotic beach desti-
nations what french fries are to cordon bleu cuisine. Nonetheless,
I have a deep, twisted love for this town, where I spent my teen

summers gaining my first real experience with work, boys, men, alcoholism, and sex with carnies and bouncers.

If you were raised in a pile of steaming cat shit, even if you eventually come to understand that cat shit is not a preferred living arrangement, still, whenever you pass a litter box, you'd sigh and think that mixed emotional thought, "Ah . . . *home.*"

Which is how I feel walking along the boardwalk, crammed with fashion felons of all shapes and sizes and ages, some wearing little more than a navel piercing, others sporting T-shirts reading THIS IS WHAT PUERTO RICAN LOOKS LIKE, or I'M RICK JAMES'S BITCH, or I'M PERFECT AND I'M A ELK, or AMERICAN BY BIRTH: TEAMSTER BY THE GRACE OF GOD. Up and down the boards they parade, accompanied by the cacophony of seagulls, game barkers, and a looped recording: *Watch the tramcar, please! Watch the tramcar, please!*

But my white trash nostalgia is interrupted soon enough. Once I meet up with my siblings, the Unalterable Family Dynamic kicks in. All the techniques I learned in therapy, all the deep breathing, and all my vows to otherwise remain calm fall by the wayside. As it was in my childhood, so it remains. I bury myself in a book to relax and escape. They eye me suspiciously for bringing written materials into the house. *What—TV's not good enough for you?*

The vacation plan is that Henry will stay with Mare, to maximize his cousin time with her kids. I am to shuffle from Mare's to Kit's, for a couple of reasons. The first has to do with that old saying about how company, like fish, stinks after three days. The second reason is that I want to avoid my sister Sue and, more precisely, her husband Luke, who stay at Mare's on weekends. Last time I saw Luke, he ran his hand over my ass, glinted at me, and sleazily asked, "How ya *doin'*?" right in front of my mother.

I have decided that if I see him again, I will punch his teeth in and tell him it's fitting that he got colon cancer. So I'm trying not to see him again. Because even though my anger at Luke is totally justified—he has always been an ass, he has always been mean to my sister, and he has always been a creep to me—Luke helps me understand the concept of walking away. He makes me know the blessing of avoidance. And because I am certain beyond certainty that he is a complete idiot, beyond change, not even humbled by a near-death experience, I have no impetus to stand around waiting for him to see the light and start being decent.

Luke hasn't arrived for the weekend yet, so I'm staying at Mare's. While I'm there, I get a call from my old friend, John, who lives a few hours away. We've been friends for seventeen years. He's calling to confirm our plans—I've invited him to the beach for a couple of days. I love seeing John under any circumstances, but in this case, I feel a sense of urgency. His mother recently attempted suicide and I figure he could use a familiar face, a big hug, a cathartic talk, and a long walk on the beach.

I realize, after inviting him, that I haven't cleared his visit with my older sisters, so I ask Mare if it will be okay for John to stay. It never occurs to me that it won't be. I have lived away from my family long enough now to have accidentally assigned them great generosity of spirit, a characteristic that actually belongs to my friends at home in Austin. Mare says yes, but hesitates. I can tell she doesn't want me to have a visitor, though I'm not sure why—perhaps it's a space issue?

I call Kit to see if we can stay at her place instead. Kit, whom I think of as less close-minded than the rest of my family. Kit, with whom I did bong hits in our twenties. She says yes—which is why, a few days later, on the cusp of John's arrival, I am less than prepared for what she has to tell me. She is having second thoughts about John's visit, she says, because she's afraid he might molest her teenage daughter.

As she puts this theory forth, suspended animation sets in, like we've just had a massive car wreck and I'm trying to sort my way through broken glass, twisted metal, and the details of what just happened.

"John?! *Molest* Kelsey?!" I ask. I feel a knife gutting me.

"It's not about *John*," she emphasizes. "It's just that he's a stranger. And Kelsey is so cute."

"I've known John for *seventeen years!*" I shout. And I start to cry. She's right. This isn't about John. But it also isn't about her ignorant belief that "cuteness" prompts molestation.

My fight-or-flight meter takes a few minutes to register a choice. In the interim, I foolishly engage my sister, tears choking my voice as I try to point out her ignorance. Doing this has the unfortunate consequence of exacerbating feelings evoked by a breakfast conversation I had earlier with Mare.

"Bill Cosby is right," Mare had informed me, referring to a recent speech by the self-righteous multimillionaire with the nice sweater collection and the secret love child. What Mare thought she heard Cosby say was that blacks needed to get their act together, learn the English language, and quit complaining about slavery because it happened so long ago.

I suggest that Bill Cosby may have lost touch with the reality of the ghetto some time ago, and that he might want to shut his piehole. I tell her maybe we ought to tell the Jews to quit bitching about the Holocaust. And, come to think of it, maybe she should quit fixating on the crucifixion—that happened a long time ago, too.

"You tell me," Mare says, "how God can give the world a beautiful new white baby and a beautiful new black baby, and then the black baby gets taught to hate the whites. Why do black families do that?"

"Whoa. Wait a minute." Like Sisyphus, that idiot, I attempt to interject rational thought for the ten-millionth time in my life. "You were raised in a family where our father took nine white babies and told them to hate niggers."

"I don't know what you're talking about," she says.

"Mare—go to Mom and Dad's house. There's a framed picture of Dad wearing *blackface* in a parade. His favorite expression when he was mad was to tell us we could screw up a niggers' picnic."

This is all true. There is an annual parade in Philadelphia on New Year's Day, the Mummers Parade, which for years was open only to white males; many of them wore blackface, which has since been banned but is hardly forgotten. The picnic remark? God only knows where he picked that one up, but it was clearly a favorite.

Mare disagrees with my assessment of our father's racism. She acts as if we grew up in entirely different families.

"Mare," I continue, "remember when you got mad at him and you frizzed your hair out like an Afro and said a van full of black dudes was coming to pick you up, because you knew that would piss him off the most?"

Mare doesn't remember. All Mare remembers is that God spends his entire existence smiling on our family, and that she just frizzed out her hair because she liked the way it looked. She cannot recall a single "niggers' picnic" ruined, though this is about the first thing I think of when I think of my dad, Mr. Blackface.

The combination of Mare's racism and Kit's distrust of John hurls me back thirty years, to a time when I was so skinny I had to sit on the toilet sideways to keep from falling in. Once, I fell in despite my best efforts, and called for help getting out, but the bigger girls just laughed at me, stuck in that hole. Now, again, I am sitting in the toilet. I am screaming for help, and the bigger girls are still just laughing, refusing to help.

I retire to my nephew's room, unsure of my next move. Kit comes barreling in. "We have to talk," she says.

"No, we don't," I say. "Leave me alone."

She persists. I yell at her that she doesn't trust me, or my judgment in friends. I whip up an analogy: "I am terrified of open water, and yet I allowed your husband to take my son out on a boat. *That's* trust." And then I tell her to go away. "I'm going to get a hotel room for John and me," I say.

But I can't get a hotel room. I have no money. And it's beside the point. What will I say to my friend when he arrives? *Sorry, you can't stay with my family because they're afraid you're a pedophile?*

I wake up first the next morning and leave a note: *Out walking. Back tonight.* I head from Kit's bay house due east to the Atlantic, along which I walk south for over an hour. At the beach's end, I continue along the street, crossing one tiny bridge, and another, and another. The bridges aren't pedestrian friendly, and their inches-wide catwalks leave me feeling like a drunken gymnast about to tumble into either oncoming traffic or the bay far below, where I will surely break my neck on impact, and then drown while crabs pinch away at my flesh.

Eleven miles and four hours later, I reach the little Victorian village of Cape May. My feet are screaming, my crippled arthritic big toe pulses with agony, and my heels are so torn up I won't be able to walk again without limping for another week and a half.

At the Acme I buy a bag of cherries, trail mix, and a lot of water. Across the way is a yarn shop; knitting being my personal Valium, I spend still more of my dwindling petty cash on supplies I can't afford. I hobble toward the beach, which costs money to step onto. I find a bench on the promenade instead, sit down, and stare at the ocean.

For five hours I knit and read and think. *What is wrong with these people? What is wrong with me? Why did I think I could visit and it would be okay?*

Now and then a family shares the bench with me. My knitting is an icebreaker. Everyone likes the yarn I've picked, chunky and red with flecks of orange and yellow and bluish purple. I am knitting a fire. The kindness of strangers who seem genuinely interested in me makes me want to cry. *How come these people can be nice to me? How come they can see the good in me and my own family can't?*

Around five, I head over to the bus terminal after bidding fare-well to a sunny, cheerful vacationing Vermont mom and her gaggle of teenage charges. The bus driver is a chunky woman with a very large homemade tattoo identifying her as Vampress. Some teens uncork a bottle of nail polish, and the fumes circulate through the closed air system.

A crotchety old lady, on her way to lose some more of her life savings in Atlantic City, yells, "Shut that nail polish. You go to the beauty parlor if you want to do that!" Vampress hopes out loud she won't pass out from the vapors. Part of me wants to laugh, part of me wants them to all shut the hell up, and part of me is still in shock and disbelief that I came from this place. No matter how hard I try to explain my roots to my friends, to accurately depict the characters who inhabit South Jersey, I never can do the tale justice. Back in Texas, some people find me abrasive. Compared to my fellow passengers, I feel like a continental finishing school alumna. *How do people get to be like this?* I marvel. *And how did I manage to escape?*

Back in Wildwood, I limp to the boardwalk and get some pizza. I sit on a bench and stare at the nighttime ocean. A man approaches me and asks if his family can share the bench. It registers in my mind: He is a black man; this is a black family. I have been raised to be racist and have counteracted this to a fault, making me still racist, but in a new way. I cannot escape my father's legacy, his screwed up "niggers' picnics." I am as bad as my family is. I want to call them and, in my most sarcastic voice, say, "Hey, guess what? I'm sitting on a bench with a *black family*. And they're *nice*. And they speak *good English*."

When I get up to go, the dad looks at me. I know from the way he looks into my eyes that he can tell I'm having a very hard time. He gently tells me to have a good night, to take care of myself. His kindness in that moment is so deep and palpable, it is almost more than I can bear.

I call a friend and procure several hundred dollars, to be deposited into my account at home, which I will use to get me out of this place five days ahead of schedule. I feel sleep deprived and shaky and like my mental health is rapidly deteriorating. Getting out doesn't feel like option A. Getting out feels mandatory to survival.

I call my son and let him know we're leaving, and he does not receive the news well. I call my sister Mare and tell her I will arrive by cab to retrieve him at 5:30 the following night.

I sit on another bench and turn up Rufus Wainwright on my iPod; he's singing "Oh What A World," with its no-place-like-home theme. I watch the lights on the Ferris wheel blink an elaborate dance. I limp back another mile to Kit's house on the bay, because I have nowhere else to go. Thankfully, she isn't home. I see her Bible on the table. I shower and climb in bed. In less than twenty-four hours, this nightmare will be over. I will never visit again. I have to break this cycle.

Before sunrise, my eyes pop open. I try to go back to sleep, but my head is urging me to run, run, run. I wash my face and gather my luggage. My backpack is heavy, and my little rolling duffel bag makes a racket as I drag it through the sleeping streets over to Mare's house. I want it to be with Henry's stuff. I want everything ready when the cab comes. I leave the luggage and walk, once again, to the boardwalk, that place I regarded, as a child, as some sort of nirvana, a destination one could never visit enough. I have another twelve hours to kill.

I walk for a mile, then stop, stare at the Atlantic for a long time, and remind myself I won't be back any time soon. I take a mental picture of the water rolling in, receding, rolling in, receding.

"Hey, how's it going?" The familiar voice startles me. I look up. My sister Mare. On this five-mile long, vastly wide beach, I have run into Mare. And her husband. And Kit. And her son.

I respond that it's going shitty, and I keep walking. After five minutes or so, I feel a hand on my arm. Kit's been chasing me.

"You need to tell me why you're so mad," she says.

"I do not," I answer. "Leave me alone. In two hours I'll be gone. No longer a part of this family. You won't ever humiliate me again."

"Humiliate you?"

I take the bait. "Yes, humiliate me! How do you think it feels for me to call my friend and uninvite him?!"

Missing the point entirely, she says I could've taken the extra money I'm spending on changing the plane ticket and used it for a hotel room. I yell at her that this is about her not trusting my judgment, and about how insulted I am.

My sister Mare, who has also been following, wants me to lower my voice, be more discreet. I refuse. This is New Jersey. People are loud and obnoxious. And they yell. A lot. These are my roots, and I am yelling. I don't care who sees or hears this altercation. Let the world watch. I demand to know why they took my son to mass that morning when they know I think the Catholic Church is full of crap.

Kit then hurls at me what will, I'm certain, become the most unforgettable line of my lifetime. "You know what this is about?!" she yells. "This is about your *internal struggle with Christianity!!*"

I am so stunned by this accusation—my internal struggle with Christianity? *What the . . . ?*—that I feel momentarily verbally Tasered by her and am unable to reply at all.

I quickly regain my footing. "No," I say. "This is about the fact that you people are a bunch of racist, sexist, homophobic, narrow-minded . . ." I am grasping for the word *ignoramuses,* but Mare interrupts.

"I have gay friends. I have black friends."

I limp away.

Back at the house, my sister is late returning with my son. I am fully paranoid now, expecting they won't hand him over, that they'll do some weird Christian intervention.

But they don't; they arrive, and we leave. I take Henry by cab to the skanky bus station and he sits beside me, sobbing inconsolably, unable to see my side since he has not grown up in this dynamic and he is forever the faraway cousin who is only ever showered with love on his rare visits to see my family. I have ruined his vacation. I am ruining his life. In this sense, he is one of them now: another member of my family who, if only for this moment, thinks I am entirely wrong. About everything.

But I hold steady. I tell him my mental-health needs trump his desire for cousin fun. I tell him I can't be a good mother if I'm falling apart. He gets less mad at me as the bus, a local, takes four hours getting us to Philly. We listen to the mouth on the fat girl in the seat behind us, her belly spilling over the top of her low-cut pants; she swears nonstop into her cell phone. *Fuckety fuck fuck fuck* is what it sounds like. Henry becomes one with me, huddling closer and comparing notes when a fight breaks out in the front of the bus between an older black woman and a young white mother. This bus is moving too slow; I think it is the weight of so much anger.

Our flight from Philly doesn't leave until the morning, and we still can't afford a hotel. On the floor of a catwalk between terminals of Philadelphia International, we find some large potted plants to hide behind and curl into each other for safety and comfort and four rough hours of semisleep before we catch one plane, and then another, returning me to sanity, delivering me from my family and from all the anger that I came from.

chapter 2

Thinking and Drinking:

Memory and Booze

Memory is one of the most fascinating things for me to contemplate. My own has begun to show holes, the result of me being in my forties. Stuff wears out. But prior to forty, my memory was accurate enough to annoy people. I could recall in meticulous detail the clothes I wore and the conversations I had at a party ten or fifteen years before. And when I try to wrap my head around the idea of memory—*What is it? How does it work? Why does mine haunt me?*—I wonder how it relates to some of the things that defined me most over the years: namely, my anger and my drinking.

When I began working on my first book, back in 1997, my family more or less cut me off en masse. They hadn't read a word of the manuscript—hell, at that point I had barely written a word. But they suspected I was going to write a scathing memoir, and we all knew I had no intention of sparing my father. Sure enough, this came to pass.

Then, an odd thing happened. By the time the book actually came out, three years after I got the contract to write it, my family had simmered down some—in part, I believe, due to a couple of major illnesses that put our petty differences into sharp relief. In the spring of 1997, I learned I had a malignant ovarian tumor, which was successfully removed along with the ovary to which it clung. Meanwhile, my mother, during a stress-related illness, witnessed her hair first turn white overnight and then fall out completely. (This occurrence was odd enough to deserve the following aside: Though my mother and I weren't speaking when all this went down, we remained deeply connected psychically. Several months post-tumor, I had a vision of her in which she appeared very old and ill, with white hair. We talked on the phone soon after this, and came to a not-totally-spoken agreement that we'd never again allow something to come between us in such a way that we'd cut each other off. In the seven years since, our relationship has grown much stronger.)

Since my family was speaking with me again when the book came out, I stopped to see them as I took an informal book tour. When I reached New Jersey, I left Henry with one of my sisters and went to New York for a couple of days.

When I returned, I sat in my sister Mare's backyard with her and another of our sisters, Rose. I nearly choked on my sweetened iced tea when both sisters announced that, in my brief absence, they'd read my entire book. I'd been hoping they wouldn't—not because it was inaccurate or because I wasn't proud of it but because I figured they'd be pissed off all over again and disagree with what I'd written. Hearing the news, I was seized with an urge to get up and bolt. Instead, I sucked in my breath and sat, waiting for their verdicts.

Rose, in classic Northeastern sarcasm mode, said, "Maybe if we had hugged you more as a kid, you wouldn't have such a bad life."

Mare said, "I just felt so bad for you. I didn't even remember a lot of that stuff until I read it. Your memory is too good."

Yet neither disagreed with the actions I attributed to our father. The things I described him doing to us—to me, specifically—were not a bone of contention so much as my assessment of the events. Rose thought I was interpreting as abuse what she classified as acceptable grouchiness. Mare wished that, like her, I could just forget it all and put it behind me. Which is to say that both thought I was "too sensitive," a label I've been slapped with my whole life.

Up until fairly recently, being called too sensitive hit me a certain, visceral way. Anger welled up that I had difficulty deconstructing. No matter how much I hated the accusation, on some level I bought it. How could I not? To react strongly against the suggestion was itself proof of my hypersensitivity, wasn't it? To this day, when I am feeling particularly vulnerable or raw and I'm caving in to the urge to have a pity party, I'm tempted to blame whatever's bothering me on what I'll call my Too Gene.

The best example I can offer to illustrate the Too Gene, and its insistence that I feel sorry for myself, relates to dating. I've had little success with dating in my life. No romantic relationship of mine has lasted more than four years, and most have been much shorter. None have held anything resembling the calm contentedness I dream of when I dream of being with my elusive, perfect other half. During the worst of my relationships—and times in between when I felt I couldn't get a date—I succumbed to self-blame, telling myself I was *too much*. Too loud, too fast, *too sensitive*. Too, too, too.

Only recently have I come to recognize that my Too Gene is as much a part of me as any other trait. It's not something I can simply eliminate, nor is it something I wish to eliminate, though there've been times when I've wished that very thing. I've come to appreciate my sensitivity, and to look at the other side of the coin: Could it be (yes, of course!) that people who level the "too sensitive" accusation are, in fact, too insensitive?

The truth is, I *am* sensitive. I'm incredibly sensitive. But I know now that very sensitive people are receivers, far more open to the energy other people give off, for better or worse. I had a meeting, many years ago, with a terrifically gifted psychic who looked at me and instantly noted that my aura, unlike most folks' auras, had a pointed quality—which, he said, acted like a magnet, pulling in the energy of others around me. Whether you buy into psychic phenomena or not, I can give you a thousand examples of times I was standing around, minding my own business, when a stranger accosted me and started telling me his or her life story—usually all

Thinking and Drinking

25

the tragic parts. People are drawn to me. They love to pour out their roughest stories and most painful moments.

Only after experiencing this repeatedly, over decades, have I learned to recognize the pattern, and also the need to protect myself. I don't mind hearing other people's sad stories, helping them process, and helping them bear their burdens. But you can take in too much, and you can overload.

Growing up in a house with ten other people—all of them high energy, loud, and dramatic, with my dad spewing constant plumes of negativity—I can see now how I was on constant overload as a child. This is why, even though I go to big parties and crowded concerts and other places where I'm exposed to large numbers of people, I also spend an incredible amount of time alone. I have to shield myself from other people's energy.

I didn't know any of this as a child, and even if I had known, there was nowhere to escape to. Our house, my father's ongoing building project, featured rooms tacked onto one another without doors. There was no privacy. You were part of the team, whether you wanted to be or not. There was no closing yourself off from all the energy bouncing off those walls.

This past summer, I was helping my friend Reggie through a hard time. His wife had died, he had two little kids to raise, and he had his own grief to deal with. I helped with the kids nearly every day, until one day Reggie told me, bluntly and in front of them, that the kids wanted to see me less. I winced and made one of my famous sarcastic remarks before I could stop myself, process the information, and recognize that this wasn't about me (and it wasn't—it was about the kids missing their mom, and about the fact that often, when I showed up, their dad went away, so that my presence came to represent his absence).

Later, referring to my wince, Reggie said I was being too sensitive. I clobbered him. "Of *course* I'm fucking sensitive!" I said. "How the hell do you think I've been able to be around three grieving people every day?" Still later, I accused him of being insensitive in his delivery of the information.

One problem with being too sensitive is that I'm hyperaware of what might offend others—whereas those who lack the Too Gene (like my sisters) don't understand this heightened sensitivity. And that failure to understand can make the sensitive more sensitive still. At some point, you have to break this cycle, or it will either kill you or break your spirit.

As I explained to Reggie, the widower, sensitive people are also sensitive to their own needs; to survive being sensitive in a world that often feels built upon insensitivity, I told him, you have to adapt. Which means that while I might initially respond hypersensitively to a remark, I'll then withdraw, process, try to see the other person's perspective, and attempt to carry on from that point. It's much easier said than done, but that old adage about practice leading to perfection comes into play here.

Unfortunately, my initial hypersensitive response often manifests as anger, which is actually me putting up a hastily built wall of defense to shield myself from what feels like an assault. This wall of anger can be effective on one level—if it drives away the other person, then I am momentarily safe. Ultimately, though, I'll replay the event on an endless loop, which is where my memory for tiny details becomes problematic. I can't, as my sister Mare suggests, simply let things go and move on. My memory seizes upon painful events the way my dog Satch obsesses over his Frisbee. He wakes up in the morning wanting it, and he goes to bed at night thinking about it. If you threw it for him twenty-four hours a day, he'd go after it until he died of exhaustion.

That's what my memory has been for me. Exhausting. But I have a theory about why my memory is so good, why just forgetting past incidents hasn't been an option. A former colleague of mine at the *Dallas Morning News* published a long essay about how she had been sexually abused as a child. She'd had no concrete memory of the incident, but for her entire life she felt something was amiss. Finally, as an adult, she confronted her mother, who—in a heart-rending scene where Mom is making tortillas by hand, tears streaming down her face—explained that yes, her daughter's subconscious memory was correct; she had been abused but her parents didn't know what to do and so they chose to not reveal the information, hoping she would forget.

After I read that piece, I sent my colleague a very long letter in which I put forth a theory: Perhaps we'd grown up to be writers because we'd been abused. Maybe at the time of the abuse some little voice went off that said, *Memorize this. This is wrong. Remember the details. Find an adult who believes you. Tell them.* And maybe, in honing our mnemonic skills, we wound up with talents that would serve us well as journalists—an eye and an ear for details; an ability to absorb and process piles of information, even painful information; and a way to deliver it.

This is a very catch-22 theory. It is entirely possible that I didn't memorize my pain in hopes of finding a witness (though those would come later in life, in the form of some good therapists, some dear friends, and one sibling who finally broke down and confirmed for me that I had indeed been abused). Maybe I just had a damn good memory, and that was what left me feeling so abused. I simply couldn't forget the countless painful moments.

Now the truth is that I've forgotten plenty of things—no one could remember everything without going totally batshit. But the things I remember, the emotions of those memories, are palpable, like acid flashbacks. Not like, *Oh, I remember I felt sad then;* I feel actual pain in my stomach, as if I'm back in the awful moment I'm thinking about.

I only recently found out that such visceral reactions are a symptom of post-traumatic stress disorder. I already knew I had PTSD—I was diagnosed in 1997, while being stalked by my ex-husband. But it never occurred to me that I might've had PTSD long before that stalking. The intense feelings that visited me when I thought about certain events in my past suggested I did. It makes perfect sense—I've suffered a lot of intense trauma since an early age.

All of us experience trauma at some point. The level of intensity varies, and not everyone succumbs to PTSD. But those who do succumb can expect to experience a spectrum of reactions which, besides those flashbacks I mentioned, also (according to PTSD experts Bessel A. van der Kolk, Alexander C. McFarlane, and Lars Weisaeth) include hypervigilance, an exaggerated startle response, and a tendency to "move immediately from stimulus to response without often realizing what makes them so upset." And yes, this includes anger. Not to say I get to blame my PTSD for my knee-jerk responses, but it's helpful to recognize it as a potential source and to know that treatments and coping mechanisms exist to get past the worst of it.

Another manifestation of my memory's persistence has been my grudge holding. If you took a survey of fifty people who know me, and asked them to name the biggest grudge holder they know, at least forty-nine of them would unhesitatingly award me top honors. I find it nearly impossible to forget or let go of a slight.

My friend John was kind enough to point out to me once that the flip side to grudge holding is fierce loyalty. I appreciated that observation, because I'm well aware of just how far into the earth I can grind my heels. My Japanese friend Makoto once said to me, "I never want to be on your shit list." It's a good wish. Because people on my shit list can count on being cut off permanently. I don't suffer fools gladly.

Even now, as I'm striving toward a place where I don't get bogged down in anger, where I get past stuff and move on, the best I've been able to manage when someone crosses me is to send them packing, put them out of my mind, and try to avoid shooting mean vibes and wicked thoughts down the path behind them. I still don't have the patience to try and patch it up if someone does me really wrong.

For example: I was talking to a friend recently about an editor we both know. "Can't stand him," I said, and began to detail why the guy got on my nerves and how, as far as I was concerned, he could go to hell and I would never speak to him again.

My friend laughed. "You cut off X? Nice career move."

I thumped myself in the chest. "You know," I said, "I'm true to myself. It's the best I can be."

The problem is, when we make these decisions to cut off others, often the decision is made in haste and heat, and we can't always know that a decision is right when rage blinds us. Sometimes a decision is wrong, and we spend forever trying to patch things up, or we simply miss the person we've cut out. Other times it's the smartest, rightest thing in the world for us to put a distance between ourselves and those who are bad for our spirits. But the method we choose to end such relationships can be self-hurtful. Just as screaming at someone in traffic doesn't change that person's behavior and doesn't make you feel any better for the screaming, grudges don't feel good and they require an awful lot of energy to sustain. Better to just drive off, so to speak, and hope you never see that person again.

It's been six or seven years since I stopped working with that editor. I like that I was true to myself and my values when I stopped working with him. But I don't like that I've invested part of myself in staying mad at him. And I also know that being true to myself can involve more than a little self-righteousness. When I think about my self-righteousness and the things I've done in the name of it—well, let's just say I've been more than a little over-the-top. But before I get to those examples, I need to talk about the drinking, because I think many people turn to drinking as some sort of antimemory suppressant.

I'm sober six years now, after binge drinking through my teenage years, sloppily slurping my way through college and my twenties, and getting halfway through my thirties with a pattern that usually involved a six-pack or several pints of Guinness every night. In the end, I wasn't a falling-down drunk or an overly social drunk. I just drank every evening out of habit and addiction, and to block out things I didn't want to feel—mostly sitting on my porch, throwing them back until I was sufficiently buzzed, then collapsing into bed.

Sometimes I was aware of a specific pain I was trying to numb—when G2 was off fucking some other woman, for instance, I would amp up my drinking, maybe bust open a bottle of wine and have most of it for lunch. Most often, I drank to quell the low-level anxiety that traveled with me from childhood, the fear that I could do nothing right, that I was doomed to failure.

Just about anyone who has confronted a drinking problem can tell you that even if you're blocking one set of pain and emotions, another set is waiting to leap out at you, like the little robot moles that pop up from their holes in that Whac-a-Mole game you find in arcades. So I might forget, for a few hours each night, the things in my life I didn't like, but I'd wake up with a pounding headache, a sick stomach, and a sense that I was quite the shitty mother. Those thoughts would bother me all day, and then, like the side of the shampoo bottle says, I'd rinse and repeat, cracking open a brew at suppertime.

There was nothing original or unique in my drinking to excess. When you drink, you keep friends who also drink, because they'll join you when you want company and they won't judge you when you prefer to drink alone. You can compare your drinking to your friends' drinking and you can tell yourself, *I don't drink too much because X drinks the same amount.* Even better, you can tell yourself, *Shit, X drinks a lot more than me. I don't have the problem, she does!*

I chose to get sober on my own, but I have plenty of friends who've gone the Alcoholics Anonymous route, and it was one of these friends who taught me a term often used in meetings: *terminal uniqueness.* Let me set my "too sensitive" side in the corner here and bluntly say that terminal uniqueness is basically when you feel like you're different from everyone else, that your circumstances are somehow more special or important, and thus warrant special dispensation. Terminal uniqueness is a way to rationalize addiction and other inappropriate behaviors. I'd be lying if I told you I don't still succumb to TU on occasion (though I no longer use it to rationalize having a drink).

Today's papers are so full of reports—some of them conflicting—about depression and drinking and the sundry mental health issues of Americans that one can easily get dizzy or overwhelmed, or cynical and dismissive, and start believing that school of thought that says we're all looking for someone or something to blame for our ongoing discomfort. I get sick of hearing about the statistics and causes and cures and triumphs and tragedies of addiction and mental illness, despite the fact (or maybe because of the fact) that, for a long time, drinking and depression were as much a part of my life as sleeping and breathing.

That's one problem with healing, with moving from point A to point Z. No matter how much you vow never to forget where you came from, no matter how accurate your memory, there is a slipping that occurs. *Was I really that messed up?* sometimes flashes through my head when I think about things I've done, because it's been a long time since I really *was* that messed up.

I feel that way about my past anger, too. While I've given up drinking, I haven't totally given up anger—partly because anger is sometimes a powerful tool, and partly because unlike alcohol, anger is not a concrete thing you can physically remove from your life. Still, I look back on my worst bouts of drinking and my worst bouts of anger in the same way. *What made me do that?* I wonder. *How is it that I got so drunk/angry?* What an amazing form of torture it would be were I forced to watch videotapes of myself in either condition. The thought makes me want to curl up in a fetal ball under my desk.

My anger and drinking often went hand in hand, one spurring the other. The combination dates back to my very earliest drinking days, when I learned the art of underage drinking at the Jersey Shore during the summers when my parents—in an odd loosening of my otherwise very tight leash—let me live, unchaperoned, in their beach house.

The summer when I was fifteen, I worked on the boardwalk in Wildwood, at a place called Mack's Pizza. Joe, one of the owners, was probably only in his forties or fifties, but to me he seemed *really* old. He was a cheerful, wiry little guy with a big grin, like Curious George. One night, he invites my roommate, who is sixteen, and me for a night on the town. Wildwood is a small place, and everyone knows everyone else. If Joe Mack, owner of a famous string of pizza restaurants, wants to bring two minors into a bar, no one is going to stop him. At least, not back in 1979.

I am wearing my knockoff Jordache jeans and a purple shirt with blue stripes and a white collar. My face is blistered, healing slowly from sun poisoning I'd suffered when I fell asleep on the beach one day. I'm not big—I weigh perhaps 110 pounds—and I have little experience drinking, factors that mean I have a low resistance to alcohol. We go to several bars and drink a lot before finally making it to a disco called the Stardust, where I stumble up the stairs. I loudly demand that the bartender pour me another, and another. At some point, he is serving me soda water with cherries in it, but I am so blind drunk I don't have a clue. (My roommate will tell me about it the next day.)

And then it happens. First one guy and then another comes over and starts making out with me. These are Philly guys, regular guidos, with greasy, slicked-back hair, gold chains, and punk attitudes. There are four of them in all. Granted, this is not a gang rape, but the violation I will feel later will rip through me repeatedly, on a burning loop, for decades. But right now, in the moment, it's not about shame. Even in my falling-down drunkenness (and I will fall down and I will throw up), somewhere in my mind a voice is saying, *He likes you. Oh, and he likes you, too.*

Only the next day will I piece together that nobody had liked me. I'd been an easy target, and no doubt a dare. *Look at that ugly chick over there with the scabs on her face. I dare you to go make out with her.* A couple of weeks later, walking down the street, I run into one of the guys. "Hey, I know you," he says. And I know then who he is, though his face had been a blur that night. I stand there on the street—me, the worst liar in the world—and deny having ever seen him before. But we both knew the truth.

When I woke up the morning after that night, I was very sick. I put on my black cardigan and curled up in a ball and tried to decide what to do. Though it pained me, I knew I had to call Joe Mack and apologize for my behavior, so I dialed his number. He said that my apology wasn't necessary.

Not until many years later did it occur to me that Joe Mack should have apologized to *me*. Or, better still, Joe Mack never should've taken a fifteen-year-old girl out drinking in the first place. There is no rationalization for it. None. But how could I have known? I was a dumb girl, inexperienced, with a free ticket to the nightlife of a white trash Jersey Shore town. You can't know what you don't know, right?

I wish I could say that night cured me of something, but it didn't. By then it was already too late: The seeds of drinking, for whatever reasons I was drinking, were taking root, and I wouldn't be able to eradicate them for a very long time.

I have many more stories like this, from Wildwood and later in college. For now, I want to share just one more:

Despite the drunken make-out sessions I would pursue summer after summer, despite the finger fuckings from drunken Irish carnies and the barely clothed groping on the beach and in dark corners of Wildwood bars and surfer cars, I somehow managed to keep my virginity intact until I was nineteen. By then it was a burden, but one I was unsure how to handle. I was still a practicing Catholic, raised to believe I was constantly sinning, and I was forever terrified of hell. Having sex was bad. So was using birth control.

But I was also a teenage girl with teenage girl hormones, in a town that I realize now has been the home to more lost virginity than most other towns. I wasn't thinking of the big picture then. I wasn't thinking much at all. Dry humping this boy or that boy filled me with longing and shame. I didn't know what to do. So I went with the usual solution. I got drunk and let the cards (and clothes) fall where they might.

Surely I'm not the first human unable to clearly remember the first night, the first penetration. But I wonder how many other kids felt rage mixed in with their initiation to the world of sex. I'm sure the answer is, *A hell of a lot.* And I know—from magazine articles, conversations with friends, talk show episodes, radio programs, and all other forms of pop culture—that sex and rage remain intertwined even in adulthood for an overwhelming number of people. We're angry with our sex partners, or about our lack of sex, or about our lack of sexual satisfaction, or about our lack of compatibility. Sex soothes and enrages, enrages and soothes. Some people pick fights to provoke apology sex. Some people withhold sex as a punishment.

For me, the sex-and-rage cycle began with the man I allowed to deflower me, a sleazy, bug-eyed bouncer named Tim. There was nothing tender or loving about him. He had a hard dick; I had a place for him to stick it. I would get wasted, and he would take me home and fuck me. This might have happened twice; it might have happened ten times. Maybe the booze is what keeps me from remembering, or maybe the trauma turns my mental screen blank when I try to conjure up the specifics.

I have only two solid flashes of memory when I think of Tim. Once, midfuck, I had to puke. Tim led me to the bathroom, let me heave, handed me his toothbrush (shaped like a naked lady), had me brush, and then brought me back out to finish what he'd started on the hard floor.

I didn't protest. I let Tim finish what Tim started. *Men's needs came first*—this was the lesson I'd been taught from birth. *Make boys like you* was another big lesson, learned not just at home but everywhere: school, TV, billboards, magazines. There was no thought process there, just a doing. Or an allowing. Being drunk allowed me to allow him to do something that, in my mind, I might try to translate into affection. Twisted thinking? Absolutely. Am I the first one to ever have used booze as a teenager to let myself do such a thing? Oh, how I wish.

The rage surfaced after that episode of sex with Tim. We leave his house and I'm too drunk to know where I am or where I'm going; I only know that I suddenly have to use the bathroom and it is extremely urgent. Tim ushers me into a pizza place and steers me to the employees' restroom in the back. A string of expletives pours from my mouth. People are trying to shush me.

There you go: the cartoon me. A large, drunken, wide-open mouth: *Fuckety fuck fuck fuck.* Just like that South Philly girl I would encounter on the bus so many years later as I swept my son away from my family and their anger and religion. That was me. A mouth. A mess. A drunk. Angry, angry, angry.

Pissed off.

I can't even tell you all the things that made me angry. My father's crushing dominance. How desperate I was to get out from under his fist and his fury. How I wanted a boyfriend, or, more accurately, some pure source of love as I fantasized love could be—bright and healing and joyful. How I craved freedom. How I needed very desperately to be loved, fully and wholly, for who I was, thinking that the source of this love existed outside of me.

I don't know that any teenager feels truly loved. I have a teenager now, and, despite my daily conscious efforts to love him as hard as I safely can without screwing him up, there are moments when he seems completely pissed off at me. Maybe it's a hormone thing. But for me, it was more than that. I was swinging my fists at God and everyone else, throwing back the booze, and praying furiously for someone to rescue me—from my father, from myself. And I was begging for someone to love me.

For a very long time, I felt like no one ever did.

part two

Portraits of Anger

introduction

Losing It

Just as anger itself has come to me in flashes and overtaken me, memories of anger pop up, triggered by events that flash me back to a bad place. The other night I went for a little boat ride on Town Lake, which divides Austin in half, north and south. I was on a tour boat, and our driver was tossing out little informational tidbits for the out-of-towners. He mentioned that on the shore of the lake there used to be an annual celebration called Aquafest. His point was to recall the tug-of-war competition between the north and south, across the river. But as soon as he said "Aquafest," I had a flashback.

When Henry was very little, I took him to Aquafest. Rides at these carnival events are always questionable at best, and I'd spent enough time around carnies in my teenage summers to know that they weren't applying specific engineering techniques, or adhering to safety regulations, if they were assembling these rides drunk or hungover.

You'd think with this insider knowledge, I might've taken my son to a Disney movie instead. But no. We went to Aquafest, we bought our tickets, we took our chances. One ride in particular looked a little scary. I'm no fan of spinning around at breakneck speed for the purpose of getting excited—my interior landscape is dramatic enough that I can sit in a chair all day thinking, and that's plenty thrilling. But Henry expressed interest in the ride, so I approached the ride operator and began to question him. Did he think it was okay for my kid to ride? He grunted and gestured to the sign indicating the mandatory height requirement. I explained that Henry was the right height, but that I was attempting to gauge the scare factor. Would it be too rough? I wanted to fulfill my son's desire to go on this big-kid ride, but I also wanted to exercise a little common sense.

At this point, the carnie got sarcastic, but I decided we would take our chances. We got on, and the thing went totally out of control. Henry was smashed up against the side of our car, and the g-force threw me against him. He was freaked out and so was I, but it was my job to reassure him; I tried, though I was on the verge of tears.

I thought to myself, *This guy did that on purpose.* Then I thought, *No, you're being paranoid. He couldn't have done it on purpose. How could he?*

I was shaken, sick, and scared by the time we were let off, and dealing with a little kid who was traumatized. I tried to salvage the evening. But as we worked our way through the crowds, a man approached me. He had witnessed some of the exchange, and he had ridden in the car beside ours. He was convinced that the ride operator had purposefully adjusted our car to make our experience upsetting, and he confirmed that I wasn't merely paranoid. Our car had been spinning at an alarming rate.

You recall that I mentioned my self-righteous streak. I went ballistic. Totally, completely, 200 percent out-of-my-head insane. I freaked out. I hunted down the manager of the rides and I let him have it. *Fuckety fuck fuck fuck!* I said. *Your goddamned motherfucking cocksucking son-of-a-bitch ride operator practically killed my kid! I want his fucking head on a platter! You fuckers!*

This manager looked at me. He denied my claims. He insisted I speak more politely. You have to have a pretty filthy mouth to alarm a man who supervises carnies for a living, but I had no trouble clearing that bar. *I will not speak more politely, you motherfucker. I want my money back! I want an apology! Fuckety fuck fuck fuck!*

A cop was called. I refused to back down. We were ushered to the Aquafest headquarters, housed in a trailer on the premises. Apologies were delivered, free passes were handed out, and things got straightened out. Sort of.

The thing is, my anger didn't subside. I was angry that I'd been tricked. I was angry that a skanky man had preyed upon me. And I was angry, above all, because he hurt my child. Aquafest lasted a couple of weeks, and each day, during my daily workout, I walked past the fairground and past that ride. It was daytime, so things were closed down, but I hoped to see that carnie. I wanted to throw a rock at his head. I wanted to shove a dagger into his heart. I hated him fiercely for what he'd done to me and my kid.

On the other hand . . .

Viewed now from the distance of ten years, I still understand why I got angry. It's in our very core to become angry when someone hurts our children. We are hardwired to protect them. But really, what was I thinking, approaching a stupid, disinterested, job-hating ride operator and asking him about the psychological effects his ride would have on my child? I'd approached him as if he had an advanced Harvard degree in child psychology. Flawed thinking, I now know. And worse, a big red flag to the guy: *Here's someone you can fuck with. Here's someone who is tentative and scared. Take out all of your mean-spirited anger on her. Have fun with it. Watch her turn green.*

As in: Yes, it is understandable that I was angry at the carnie. But I could've just skipped going on that ride, letting my doubt about its safety and the warning signal of his sarcasm be my intuitive guides. Instead, I second-guessed myself, and in doing so, I set myself up.

Likewise, repeatedly (oh so repeatedly), I would put myself in a position, intuit a bad vibe (from a man or a situation), override that bad vibe, convince myself an obvious wrong choice was the only right choice, and immerse myself further in chaos—and further, until I was on fire with rage, ready to kill (or at least feeling ready to kill).

Following are random portraits of this rage, these bad choices, and the things that manifested as a result. These pictures aren't pretty, though some are amusing if you contemplate just how angry I let myself get, for the most ridiculous reasons. Some will hopefully be helpful—some of my anger was justified, and sometimes my anger was like a faithful sidekick, catapulting me to a better place. There is no chronology here—just flashes that occurred to me, in much the same way that the anger reared its awful, ugly, persistent head.

Now that I'm less angry, I have to say that offering this compilation is a bit embarrassing. Considering the montage will not be tempered or balanced with palate-cleansing word pictures of moments when I was happy and cheerful, I know I run the risk of presenting myself as a perpetually rage-filled maniac. But if you buy into that saying about misery loving company, well, let me just say that, over the course of writing this book, I talked to a slew of women about their anger. Many of their stories are in here, too. And I take consolation knowing that I'm not the only one who has succumbed to road rage and in-law rage and coworker rage and professional-jealousy rage and what-did-I-ever do-to-deserve-living-with-a-teenager rage and I-hope-this-customer-service-representative-comes-back-in-her-next-life-as-a-dung-beetle rage and why-are-men-so-fucking-stupid-especially-in-relationships rage and all the other rages I'm about to detail.

portrait 1

Dave Eggers

A lot of people know who Dave Eggers is. In case you don't know, let me tell you. He put out a magazine in the '90s called *Might*. *Might* was wacky and ironic and dripping with the sort of sarcasm I grew up with. *Might* got Dave a lot of attention and he parlayed this into a big gig with *Esquire,* which he hated, and then a $100,000 contract with Simon & Schuster to write a memoir, *A Heartbreaking Work of Staggering Genius.* Many book critics—among them the notoriously finicky she-won't-like-it she-hates-everything journalist Michiko Kakutani, the top book reviewer for *The New York Times*—lined up around the block to give *A Heartbreaking Work* the equivalent of a book-review blow job. Everyone wanted a piece of Dave, who went on to sell the paperback and movie rights for a reported eleven gazillion dollars.

I became acquainted with Dave back in the mid-'90s. I've had more than a few odd jobs, and at this particular time, I was managing a comedy club in Austin called The Velveeta Room. One night, we had a comedian in from San Francisco named Harmon Leon. At the end of the night I was tired and irritable, and Harmon wanted to be paid. I don't recall our exact exchange, but I hardly left a good impression.

Somehow, though, we got on the topic of magazine articles—managing the club was one way I was supporting my fledgling freelance writing career—and Harmon said that he wrote for a magazine in San Francisco called *Might*. He'd be glad to hook me up, he told me. Which is how, quite randomly, I came to be a semiregular writer for one of the hippest magazines in the country.

There was a catch—there always is. And the catch in this case was that no pay was involved. On the other hand, I could write whatever I wanted, such as a piece called "People I Hate," which was illustrated with a photo of Henry and me posed in front of a gravestone that said LOVING on it. I got to say I hated Jesus for demanding that I be forgiving when I didn't feel like it.

At the time, I went out to San Francisco, where *Might's* office was located, with some regularity. From time to time, I'd visit Dave and the rest of the staff. I was even in attendance at a now-notorious party, detailed in Dave's bestseller, that unveiled a hoax the magazine had successfully pulled off suggesting that mid-'80s child TV star Adam Rich (from *Eight Is Enough*) was dead (he wasn't).

To say I was close to Dave Eggers would be quite the crock. I knew him. He knew me. He was raising his brother. I was raising my son. One of my lawyer friends got one of his friends out of a speeding and pot-possession jam once. We eventually drifted and lost touch. In 1996, Simon & Schuster contracted me to write my memoir, *All the Wrong Men and One Perfect Boy*, in which I detailed my ongoing, inappropriate crushes on unavailable men, my anger toward my father, my love of my son, and my life as a single parent. That book came out in 1999. It was hardly a bestseller, which was fine, because an awful lot of the folks who did read it took time to send thank-you notes and share their own stories. That felt very good.

That would be the end of the story, except . . . I guess it was maybe early 2000 when I was in Austin at BookPeople, my favorite bookstore, and, as I was in the habit of doing, I wandered over to the biography section before leaving to make sure copies of my book were in stock. Vain, but true. As I was glancing at the titles, looking for mine, I saw Dave's book, and I thought, *Oh, wow! Dave has a book out! Good for him!*

Though I am typically a major news junkie, I must've been in one of my antinews phases, because I had somehow missed the blaring news that Dave Eggers was being hailed as Gen X's next James Joyce–T.S. Eliot–Jack Kerouac–William Shakespeare–Tennessee Willams–Jay McInerney sensation. Being someone who personalizes most things (not so much out of vanity—though that accusation gets hurled at me regularly—but because I lack overview), I thought, *Dave must be so excited and nervous! Gosh, I wonder what he's thinking!*

When I got home, I shot Dave an email. Not that we were regular email friends. But I had his address at *Esquire*. Come to think of it, maybe he wasn't even at *Esquire* anymore. Maybe he never got the email. But I sent it, and he didn't respond, and that was the beginning of the end for me. Actually, it was the beginning of the beginning of some pretty unfucking bridled anger that would last for a good five years.

I remember with great clarity that I congratulated Dave, told him I knew what it felt like to have a memoir out, wished him the best, and specifically noted that I guessed he was very busy and there was no need to respond.

Hint: That last part is where I was full of shit. Of course I wanted him to respond. Not because he was a big famous writer. I didn't know he was a big famous writer. I just thought of him as an old colleague on a new adventure. I wanted him to respond because to me, lack of response equals rejection, which is the thing that most makes me think of my dad, and which makes me shake my fist at God.

After being rejected (in my mind) by Dave, I then read the book. And here is where my anger grew a hundredfold. For starters, Dave was allowed to get away with writing a perceived-as-absurd cutesy metacognitive opening, weighed down with countless parenthetical asides and enough self-consciousness as to make Narcissus seem humble. My thought on this (and you may hear it in your head as a whine, because that's what it was) was, *I never would've been allowed to get away with something like this* . . . I probably also added, *because I'm a woman writer.*

Next, Dave bitched about how he only got $100,000 to write the book. Bear in mind, Dave and I had the same publisher, we were writing on similar topics, and yet I had received a fraction of that amount for my advance. What the hell was his problem, complaining about six figures?

Then came the part in the book where Dave recalled the making of *Might* magazine. By this point in my reading, I was aware of the publicity Dave was generating, how the world was kneeling before him, mouths agape, ready to do anything he desired. I guess the words *professional jealousy* capture a good part of what I was experiencing. Exacerbating my irritation was my perception of his description of the people who wrote for *Might* for free, among them yours truly. I felt like he was mocking us for being so stupid as to do his bidding sans pay. He probably was, but doubtful to the extent I felt it. Whipped into a frenzy, I felt no more joy for Dave, only a blind rage. Fuckety fuck fuck him.

I invested a good amount of energy in my Dave anger. I invented a nickname for him, to make fun of him for exploiting his parents' deaths to become a millionaire. I called him Dave "My parents went to heaven and all I got was this lousy kid to raise" Eggers. I told anyone who would listen, and more than a few people who didn't want to, that Eggers was full of shit and that his sister was rumored to have done most of the heavy lifting when it came to raising their little brother. (This was a rumor that surfaced on the Internet briefly and then was quashed, which I attributed to Dave coming down hard on his sister.)

When Dave wrote an op-ed piece for *The New York Times* dictating that all college students should be forced to participate in mandatory volunteer work, I spent a good bit of time writing a rebuttal to this oxymoronic notion. My letter to the editor, as you might guess, was never published.

I think it is safe to say that while all this was going on, thoughts of me never crossed Dave Eggers's mind. I was investing enough energy to power a Malibu Barbie condo around the clock for a decade (at least), and he was carrying on with his life. I created a narrative that could only have one plotline: Dave Eggers didn't email me back, after all that free work I did for him and after he'd acted like he was my friend; ergo, Dave Eggers is a pompous asshole.

Two things happened that made me rethink my attitude toward Dave. For one thing, his sister committed suicide. I've been closely touched by suicide on more than one occasion in my life, and Dave's loss reminded me that, no matter how much of a god the media made him out to be, and no matter how much public strutting he was doing (and it seemed to me that he was), he was mortal, capable of being as wounded as the rest of us. I thought of his dead parents, too. And I thought, *Wow, this guy has been pretty screwed.* Me being me, I still wished he would've returned that damn email, but I backed down off my bitchy soapbox just a little.

And then came an email from San Francisco columnist Jane Ganahl. Jane was editing an anthology of essays by women of a certain age who were single. Jane wanted me to write a piece, and I asked how she had found me. Here was the kicker: *I got your name from Dave Eggers,* she replied, *who raved about your work for* Might.

I haven't yet talked about my anger with the Catholic Church, and all the residual fallout from that anger. But Catholic guilt is a real and devastating thing, even though I joke about it as if it were simply a chicken crossing the road. *She got my name from Dave? Who raved about my work for* Might? Oh, God, what a shit I was, going around for five years bad-mouthing the guy who's recommending me to people.

By then my brain no longer had time to sustain the fictive narrative about how Dave Eggers was out to reject me. Otherwise, I might've thought this to be the ultimate prank—*Dave gets even with Spike by being really nice to her.*

Adding humor—or sadness, or irony (let's call it irony, since that's Dave's middle name)—is that the piece I produced for Jane is one of the best I've ever written. It was excerpted in *The New York Times,* which netted me a landslide of fan mail and interest from other big editors and, get this, *The Tyra Banks Show.* I'm not saying that Dave's support prompted genius prose on my part. I'm just saying, *It figures.*

Later, I'll tackle how Buddhism has been influencing me to back down off my pit bull hind legs and unsink my teeth from the asses of people like Dave Eggers. For now, suffice it to say that even though I still had mixed feelings toward Dave, and even though I still think the *Heartbreaking Work of Staggering Genius* publicity was wildly overblown, I decided I should apologize to him and thank him for recommending me.

And so, circle of life and all that, once again I sent Dave an email. I briefly fessed up that I had trash-talked him for years, I sent my condolences regarding his sister, I thanked him for the reference, and I apologized for my misbehavior. I didn't feel entirely sincere—what I mean is, I'd invested so much in being angry that I felt a little disingenuous shooting out an apology as if it were a casual thing and as if a few electronic lines could undo all the bad juju I'd sent out over the wires. But I thought of it as a baby step, and let it fly.

Dave didn't write back. I admit, that sort of pissed me off. But I reined it in.

We've all had our own Dave Eggers experiences. Maybe yours was in kindergarten, when you headed off for the first day, convinced you had the best dress or lunchbox or barrettes in the world—only to be upstaged by Maribelle, the wunderkind, who had natural ringlets and shiny red shoes to rival Dorothy's in *The Wizard of Oz.* Or maybe it was in high school, when that kid beat you out for valedictorian. Or maybe it's right now—you're doing all the shit work at your job, *and* you're generating ideas, *and* yes, you noticed when someone stole one of those ideas and presented it, at the last big meeting, as her own.

Or maybe you've been working on your writing (or painting, or filmmaking) for the past ten (or twenty, or thirty) years, and every time you open the Sunday *Times* Arts & Leisure section or turn on the TV or flip through *O* magazine, you find someone whose work *sucks,* or at least can't hold a candle to your own, and yet there they are, sprawled out across an expensive couch in a fancy house, these things being just small spoils of their big-contract windfall.

So you get jealous. And you get mad. It's very difficult not to. I'm reminded of one of the stories my yoga teacher tells during end-of-class visualization and relaxation time, about a man who wishes for all the great luck that his brother has. While the man making the wish struggles, everything seems to come easily to his brother. Somewhere in there there's a big fire, possessions are lost, and hell breaks loose. Because I often fall semiasleep during this part of class, the details escape me. But the moral does not. Luck, goes the story, is something we're allotted. We have a lot of it or we don't, and there's no use bitching to the high heavens if it's the latter.

I have two problems with that theory. The first is—and maybe I'm naive here, but—I think luck doesn't do much unless it's paired with persistence. The second problem is that, while I love a good parable at least as much as the next yoga student, real life application is much more difficult. Accepting our lot—or just buying the concept that our fate is what we're given—is a tall order.

And besides, jealousy—particularly professional jealously—can, if channeled correctly, inspire you to do what you need to (hopefully within reason) to catapult past the person of whom you're jealous. Ideally, you turn the situation into a swim meet—one where you're competing against yourself and your own best time, but where it's also okay to notice the swimmer in the next lane as you pass by.

I don't know that any of the energy I wasted being mad at Dave translated into a particularly good query letter composed or writing contract secured. I do think it's possible that I felt at least a little nudged by his success to find my own. Which I have. And, ironically (again with the irony), it turns out that Dave and I both have grown up to spend a whole lot of our time doing nonprofit work to help kids with writing and other projects.

Maybe that's why he's too busy to return my notes.

alyssa harad

I.

I was working at the mental hospital—that's where I met her. She was a frequent visitor. First, there were the suicide attempts. Later, there were visits to bolster her fragile, stubborn recovery from a lifetime of terror and torture, at the hands of her father and then, as such things go, a series of other men.

I was supposed to make sure she walked a certain amount every day, so I walked with her, and she told me stories like: Once, in the middle of a hospital visit, she learned her grandmother was dying. She fought hard for a special pass so she could rush to her grandmother's side. When she arrived, her family greeted her with disgust: *Too late, you screwup.* But when she walked into her grandmother's room the old woman rose up on her bed, pointed a long bony finger straight in front of her, and, with a death rattle in her throat, cried, *I know you! You're the one who can't keep a man!*

One day, while we were walking, she told me about her doctor, and how he had warned her not to read a self-help book she'd been enjoying. He said it would give her lesbian tendencies. Did I think this was true? she asked me. I didn't know, I said, but I thought there were worse tendencies a person could have. For example, the tendency to get beaten up every night by her husband. We agreed on this. And then, because I was very young and freshly outraged at the ways of men and the world, and couldn't tell her what I really thought of the doctor's reading recommendations, and was sure she knew far more about survival than I ever would, I went on. And on. I told her about all the things I thought were making me angry—the starving girls, and the magazine covers, and all the usual blather. And she asked, really wanting to know for herself, What do you do with all that anger? And I said fast, without thinking, This job.

II.

I don't have that job anymore, but I am still angry. It's a slow burn, this very womanly anger, three parts stone to one part fire. And I am no more coherent. If you ask me what I am angry about, I am just as likely to stare at you, unable to speak, as I am to talk and talk and talk until neither of us can keep track of what I'm saying and we're both a little sorry and embarrassed. For example: I am angry at the violence done to that woman by her father, and the men it led her to, and the grandmother who taught her father how to think about the world, and the bigoted doctor paid to heal her, and the structures of mental health that employed a twenty-three-year-old English major to be her first line of defense, and at my twenty-three-year-old self-centered talk, and all the things that separate women from each other in what, I came to believe at that hospital, is an all-too-literal war of the sexes, sometimes subtle—a joke, a nervous twitch, a shadow at the door, a bitten tongue, a hesitation, a flinching away—but just as often crude and vulgar—a blow, a scream, bodies laid across the floor.

By now it is an old story. We have statistics now. Someone counts the women and the violent trespasses against them, and the numbers say it isn't strange, my knowing so many. But that doesn't make it any less uncanny as they mount up, all my numbered friends, until I wonder about myself, and how I came to stand in this circle.

Because first there was T, who never told me in person, but who announced it, and announced it, with her life. And then there was O, who gripped my shoulder in the middle of a class and included me in the circle. And then there was J, who was only trying to explain the difficulty of having to leave her newly found home. And then there was A, who only hinted in private, but made her story into a brazen, public performance. And then there was C, who was only sometimes sure, and her sister, too. And then there was R, who was too professional to tell me straight out—I knew, but didn't know, until I read the introduction to her book. And then there was B, who still goes home to visit, far more often than I do. And then there was D, who told me to explain something else, some other point that I dearly wish I could remember, since surely it was important to her. She was just five years old—that is what I remember instead.

And there may be others I have forgotten, because that is how the story works.

And there are others who haven't told me, because that is also how the story works.

And I am furious, even though it is not my place to be angry for them. Their stories are their own.

So what am I doing with my anger now?

Telling you this story.

Alyssa Harad is a writer and independent scholar currently working very hard for a glamorous nonprofit agency. She thanks all the friends who taught her how to bear witness with a toast, a joke, and a certain amount of silence.

terry galloway

On Being Told "No"

Two incidents in my life continue to piss me off royally.

One: I'm a senior in high school, a hardworking A student full of dreams about what a clever success I'm going to be. Then, one day, my guidance counselor calls me into his office. I think for sure he's going to give me the brochures of the top-notch colleges he's been passing out to all my friends. Instead he gives me one that reads, FACTORY WORK MAKE GOOD JOB FOR DEAF.

Two: A year later, I've won a scholarship to study theater at the University of Texas, Austin. I've arrived for my interview, only to be informed that I'm deaf. Now, clearly this isn't unknown to me, but my interviewers seem to think the word *deaf* covers a lot more territory than I think it does. For me, being deaf means that I wear two hearing aids, I'm an expert lip-reader, and I've spent most of my young life working to make my speech precisely enunciated and nicely inflected. I've come to UT thinking I ought to be allowed to pursue my passion and hone my craft.

They seem to think that my being deaf means no, there isn't any room for me in theater, even in theater created under the guise of education in an institution of learning. I'm not allowed to audition to perform or direct, they explain. But I am given an option: costuming. I'm not sure why they think my deafness qualifies me to wield a needle. In high school home economics, I was ostracized for having sewn my thumb to the hem of a skirt. The costume shop looms cold as Siberia. I politely decline and walk out of the interview fuming, thinking, *I'll fucking show them.*

That fury, that bitterness, has been one of the driving forces of my life. That fury pushed me in nontraditional directions, pushed me to discover, participate in, and create new alternatives to old theatrical ideas. Instead of playing the same old tired roles for women on the University of Texas drama department's mainstage, I played Falstaff, Puck, Dogberry, and Bardolph in the wonderful old theater barn that hosts the University's Shakespeare at Winedale progam. Instead of being in a chorus line on Broadway, I toured England with a P.S. 122 Field Trips troupe that included Blue Man Group and Laurie Carlos from Urban Bush Women. Instead of playing a maid or an extra in yet another theatrical revival, I cofounded *Esther's Follies,* a now-legendary cabaret still going strong on Austin's 6th Street. Instead of the same old same old, I created my own one-woman shows and toured all over the world. And I got to work with the late Heiner Müller, the iconic director of the Berliner Ensemble; work at the TransAct Theatre when it was giving birth to *Greater Tuna;* perform at WOW alongside Holly Hughes, Peggy Shaw, and Lois Weaver; and get my longer play produced and performed by the Rude Mechanicals of *Lipstick Traces* fame. And now, at age fifty-five, at a time in my life when the roles for a woman in traditional theater would be drying up, I'm still working—writing, producing, directing, and performing for stage, radio, video, and film. But even more satisfyingly, much of the work I'm doing is with people like me, who, for whatever reasons, would have been rejected by the wicked old university that first told me no. In Austin, Texas, those people are part of Actual Lives, a writing and performance workshop for people with disabilities. In Tallahassee, Florida, those people are part of the Mickee Faust Club, a "community theater for the weird and queer community." I have the great satisfaction of training other people how to do as I did, and say "No" right back.

Terry Galloway is a fourth-generation Texan who now lives in the part of Florida that is not Miami Beach. *The Performance of Drowning,* a chapter from her memoir-in-progress *Mean Little Deaf Queer,* was published in *Sleepaway: Writings on Summer Camp* (Riverhead Books).

Panic Attack

I have written about Henry since before he was born, detailing at length the near-constant joy he has brought me. We have done a million things together in the sixteen years since he was conceived—even when he was in utero, I took him to shows (once making some bouncers at a Poi Dog Pondering concert very, very nervous as, nine months pregnant and crammed into a vintage minidress, I danced my ass off). I rarely left him home, typically taking him anywhere I went—on errands, to concerts, even on dates.

Henry has been easy at least 90 percent of the time, has thankfully not developed an Alex P. Keaton streak, and has a charm and disposition so sweet that more than a few strangers have felt compelled to approach me and heap praise upon him after observing us out in public. When I stop to think about what he has meant in my life, what a healing force and source of joy he's been, I'm left breathless.

That said, nobody escapes parenting without having to clear plenty of hurdles, and I certainly have had mine. A major one is that, though I have striven to be the opposite of my father, there are moments when I channel him so thoroughly it makes Linda Blair's performance in *The Exorcist* seem like a trite outtake from the *Teletubbies*. Having been raised with rage, I am fluent in the language of rage. I don't have to think twice—hell, I don't have to think at all—to cut someone down if I am feeling angry or threatened. And if the someone in my way happens to be my child, the little guy I vowed, from his first days in the neonatal intensive care unit, to only ever love and adore . . . well, let's just say sometimes promises get broken. So it was on a hot summer night in 2004 in downtown Austin when my anger at Henry resulted in a trip to the emergency room.

You need a little backstory here. In September of 1991, when Henry was just ten months old, we moved from St. Louis—a city I wanted to escape—to Austin at the urging of Paula, my college roommate, who'd moved to Texas the year before. I didn't know much about Austin, didn't have any work lined up, and only had that one friend there to help me. But soon enough, I made new acquaintances.

I met Angela at a little park near my shitty apartment on a sunny autumn afternoon. We quickly figured out that our sons were both born-at-home bastards, with the same birthday. The boys even looked alike. Henry and MarkHenry became instant buddies, and to this day remain best friends—actually, more like siblings—who have celebrated every single one of their birthdays together.

Over the years, Angela and I went from our own close friendship to a major falling-out. But we never tried to separate the boys, and that has been made easier because one man, Ross, who married Angela when the kids were very young, has acted as father to both boys since soon after they started walking.

Early on, Ross and Angela and I decided to coparent the boys. This experiment was not entirely successful. MarkHenry and I often clashed. As a child he was prone to temper tantrums and often didn't comply with my rules. Ross and Angela and I each also had different ideas of what was okay and what wasn't. It often chapped me to see MarkHenry get away with behavior I would never tolerate in Henry.

Voicing my discomfort at this getting-away-with stuff only ever caused conflict among us adults. And I was often left with the feeling that my requests and desires for how the boys should be raised were either dismissed or taken with a grain of salt. This pushed the same buttons in me that my older sisters pushed whenever they dismissed my ideas, lifestyle, or beliefs and insisted their own way was better. Talk about ancient wounds.

When you let something like this build up over a dozen years, the cumulative effect can be explosive, which is precisely how it went down. One broiling evening in 2004, Henry and MarkHenry and Ross and I went to see Robert Altman's *Nashville* at the historic Paramount Theatre. This wasn't the first movie the boys had seen at the Paramount that week—there is an annual summer movie series as beloved for the theater's icy air-conditioning as the classic selection of flicks shown. A few days prior, at a different show, one of Henry's friends had irked the projectionist when he stood up and, either by accident or prankish purposefulness, stretched in front of the projector, blocking the credits with the shadows of his arms.

For this return trip to the theater, the boys again sat in the worst seats in the house, at the top of the balcony, directly in front of the projectionist's booth, while Ross and I sat a couple of dozen rows below. At the end of the show, Ross and I headed out ahead of them. I looked up, saw the boys running around in the balcony, called to them to stop, and kept moving. Ross laughed at me and I backed down, trying to be cool with Ross's less strict attitude. But you can't have it both ways, and I really should have stood my ground.

Ross and I reached the sidewalk first. Five minutes later, the boys were escorted out of the building by the manager, who informed them that if they couldn't behave, they were not welcome back. Ross felt like the lecture from the manager had been lesson enough. But something inside me snapped.

This debacle came on the heels of Henry having confessed a few days prior that he'd ingested a couple of pot brownies. I'd told Henry, from the time he was young, that if he ever fucked up, he needed to tell me and I would promise not to flip out. I did my best to honor that promise when I found out about the pot brownies, though the experience left us on shaky ground. I had hardly started to get a handle on the issue when the incident at the theater occurred.

Ross and I argue very rarely. We have disagreed on many things over the years, but for us to yell at each other is highly unusual. Yet here we stood, outside the Paramount, Ross telling me to back down as I mounted an increasingly hysterical verbal assault on my son, the culmination of my fears that, with the pot incident and now this acting out in public, the previous thirteen years of happiness and relative calm had taken a brisk run down a class IV river in a wobbly handbasket.

"He learned his lesson from the manager," Ross repeated.

"I am so fucking sick of this," I responded. "He's still on probation from the pot brownie incident!" (I meant mom probation.)

We went on, and our yelling at each other scared the kids. I was scared myself. Not of the yelling—I was raised yelling, and even though I'm working now to give up yelling, it wouldn't surprise anyone if I died yelling. But I was scared of this new rebelliousness rearing its head in a child who, up until a month before, had been almost exclusively pleasant and stayed inside the boundaries I set for him. I was also embarrassed that he'd been disrespectful, been caught by the theater manager, and pissed off the projectionist to boot. I felt like Ross was condoning their behavior. I felt ganged up on. And though I knew losing control wasn't going to fix anything, I couldn't get a grip.

In the car, I lost it.

Now, when I say *I lost it,* I am not saying I raised my voice slightly or momentarily. I am saying that thirteen years of feeling like I'm the last one anyone listens to (forty years, if you consider my childhood too) came crashing to the surface, and I fucking flipped out. I can't give you a verbatim report of what came out of my mouth, but it probably made what I'd said to the carnie manager years before seem like sweet nothings. I have this absurd memory of trying, as I screamed, to incorporate some of what I'd learned in therapy, missing the point that if you're screaming, you're not really using pointers picked up in therapy. Still, I made sure I didn't say, "*You're* stupid," though it's entirely possible that I said, "*This* is stupid!" But of course Henry wasn't picking up on whatever subtleties I was aiming for, because he quickly went from being horrified to terrified, and then he succumbed to a full-blown panic attack.

I guess that will happen when your mother is bashing her hands on the steering wheel, alternately screaming and crying. The only thing I didn't utter at full volume was this half of a sentence: "*If this happens again . . .* " It was in the context of the phrase, "If this happens again, you will never see Mark Henry again. *Never!*" That first part was the one thing I said softly—no doubt purposefully, so that I could tell myself I had said it but also instill the fear of my having not said it.

Because he didn't hear me qualify the remark with "*If this happens again . . .* " Henry was under the distinct impression that this was it—I was cutting him off from his best friend. I didn't mean to be so cruel, but surely my subconscious caused me to tone down that half of the sentence and give the impression that it really was over between them. I wasn't thinking about Henry or his feelings. All I was thinking was, *Nobody ever fucking listens to me until it is too late! Why won't anybody fucking listen to me?!*

And there was the root of it. I was yelling at Henry. I was yelling at his long-gone father. I was yelling at my long-gone father. And my sisters. And all my ex-boyfriends. And all the shitty bosses I'd ever had. And every other person on the fifteen-thousand-mile-long list of People Who Won't Listen to Me.

Henry started breathing funny, and I told him to quit being so fucking dramatic. He then yelled, very dramatically, that he wasn't being fucking dramatic, which would have been very funny except that in addition to the breathing difficulties, his legs began to shake uncontrollably.

That's when it got truly scary. His breathing grew very shallow and he couldn't stop crying those big, gulp-for-air sobs where you think your chest is going to cave in. It crossed my mind that I had induced a heart attack. I wasn't sure what to do. I drove home, found a paper bag, brought it to Henry, and demanded that he breathe into it. This did not have the desired effect. Now his arms were shaking, too. I, too, began to panic, but willed myself to remain outwardly calm.

I called my friend Sarah, a solid midwesterner and voice of reason in my life. I am not the sort of person who downplays the truth with any regularity and so on this night, when Sarah arrived to find Henry shaking so badly he couldn't stand up, I didn't mince words. I copped to the fact that my yelling had induced this response, and even Sarah couldn't find soothing words to reassure me. "Take him to the hospital," she said.

The only thing that kept me from feeling like the Über Shit of the Universe as I limped my nearly six-foot-tall "baby" into the ER that night was the fact that I had to focus on keeping him from falling over. There would be time later to hate myself. The ER personnel, notorious for leaving you sitting in the waiting room until you're pretty sure you're going to bleed to death, did not hesitate to rush Henry to the back. They wanted to know if he had taken any drugs.

Good question. I was still in my paranoid stage, the pot brownie incident being relatively recent. Had Henry, with his rambunctious friends, taken something at the theater? This required a call to Ross, who was already furious with me, and who grew no less furious on learning that my anger had landed Henry in the hospital. He checked with MarkHenry, who insisted no drugs had been taken. Nope—this was all courtesy of my temper.

The ER doctor diagnosed the problem as a panic attack that could be resolved with some tense-and-relax exercises. Somehow, she got him to listen to her instructions. He tensed. He relaxed. He tensed. He relaxed. How long did this go on? I'm not sure. Long enough for me to assess the rest of the situation and wonder if somebody was going to call Child Protective Services on me.

I can't even remember all the feelings I felt. I felt stupid. And bad. I felt angry with the boys for doing what they'd done, angry with Ross for not reinforcing me, and angry with myself for causing the attack. I felt apologetic. And I felt defensive, too. Even though getting as angry as I'd gotten wasn't anything I would ever be able to rationalize, this hadn't been some bolt from out of the blue—it had been preceded by Henry breaking rules.

The next day, like a couple who've had a horrible fight and can't bear to be together but also can't bear to be apart, Henry and I faced each other. There was a lot to sort through, but we both felt too raw to speak. We retreated to our out-of-town friends' house—we were on mail duty—and sat in this neutral territory, in the freezing cold air-conditioning (our own air-conditioning sucked), and barely spoke a word. We just watched TV, hypnotized by a poker tournament, wondering where to go from there. Kids aren't like spouses—you can't divorce them, and you can't hold stuff against them forever. Actually, you can—I always felt like my dad held everything against me, from my birth right on through every milestone I ever reached. But I didn't want that for us. I knew Henry and I needed to resolve this. We had a lot more living together to do, and I was the adult who had to steer us through. How? I had no idea.

The sitting was meditative. Slowly we thawed, still wary, still hurt, each still shocked at the other's behavior (his breaking rules, my loss of control). Eventually we got back to who we'd been before, though I can't ever go back and take away that moment in the car. The thinnest silver lining is that going through that experience was a really effective way of learning that I never wanted to go through it again. And now, when I tell Henry and his friends to quit screwing around, they typically respond more quickly, though I worry that's more out of fear than genuine respect.

I don't know where a child's capacity for forgiveness originates, but this capacity is real and incredibly stunning. Henry had no choice but to continue living with me and dealing with my fumbles. I still think I make more good decisions than bad ones, but seeing him that night in the hospital was more than a little humbling.

When Henry was very little, maybe one or two, we were splashing around at one of Austin's community kiddie pools. I was right there with him, and couldn't have glanced away for more than a second when he slipped and went under. We're talking a foot of water, a parent one inch away, and no time at all between him slipping and me grabbing him. But the incident surprised and scared both of us. For me, the surprise was a reminder of just how quickly something undesirable can happen.

Another mom approached me and smiled gently and reassuringly. She said, "I remember when that happened to me." A simple statement, but also powerful, leaving me with a feeling I've never forgotten. Not only wasn't she judging me or chastising me, she was consoling me. *This happens to all of us.*

I've always tried to pass on that compassionate sentiment when opportunities arise—a screaming baby in a supermarket, a kid falling down, any of the million moments in parenting that do not fall under the *Gosh, this Kodak moment makes me wish I had six more kids* category, which is to say a *lot* of moments in parenting. I'm not always successful in passing along the good feeling, and there are times (many) when I succumb to the commands of my holier-than-thou inner asshole and judge some fatigued, angry, nonwatchful parent as if I had never erred myself. But when I'm getting it right, I'm offering a knowing nod or glance, a few words of consolation, the camaraderie of being in that club none of us are proud to be in: Not Even Close to Perfect Parent Club.

When I teach journal writing for health, I give those in attendance little on-the-spot writing assignments to prompt spontaneous writing. Often, I ask them to list five things they love and five things they "unlove." One woman noted how her teenagers had made both the love and unlove list, and I appreciated her candor. Because that's what parenting is. When they're in utero, we can't wait to meet them. When they're brand-new and squishy and floppy-necked, we wonder how anyone could ever yell at a little baby. And then they grow up, and they turn ornery and don't follow every rule, and things get cranky and words get exchanged, and sometimes, unfortunately, the words get exchanged very, very loudly and laced with hostility.

I have certainly yelled, at times loudly, since the night of that big incident. These times, my perspective is that my son has pushed every button I have and then some. He is a genius at this because he knows me better than anyone and, with the exception of my parents, he has lived with me longer than anyone. We are separate, but we weren't always that way, and we've maintained a relationship so close it astounds others. Likewise, I know how to get right in there and piss him off. (Considering he's a teenager, this is fairly easy and can be accomplished with certain three-word commands: "Clean your room." "Change your clothes." "Do your homework.")

I know other parents go through screaming bouts with their kids. I hear about it all the time. I don't find such news as consoling as those words that came from the nice lady in the baby pool, but still I gather some comfort knowing that we aren't the only family out there that sometimes struggles with anger. When Mary Karr was on tour for her bestseller *The Liars' Club,* she reported that one thing she'd learned along the way was this: A dysfunctional family is any family with more than one member. Possibly the greatest truth ever spoken.

cathy chapaty

I never get angry.

That's what I thought for years. And in part, it was the truth. I didn't get angry. I became enraged. There was never any middle ground—and never any warning that my internal volcano was about to blow.

It was always the little things that got to me, too— like the time my cat tore the foam out of my Walkman headphones. Nothing could have prepared him for the rampage that followed. And nothing could have prepared me, either. I don't remember having had a particularly bad time at work that day. I wasn't going through a breakup. My bills were paid, I had food in the fridge, and my little Hyundai Excel was running smoothly. Nothing major seemed to be wrong, but when I walked into the living room of my town house that day after work and saw those little pieces of black foam all over my teal carpet, I flipped out. I screamed at Pica, chasing him from room to room, upstairs, downstairs, and back upstairs again until I was out of breath and in tears. If I could have caught him, I would have killed him. But God bless Pica, he was always too fast for me.

It didn't matter whether it was spring or fall, morning or night. I didn't act any different when the moon was full or new. Rage periodically peaked, out of nowhere. Once, for example, I brought a Christmas tree home and flew into an anger fit because the trunk was too large for the stand. My solution to this dilemma was innocent enough: I marched into the kitchen and grabbed the big, honkin' knife I'd used to carve my first Thanksgiving Day turkey, just a week before. Whoever heard of taking a Christmas tree back for exchange, anyway?

In the middle of that same town house living room, I began shaving the bark off the trunk.

Shaving, shaving, shaving, shaving.

I was focused. The knife was sharp. The bark sliced off easily. After a while, I stopped, lifted the tree, and again placed it in the center of the stand.

It still didn't fit.

I let out a huge sigh—and then began shaving again, this time at a quicker pace.

Shaving, shaving, shaving, shaving.

I was starting to resent the tree, the holiday season, and my father for having come home drunk so many times on Christmas Eve.

Eventually I stopped again and tried once more to place the trunk into the stand—hoping, praying, that it would fit.

It didn't.

"Damn it! Shit!"

I grabbed the trunk and attacked.

Shaving, shaving, shaving, shaving, shaving, shaving, shaving.

Screaming, screaming, screaming, screaming, screaming, screaming, screaming.

I'd turned into a potty-mouthed Tasmanian devil. And it wasn't until the sight of blood caught my eye that I stopped. In my rage-daze, I had sliced my thumb wide open. There was blood—and sap—on my hands, my clothes, and that beautiful teal carpet.

And in the end, the tree still didn't fit.

I opened the patio door, hoisted that freakin' tree over my shoulders, and hurled it outside, where it stayed—

looking rather healthy despite the warm tropical temperatures—until mid-January.

It took me years to understand that the numbness I had lived with for years was called depression, and that those little rage attacks happened because I was unable to appropriately express anger.

And it took me years to realize that I usually lost my temper and sanity when I realized I'd spent money on something I didn't want, or when someone didn't listen to or acknowledge my expressed needs or wishes. For instance, one time I ordered a chili cheese dog from a fast food joint and specifically told the counter boy not to put mustard on it. As I climbed the stairs toward my new apartment, I could smell the odor of French's permeating the bag.

When I sat down in my favorite living room chair to eat my dinner, I opened the bag, and I was right: There was mustard on my dang chili cheese dog.

"Damn it! Shit!"

Seething, I wrapped my palms around that hot dog and squeezed, trying to choke the mustard-laden life out of the bun, the wiener—the fast food joint itself. I screamed. I tore at the bun. I shook the wiener. And it wasn't until the sight of chili on my walls caught my eye that I realized I'd done it again.

While cleaning chili off my chair and the walls (chili, by the way, is a bitch to get off eggshell white), I realized it was unwise for me to continue to spin off at will. I had been lucky so far—no one had ever been present to witness my ugly rage attacks, or been the target of my wrath. I meditated about it at my prayer table that night, and then tried to get some sleep, despite the fact that I could still smell the chili on the walls.

Funny things happen when you speak your truth

out loud. Something amazing always happens. Someone listens. And that night, I had my first anger dream. I was yelling at my mom and sisters for not saving me a seat at a restaurant table. They'd forgotten all about me. I was so hurt, and was telling them things I had always wanted to say, but had been too insecure or scared to verbalize. I awoke emotionally exhausted, but at the same time oddly relieved.

In the years since, I've had many other anger dreams, too many to count. Many times, I've told Daddy how hurt I was that he'd spent so many years of my childhood wasted on Jim Beam. Other times, I've told Mamma to stop trying to run my life. In an odd way, the dreams have allowed me to get all the hurt, frustration, and longtime resentment toward friends and family members out of my body without ruining current relationships. And I relate to Mamma and other family members much better now.

It was ten years before I dared get another live Christmas tree, and about ten months before I risked ordering a chili cheese dog again. But I learned some important lessons. Like, if I get a huge tree, Wal-Mart probably has the size stand that I need. And if the first thing someone asks me after my chili cheese dog order is "Do you want mustard on that?" it's a good idea to thank the counter person and walk out. And I learned that as long as I had Pica, or any other animal, I should put my Walkman headphones out of reach—or start running without a Walkman.

My life is much more balanced today. I continue to have anger dreams, but now in my waking life I'm able to express frustration and anger in the moment, not years later. One of my favorite waking-anger moments was when my best friend, Susan, and I got into a fight at a boxing match. It was a petty argument that we both got over before the last punch of the evening (the boxers', not ours). But it was the first time I realized that I could be mad at someone I loved, and they wouldn't necessarily go away.

So now when I'm angry, I don't emotionally go away either.

Cathy Chapaty is a tae kwon do instructor and the owner of the Tao of Texas Martial Arts Institute in Austin. A passionate teacher who specializes in youth character development, Cathy is the author of several essays on children and the martial arts.

jill parrish

Bitch in the Blue PT Cruiser

I can often slough off irritating, annoying, or selfish
people—except, I've discovered, when they mess with
my niece and nephew. I don't have kids of my own, but
I'm blessed with an exceptionally generous sister who has
shared her children with me, literally from the moment
they drew their first breaths. Protecting Amy and Eric (and
my precious time with them) brings out the mother-bear
instinct in me.

So when the bitch in the blue PT Cruiser ignored
my signal, reverse lights, and moving vehicle and zipped
into the prime parallel parking space in front of Gregory
Gym—thus ensuring Eric and I would be late to Amy's
final basketball game of the season, because we'd have
to trudge across what felt like the entire back forty of the
University of Texas campus in hundred-degree heat—I
did what every self-respecting mother bear would do: I
got out of my car and ripped her head off. Figuratively,
of course—but if I had been sporting razor-sharp grizzly
bear claws, I would probably be writing this in a six-foot-
by-six-foot cell.

The woman knew exactly what she'd done. She
responded to my disbelieving question, "Didn't you see
that I was backing into this spot?" with a flippant "Yeah,
I did. Sorry!" Then she smiled and ran off to her destination. Of course I had to scream, *"Bitch!"* at the top of my
lungs and, feeling that the fairly tame expletive didn't
quite capture the moment, follow it with an equally loud
"Cunt!" Which was the exact point when I remembered

my sweet, innocent nephew and looked down to see him calmly sitting in the backseat of my car with a confused look on his face, staring at his hippie aunt Jill losing her shit in the middle of the street.

It's not that I'd never cursed in front of Eric, but I don't think I'd ever used the *B* word and I had certainly never used the *C* word. In fact, I don't know that I'd ever called anyone a cunt before in my life. Even in my blindingly angry state I remember debating the political correctness of the word, and I surprised myself by being willing to say it, let alone scream it, in front of fifty coeds. I was *so pissed!*

But then came the hardest part—the realization that I wouldn't be a good aunt unless I turned this into a life lesson for my nephew, who was quietly waiting for me, uncertain of what he should say or do. I took a deep breath, returned to the car, and calmly stated that there were people in this world who could be very mean and very rude, and that this was a perfect example of selfishness. And, by the way, not such a great example of how to handle being angry . . .

I parked the car and spent the twenty-minute walk to the gym (uphill, by the way, and did I mention that it was a hundred degrees out?) talking to my nephew about forgiveness and how hard it is to stay calm when you're really angry. All the while, I was strategically positioning my keys in my hand so I could scrape the shit out of that goddamned Cruiser when we walked past it. But alas, my nephew asked why I was walking so close to the mean lady's car. And he wouldn't take his eyes off me, even for a second!

Conflicting feelings of guilt and anger battled in my head. Finally succumbing to the guilt and attempting to salvage my last shred of self-respect, I walked away from the car, holding Eric's hand as we crossed the street. I fantasized about what I would say if I happened upon the driver in Gregory Gym. With a straight face, I'd walk up to the bitch and inform her that someone had keyed the shit out of her car. Her eyes would narrow with anger, and through gritted teeth she'd say, "That's a brand-new car!" to which I'd flippantly reply, "Yeah, I know. Sorry!"

Dragged to Austin kicking and screaming when she was sixteen, **Jill Parrish** is now grateful, twenty years later, for her parents' decision to uproot the family. A fan of books, music, and international travel, Jill loves returning home to her husband and four cats, all of whom happily reside in Austin.

portrait 3

In-Laws

I have a tendency to fall in love with entire families, particularly those that have produced the men I've loved. Perhaps in reality these instances were less of a falling in love and more of a desire to please these people and ingratiate myself, to somehow secure a relationship with their son/brother. Possibly it was a desire to find a new family to take the place of my biological family, from whom I distanced myself at eighteen and still feel more apart from than together with. Probably, both are true.

I'm hardly unique in this adopt-and-be-adopted-by quest for family. There is no shortage of women of a certain age who, prefeminism (and postfeminism, come to think of it), married very young to escape their biological families. Funny (not really) how, in a pattern more pronounced than paisley, so many of us spend so much time trying to get away from a family we consider the source of aggravation, and then we go out and try to find similar dynamics in someone else's family.

Even recognizing this as a repeating scenario in my life, I can still say, with seventeen years to reflect back, that when I met the O'Reillys it really was love (and infatuation) at first sight. I met Sean first, when we both lived in Knoxville, Tennessee. He moved back to Saint Louis, where I stopped to see him during a road trip. On this short stop, I revealed the longing I'd harbored for him for some time.

He responded that he, too, found me quite attractive, but he thought I was better suited to his brother. Thus began the longest, most intense, most joyful, and most agonizing chapter of my life, a chapter I'm still writing. Michael O'Reilly was tall, young, redheaded, and leaning against his parents' kitchen counter when I met him. I fell for him in fifteen minutes, possibly less.

The parents O'Reilly were out of town, a signal to their six adult children to each invite a few friends over to the house, break into the liquor closet, and throw a party reminiscent of high school, which we'd all departed years prior. I couldn't believe my luck—stumbling into six physically gorgeous siblings who shared my love of both sarcasm and heavy drinking. We drank, we snarked, we drank, we barbed, we drank, and we laughed our witty little smart asses off.

Less than six months later, I revisited that city, that house, and that man. Again, his parents were gone, the kids were having a party—this one to celebrate Halloween—and my love for all of them grew. In January of the following year—on the night of my twenty-fifth birthday—Michael came to Knoxville for my party, and we officially paired off. In February I flew to Saint Louis to see him for a passionate Valentine's Day.

On this trip, Michael's sister Annie—a woman with alabaster Irish skin, huge blue eyes, curly strawberry blond hair, and cheekbones higher than some kitten stuck in a tree—took me into her confidence. She loved me, she knew I loved her brother, and (she let me know in no uncertain words) if I ever hurt him, she would kill me.

If I'd been smarter, I would've asked her to clarify her threats and definitions. As it happened, though, I was floating on the big Cloud O' Love, and I took her drunken proclamation, processed it with drunken ears, and decided we were all in love with each other (2gether 4ever, like in a yearbook autograph).

In the four years I spent with Michael, we laughed a lot, drank a lot, and fought a good deal, though my brain chooses not to remember many of those incidents clearly. We also had a baby and named him Henry, and did our best to raise him together until it became apparent that Michael's drinking was precluding his ability to be a responsible father. Actually, we stayed together even after that, because it took me a long time to face these truths: (1) The man I loved was totally fucked up; (2) I would have to raise our baby on my own.

I'll talk about Michael's near-death drinking saga, and eventual sobriety after many stints in rehab, later. For now, I want to talk about his parents and his sister Annie, she of the threatening sort of love.

Annie had a habit of announcing she was leaving Saint Louis and moving elsewhere at least once a year. Typically these "moves" amounted to two or three months of couch surfing in another city, followed by her allegedly triumphant return to the Midwest. Sometimes it seemed these bon-voyage and welcome-home parties were the real point—celebratory excuses to drink that much more than we consumed during the run-of-the-mill stupors we pursued each night.

In 1991, fed up with Saint Louis, I decided to make a real move, which would turn out to be permanent. Henry and I flew to Austin and set up house in a shitty apartment, to be joined a month later by Michael, after he'd wrapped up some things in Missouri. Before long we moved from the shitty apartment to a shitty rental house, which prompted Annie to announce she was moving to Texas to live with us.

I don't recall much, if any, rent coming in from our new "roommate." And by this point Annie's charm had long since worn off for me. Her antics, in my house and out in public, were annoying at best and a big embarrassment at worst. A small but telling example comes immediately to mind: Out drinking one night, Annie knocked over her mug of beer and made no move to do anything about it, instead sitting and watching as it spilled everywhere, waiting for the rest of us to leap to attention and clean up her mess.

A bigger example: Mind you, my judgment was often poor (to make an understatement) and the concept of *having boundaries* was far, far from my sight line. So when some acquaintances of mine from work—let's politely call them the Very Strange Family—asked to stay with us for a few days as they prepared to leave town, I didn't know how to say no.

Our house was already pretty nuts. Besides Michael, Henry, Annie, and me, Paula (my old college roommate and the one friend I'd already had in Austin when I moved down) was living with us. Michael and Paula and I worked at the Magnolia Cafe, a twenty-four-hour place three blocks away. So the house was an ongoing circus: People dropped by at all hours with postshift cases of beer and cartons of cigarettes, plopping down on the couch to bitch about work, catch up on bad TV, and smoke.

I suppose Annie had her limits, and the addition of the Very Strange Family proved her undoing. She insisted I kick them out. Of *my* house. I was the primary breadwinner, the one person holding the place together, the most responsible by virtue of the fact that I "only" drank a six pack per night.

While on a gut level I agreed with Annie that letting the Very Strange Family stay with us had been a Very Terrible Idea, her proprietary attitude pissed me off. Who the hell was she to tell me what to do? She herself had brought at least one stranger home to spend the night without consulting me, and it was *my* house.

I was furious with Annie and the situation and, as usual, did not have the tools to deal with my feelings or circumstances. Michael, in a rare assertive move, stepped in and told the Very Strange Family they really needed to hit the road. (Thankfully, he did this before the family matriarch had the chance to force upon me the homemade tattoo she adamantly insisted would be my thank-you gift for having her. God knows, with my then-limited boundaries, what the hell I would've ended up with as a permanent souvenir.)

During this time, I came home from work one day while a major Texas storm brewed overheard. Annie and Henry were nowhere to be found. Panicked and pissed, I set off in the car to find them. Annie was a ways up the road, on a walk, with *my* son. And she was wearing one of *my* T-shirts. In the car, she lectured me about boundaries and the Very Strange Family. I wanted to yell, *You bitch. You're wearing my shirt and you took my kid without telling me, and you're telling* me *what boundaries are?*

My anger with Annie grew exponentially over the years—even after she finally left us to "move back" to Saint Louis—but it didn't come to a head until about a dozen years later, in the fall of 2004. By this point, I was sober, I'd been through therapy, and I had finally learned to recognize my limits and make choices that didn't leave me feeling constantly uncomfortable.

Part of my new mind-set meant I no longer bent over backward to seek the approval of Michael's parents—approval I'd pursued from the moment I met them until a good ten years after Michael left me to raise our son alone and without the benefit of child support. As a result, my trips to Saint Louis, which I'd formerly taken regularly (and at considerable expense) in hopes of keeping Henry connected with that side of the family, had come to a halt.

I'd be lying if I didn't admit that an ulterior motive for these trips had been to offer an unspoken *Oh yeah? Well, fuck you, I can too raise this kid on my own despite all your predictions to the contrary.* Because Michael's parents certainly had predicted I would fail, from the moment they learned I was pregnant.

It's sadly common for us to most want to impress those least impressed with us, those least deserving of our attention. And it's sad, too, the amount of energy we waste on these people. How could I have ever thought (or wished) that this family would suddenly snap to, recognize my achievements, and praise me? And yet I strove to achieve this goal, by any means necessary: passive-aggressiveness, aggressive-aggressiveness—I even once, in a desperate act of foolishness that could have easily gotten Henry and me killed, drove us from Austin to Saint Louis, through a deadly ice storm, to see Michael and his family one Christmas Day.

In October of 2004 an invitation arrived in the mail for Henry and me, announcing that Annie (whom I had by then begun referring to as the Diva) was getting married. Initially, I was excited, in part because no matter how pissed off and disenchanted I'd grown with the O'Reillys over the years, I am a hopeless (if often cynical) romantic; I imagined for a moment that this could be a joyous occasion where we could all see each other and put the past behind us.

That sense lasted about thirty seconds. Okay, maybe two weeks. Then a thought crept into my mind: I decided that Annie had only invited me because she couldn't think of a way to just invite Henry. *I mean, really, Spike,* I thought, *think about your relationship with her. You can't stand her.*

My mind flooded with countless thoughtless, aggravating things she'd done to me. Memories of everything all the O'Reillys had done to aggravate me filled my mind. Annie loved to sweep Henry away from me whenever I brought him to Saint Louis—she'd take him out, spoil him, and never give me a clear idea of where they were going or when they'd be back. I had the distinct feeling that she and the rest of the clan attributed Henry's being such a good kid to the fact that he had some of their DNA in his system, that this goodness had nothing to do with how I had raised him. Annie still drank; having been out drinking with her on more than a few occasions, I knew she'd drink regardless of the time of day, and I worried she'd drive with Henry in the car after she'd been drinking.

My old self-righteousness flared. But instead of making a swift, true-to-the-heart decision followed by the proclamation, *Sorry, we can't make it to the wedding after all,* I began to waffle on whether or not we would attend. I thought about sending Henry by himself. I couldn't decide. This led to an email exchange of which I am not proud.

Having an email fight with Annie was as close as I could get to having a drunken brawl with her. For those who are lucky enough not to know drunken arguments firsthand, allow me to shed a little light: When drinkers communicate, they'll often hurl out what they really think only while they're drinking, perhaps because they can back down the next day and deny they said anything, or at least blame their outburst on the booze. Similarly, with email, you can always accuse the recipient of not getting your tone, of misinterpreting you, and blame the whole thing on virtual miscommunication, even if you said precisely what you meant.

The exchange started out respectfully enough, with a save-the-date request. I made the mistake of RSVPing a yes without thinking hard enough about what attending would mean to me, emotionally and financially. I then backed out, and explained that while Henry's soccer schedule might preclude him attending the afternoon ceremony (for which Annie wanted him to play guitar), perhaps he could hop on a direct flight after the game and make the evening reception. (It might seem odd to prioritize a soccer game before a wedding, but as I saw it soccer had played a pivotal, steady role in Henry's childhood, whereas the paternal side of his family had not.)

Next came the discussion of finances. I told Annie I'd looked into airfares, they were higher than I expected, and that might be a problem. She offered to help pay. I set aside the feeling that I might be beholden to her for this, and responded, Yes, it would help for her to kick in some money. This was the first time I had ever asked an O'Reilly, other than Michael, for financial help. And the O'Reillys had never offered us a cent of support (outside of a little gas money when I'd drive Henry eighteen hundred miles round trip to see them).

Next, Annie told me she would call the airline and put *part* of Henry's ticket on her credit card. She was sorry, she said, but she just didn't have any cash, so this was how we'd have to do it. I explained to her that no airline would allow her to partially pay with a credit card, and then I suggested that she put the whole fare on her card and talk to Michael about reimbursing her for part of it. At that point I also considered a question a friend posed to me: *Why do they expect you to pay for Henry to go to his father's sister's wedding?*

Because I had known Annie for so many years, because I'd witnessed her, up close, freeloading, and because I knew she could finagle and flirt and diva her way into getting anything she wanted with very little effort, my irritation with her quickly expanded to fill up my days. I decided that the whole "partial payment with a credit card" deal was her way of pretending to offer help without actually offering help. More passive-aggressiveness from a passive-aggressive expert.

Bam: I was back to the bad place, the place I really had tried to move from, the place where I walked around resenting the hell out of Michael's family.

As my patience waned, my email tone became shorter—which was when Annie told me I needed to spend the small child-support check that Michael had just sent me on a plane ticket for Henry. (This child support was a new thing, something Michael had started sending when he got sober.) Again, I need to own up to something here: I feel certain that I asked Michael if he would send me extra money to help finance Henry's trip. And he did send some money, but what he sent I needed to cover day-to-day expenses. There wasn't enough extra to put toward a ticket. The $200 he sent was money I needed to put toward bills and food. I also knew that Henry's grandparents had plenty of money, and I was certain they were blowing an assload of it on their princess's wedding. And there I went, angrier still. Here is what I wrote to Annie, after explaining the situation with the child support funds:

> *I have $56 in my bank account. . . . I don't have enough
> to cover the ticket and it has to be purchased by Saturday
> morning. Maybe your parents would be willing to spring
> for it. I know you have a lot of things to deal with but I
> don't know what else to tell you. I thought my freelance
> check would be here by now. It isn't. And I added up
> my bills—when it does arrive, 90 percent of it is spoken
> for. Any solution you can come up with by Friday night
> would be most appreciated.*

By that point, I was bad-mouthing her to anyone who would listen to me, but I still hadn't fully confronted her or honestly spoken my mind. I was stuck in a trap. I'd worked very hard to be a better, calmer person, but just as my own family would send me hurtling back to ancient dynamics, I also re-entered the O'Reilly time warp without even noticing at first. I wrote:

I haven't booked the flight yet. I don't even know if I can make this happen now. Please don't try booking a flight for him, as I am particular about what airline he flies on and I also have to check regulations. Since he is thirteen he usually has to pay $80 extra for an escort, and there is no way around that. Believe me, I have tried.

Now here's where we really get into interpretation of tone. What Annie wrote next, if read by an outsider, an expert, a counselor, or a judge—really, anyone who didn't know her, or me, or our relationship—would probably be interpreted as a very straightforward note, no hidden agenda. I read passive-aggressiveness all over it:

Since you want to reserve the flight for him yourself, I will wait until you do so, so you can then send me the itinerary, if you do in fact still want to reserve a ticket. I can't really do anything here until you reserve something . . . if this becomes too problematic, do what is easiest and least stressful for you.

Exasperated—angry with Annie for once again trying to have the world bow to her feet (and for all the other times she'd tried), and even angrier with her family—I no longer reined myself in. I emailed her again:

I will know tomorrow whether or not Henry will be coming. I would just like to say I wish you hadn't made an offer to help pay only to withdraw the offer. It has caused me stress. Michael is attempting to resolve the situation. If

Henry can be there, he'll be there. I can't use the child
support check for plane tickets. As I have for the past
fourteen years (entirely at my expense), I will do the best
I can to arrange for Henry to spend time with your family.
I don't think it's unreasonable for me to expect your family
to pay for the ticket since this is an O'Reilly family event.
I have spent many thousands of dollars over the years
delivering Henry to the O'Reilly doorstep with no help
from anyone up there. I was going to attempt to do this
again for your sudden wedding. . . . I hope you can try to
see it from my perspective. . . . Since no one in your family
has offered any sort of financial assistance to Henry in
the past, I had been trained to expect nothing. But then I
woke up and decided if y'all would like Henry at the wed-
ding, I'm sure you can find a way to pay for his travel.

I knew that Annie must have thought I was being selfish and
stingy with Henry, and clearly I was harboring piles and piles of
resentment over many past pains. As with so many situations in life,
this altercation was about so much more than what it seemed to be
about. Annie responded:

I have only read the first three lines of your email and I
have decided it's in my best interest not to continue as it's
making me apoplectic, upset, and very, very anxious. Since
you're having such tremendous difficulty understanding
my intentions, perhaps we should discontinue emailing and
rather talk on the phone, where I would hope the lines of
communication will be less confusing for you.

I responded:

This is my last email. In no way am I confused. You offered
to help pay for the ticket. Then you said you would put

"some of it" on your credit card. We have both traveled
extensively by plane. And we both know you can't put
"some of" a ticket on a credit card. . . . I only think one
of us deserves "apoplectic," as you so dramatically put it.
And I don't think it's you. Please just stop emailing me. If
Henry can be there, he'll be there. If not, he'll send you his
best wishes, I'm sure.

And then, finally, the Diva showed her true colors:

Again, the confusion seems to swirl thick in your head.
In this very email that you sent me, you say that I offered
to help pay for the ticket and that I would gladly put part
of it on my charge card. While I have traveled consider-
ably I am not at all aware that airlines do NOT offer the
opportunity for more than one party to pay for a ticket.
It seems only natural that this would be an available
option, as people are very often flying when other people
pay for their tickets. And no, I don't think you should be
apoplectic in the least, and I can only imagine that you
arrived at this mental state because you are incapable
of seeing anything other than your own hysterically self-
absorbed picture. For you to be apoplectic seems bizarre
and strange given that Chris and I have offered to help
pay for Henry to come to our wedding . . . and this is no
small gesture, as we are both insolvent. . . . You're mad
that we wanted to help pay? I am truly perplexed. My
dad is looking into plane tickets . . . he told me today
that he wants to fully pay for Henry's ticket. Seeing that
time is of the essence I would heartily recommend that
you figure the out the logistics of what airline you would
like him to fly on—today, as the prices will (as you know
as a seasoned traveler) rise exponentially with each
passing day. From now on just contact my parents about

Henry's travel plans . . . I will gladly comply with your
wish to stop emailing you.

I quit mincing words:

Fuck you. For an idea of who the self-absorbed party is,
might I suggest you consult a mirror. You're probably
already in front of one.

Annie insisted on the last word:

Wow . . . "fuck you." That's not terribly original. I would
have expected much better coming from a widely published
"writer" such as yourself. Your creative juices don't really
seem to be flowing today. Good luck with that, though.
Gotta go, my mirror is calling me.

How did we get to this point? Why? What happened to the two
drunken girls sitting in a car on a cold winter night in Saint Louis in
1989, confessing their love for each other and Michael?

I really don't like reading the above exchange. It embarrasses
me. And yet my hindsight is better than 20/20 and I am trying to cut
myself some slack here. A therapist could've cut through the shit a
lot quicker than I was able to in my series of pissed-off emails. I can
see now the most obvious source of my pain: Just as I wanted pure
love for myself, I wanted it for my son. I especially wanted it from the
people least inclined to offer it to him, at least by my estimation: his
father's relatives.

I'm sure they would contest this. And here's a mixed message:
Though she's pissed me off interminably over the years, Annie has
always stayed in touch with Henry, bought him gifts, and done things
with him that have brought him joy. Thus, Henry's perspective might
well be, *Why is my mom bitching about my nice aunt? Must she com-*
plain about everything?

Because Henry was in utero at the time, he'll never fully comprehend the distress his grandparents showed at his conception. I can understand this stress now—Michael and I were young, drunk, stupid, broke, and uninsured. But his parents' disapproval and lack of support certainly didn't help matters.

And so the seed of anger rooted, deeper and deeper, and grew into a monster weed that I only attempted to pull out, too late and unsuccessfully, when Annie invited us to her wedding. Money was the metaphor, and it's possible I came off looking cheap or like a money-grubber. But money was only part of the equation. I wished things had turned out differently, and that Michael's parents were more demonstrative, and that love could be salvaged in the aftermath of my separation from their son.

And, of course, deeper still, I wished that things between Michael and me had worked out, and that the instant love I'd felt for him and his family that sticky summer evening when we drank pilfered warm Schaefer beers in his parents' driveway could have grown and transcended and kept us all together.

But it couldn't, and it didn't, and until I could put distance between myself and that wedding, I was the vision of pissed off, pure and distilled.

kathie goldsmith

It must sound evil of me to admit that I am troubled by forgiveness, but it's not what it sounds like. I have simply realized that after forty years of living, I don't always know what forgiveness is.

I thought I knew. I thought I knew how to ask for it and how to give it. There are steps: you identify the problem and your role in it; you offer a sincere apology and say that you will try to better your ways; and lastly, you remember your word and attempt to not make the same mistake twice.

Easy, right?

As a substitute teacher while in graduate school, I decided that the greatest contribution I could make to society was to try to teach my students how to solve a problem and forgive the offending party. It's hard to turn the world in a one-day subbing gig, but I attempted to teach them that if nothing else.

Almost daily, Child A (the bully), Child B (the downtrodden), and I (the sage) would be somewhere on the playground going through *the forgiveness steps*. My efforts were usually met by snickers and sneers, but I didn't care. By the end, both students would run off and laugh at me, united in their amusement of me, but united nonetheless.

As adults and children, asking for forgiveness can be a hard thing to do. Admittedly awkward at times, I personally find that eating crow can be liberating, and a great vehicle for growth.

I guess I should tell my story. The simplest version

is that my twelve-year-old (at the time) stepdaughter was having a fit over something very insignificant involving misplaced blame and threatened to let my very beloved dog out into the street. Three days later she made good on her threat, and my dog was killed by a car. This wasn't any dog. This was a dog with which I shared a major dog love. She comforted me during my divorce, the death of my father, a miscarriage, and some other pretty serious personal tribulations. This dog was family, friend, and a deeply loved companion.

I was seven months pregnant at the time, and the loss was devastating and almost more than I could bear. I still have teary-eyed memories of my swollen-bellied self in the backyard, my face buried in the freshly washed but bloodied fur of my stiff pup, wailing inconsolably while my husband dug a grave.

I could not speak to my stepdaughter and could hardly be in the same room with her for weeks.

I cannot say that we had a great relationship before the incident. When I spoke to her she would ignore me or look right through me. It wasn't bad; it was just empty. It was superficial and not much more.

If it were a pure accident, maybe things would have been different. I know that she did not mean for my dog to get killed, but she did let her out on purpose. She admitted that at first, but later changed her story and stated that she "forgot" we had dogs in the backyard.

When it happened, I insisted that she get therapy. This was not her first offense, but it was her worst offense. I did not want my pain or my dog's death to be in vain. I would never be okay with the fact that it happened, but I at least hoped that therapy would get her attention and would instill some sort of change in her. I wanted to see her learn how to manage her anger better, and blame less, and learn something about the relationship between one's actions and the consequences of those actions.

She did go to a couple of sessions, but nothing really came of them. My grief was debilitating, and during that time she became very quiet and inward around the house. Our house was shrouded in sadness and anger. It was inescapable; it devoured all who entered.

Once my grieving subsided enough that I could again function as part of the family, she went right back to being her old self. On the first day I was able to act normal, it opened the window for her to act normal, her kind of normal, too.

She was grounded for a month after this incident. Toward the end, she tried to talk her father into shortening her grounding. When that didn't work, she tried to gain me as an ally to try to talk him into shortening it. The audacity of asking me to do that was unfathomable to me.

So nothing has changed since that day twenty-two months ago. My stepdaughter usually ignores me when I greet her or ask her questions, she's still disrespectful to her father, and she still blames others for her actions. Nothing was learned from our tragedy. It was, and I had prayed it wouldn't be, completely in vain.

I have not forgiven her. I have moved on, but that's different. I don't know how to forgive her when she doesn't admit to her role in what happened, she still misplaces blame, and has now completely rewritten the story. (She recently told her father that she never understood why she was grounded when *her* dog died. Hearing those words burned my heart.)

How do you forgive someone for hurting you when they don't ask for your forgiveness? When they don't admit their actions? When you are not sure that they wouldn't be equally irresponsible with your feelings all over again?

This is my dilemma.

Despite the fact that it's been months since Molly was killed, I still cannot cross that bridge. Should I forgive my stepdaughter simply because she is a child? What is gained from that? Should I better accept that it happened because she is a child? Am I letting her off the hook for seeing it like this? Maybe. It clouds my vision and makes it difficult for me to relish the good in her—and there is good in her. I don't know how to make it right. For now, the only thing I know how to do is hope that everything will change one day. So hope is what I do.

Kathie Goldsmith is an Usborne Books consultant and recruiter in Austin, Texas. She loves music, nature, books, her town, and her family, and wants to help all desiring moms work at home.

michelle langmead

Out, Damn Spot

Let me write this right now. Right now, while I'm angry. My anger seems slippery, hard to define in retrospect. But now, in the moment, I recognize the feelings. My heart is fluttering, my stomach is unsettled, my movements are hurried and careless, my patience is poor, and I want to beat the dog and kick the cat (though I won't) for getting underfoot as I race in the front door. This anger is repetitive. I am feeling bullied by an individual. An ex-husband, to be exact. Via email.

In the past he's also done it in person, by letter, and by telephone. In every instance, I want to fling the moment away like a dying bug that has landed in my lap. I want to flee. But then I also want to scream back my defense. I feel so wronged, so misunderstood, so unjustly condemned. It all reeks of irrelevance and the rabid tirade of a crazy person.

I know what he writes and says is untrue. I can *know* that, but because it is *out there,* I don't know to whom I should defend myself. He doesn't care if he's right or wrong. My friends don't want to listen to more of the same, and could they ever really get *it* without being witness to *it* anyway? I move right into hopelessness.

There is no way to right this wrong—no way to convince a crazy person filled with hate and persecutory delusions that I am not who he thinks I am. And even if I could, to what end? I can take item by item the lies that he says and dispute each one. But then I am allowing him to be my judge and jury. So my anger becomes something

Pissed Off

akin to an anxiety attack. He is hurting me, and I can't make him stop. I am protective of myself, and yet an attempt to defend myself would fall on deaf ears.

So I should take the high road, leave these unjustices *out there,* and move on. Is my anger really a protective mechanism, then? It tells me I am uncomfortable and something is amiss, so I need to change my environment. I did that when we divorced, only not really. It followed me, and I feel stalked and bullied by his vengeful anger and assault of lies. So that leads me back to hopelessness: all this adrenaline, and no one to punch.

And then something distracts me from myself, and the anger goes away. My heart stops fluttering, my panic subsides, my arm is no longer caught in a trap preventing my escape. I'm not even angry enough to call him up and confront his behavior. The rage just goes away, until it catches me by surprise the next time. Is that adaptive behavior, as one friend says? Preventing me from living a life of misery? Or is it a sign of sagging self-esteem? Have I finally learned that nothing will change and any attempt to change things is futile, thereby marking me a pathological sap?

Michelle Langmead is the beleaguered single mother of Jack and Abby, ages six and four. By virtue of her education and years of toil, she has been deemed a licensed clinical social worker by the state of Texas. She has a thriving psychotherapy and life-coaching practice in Austin, Texas.

robin bradford

Strong

In her matching pink slacks and top, reading glasses
perched in her black hair, my mother looked like a country-
club wife after a late-night bridge game. She hugged me
close, then pushed a box of hefty-size trash bags into my
hands. She'd been dying to do this for years—how she'd
love to jam them full of Gram's pastel skeins of acrylic
yarn, her towels thin with wear, her Barbra Streisand
records, and her hand-painted Ukrainian eggs. She would
cram in the furniture if she could. It was the day after
Gram's funeral, and this was what we'd come to. Not only
were we speaking after nine months of silence, we were
rescuing my grandmother's belongings from the rising tide
of her death.

There's a sadness in objects that no longer have an
owner. What would become of this old jar of nails, plaster
still clinging to the sharp points, without my grandmother?
Who would tend to these green rubber bands soiled by the
newsprint of the papers around which they arrived? Who
would iron these scraps of foil with the flat of a hand?
Even the plastic bags, washed out and dried, air pushed
out, folded, some turning yellow because they'd been
saved so long, made me sad. They'd once had a purpose—
to protect. I imagined that years ago, one of them had
served its noble purpose wrapped around my sandwich on
a picnic Gram took me on while my mother worked.

With a loud *smack* my mother unfurled a black
garbage bag big enough for me to crawl into. Gingerly, I
dumped in the nails whose holes had been filled and for-

gotten, along with the other assorted collections that my grandmother grew, inspired at first by poverty, but later, I think, with a presentiment of environmentalism.

"Better save some of the bigger ones," my mother said as I knelt before a drawer of plastic bags. "For the yard sale."

I put aside maybe half of everything that belonged to my grandmother, the lucky half that would have a new life.

On the kitchen table my mother made a single pile of stained-glass tools and craft supplies, as if among her mother's things these alone were saintly and valuable. She told me to dial the phone number my grandmother had carefully written out and taped to the handle of her soldering iron: the Stained Glass Shack. Their line was busy. I looked at the familiar handwriting and considered that its particular slant had died as well.

"Jesus! I guess this crap'll sell!" my mother said to the pile of junk.

I hadn't visited my grandmother at the hospital. She wasn't there long before she died, and even then, according to the doctors and my aunt, she was already gone. But the reason I didn't come is that it would have meant speaking to my mother, after nearly a year of silence that had been my doing. The decision to divorce my mother had snapped into my vision when I saw her on my twenty-ninth birthday, when her impatience and disappointment and utter sadness about things that most often had nothing to do with me bloomed into a roaring rage. I was weary and weak and lame with three decades of her hurling her loss at me. But for just one moment I was strong as nails. I had written her a letter that said to please leave me alone.

My grandmother made my mother and me who we were. After her roughneck husband abandoned them when my mother was ten, she moved her small family to

Oklahoma to be closer to her sister. Gram was a single do-it-yourself mom before the era of TV dinners. She built model airplanes and climbed trees to rescue the family cat, which was always named Kitty Clover. The last time we'd talked on the phone, I'd told Gram that my mother and I weren't speaking.

"There was always something off about your mother," she said.

I knew my mother viewed these drawers' contents—neatly folded dishtowels, brand-new-looking twenty-year-old suitcases, rows of square-toed 1970s shoes that my grandmother thought might have their comeback—as proof that her mother was insane. Of all the statements my mother would repeat when I was growing up, the one that got the most use was "Well, at least I'm not like your grandmother." I agreed. They were nothing alike.

Gram wore African shirts, rode a three-wheeled bike, and played a wooden recorder in her car while she waited for me to finish cheerleading practice. In the 1950s, when the family lived in Okmulgee, she'd crossed over into "colored town" when the black doctor needed a nurse. She was a horrible cook and had little good to say about the thirty years she worked at St. John's Hospital, but she served on the city's commission on aging and was a seasoned "armchair traveler" through a film series at the library. At the age of eighty-six she became fascinated with David Lynch; the last movie we saw together was *Wild at Heart,* which she admitted was too raw for her taste (but she didn't walk out, either).

But this wasn't the Gram my mother was thinking of now. These hundred objects belonged to someone else entirely: the woman who called my single mom a whore for dating after her divorce at age twenty-six; the woman who ridiculed her eldest daughter for being "sensitive" and

"needy"; the woman who labeled my mother's single pos-
session her beauty, preventing her from taking ownership
of her good sense when she finally did discover it much
later. To my mother, this was an apartment full of weap-
ons, belonging to the person who'd made her feel stupid,
ugly, worthless, sad, and outrageously angry.

She would have liked to destroy it all. She jammed
a handful of shiny, colorful metallic knitting needles and
crochet hooks into a cheap glass vase and they clattered
with fear.

"Here, why don't you go through this goddamn
thing," she said, shoving Gram's purse at me.

When we'd started that morning, I had revered each
of my grandmother's belongings as relics, but by midafter-
noon my mother's coolness had left me feeling like a thief
sorting through loot. I sat down on the bed with Gram's
handbag and threw away a wad of soft Kleenex, half a
roll of Life Savers, a pen advertising an insurance agent,
and a pair of scratched sunglasses. I emptied the contents
onto the bed and chucked the purse itself, ugly and striped
with wear. Among Gram's things was her wallet. I pulled
out each item and examined it: first, a folded index card
on which my grandmother had recorded every medical
condition and prescription she'd had since 1970. I showed
it to my mom because I knew it would piss her off; she
crumpled it, tossed it at the garbage bag.

"Goddamn fucking bitch!"

I threw away photos of me, worn soft around the
edges. I tossed identification cards and membership cards
from all sorts of organizations. For someone who knew
no one and did nothing (at least according to my mother),
my grandmother was very involved. Then I pulled out a
rectangle of clear plastic taped around a yellowed piece of
paper with something typed on it:

The weak can never forgive.
Forgiveness is the attribute of the strong.
—Mahatma Gandhi

I'd never known my grandmother carried this with her everywhere she went. I wondered if she'd wished to forgive or if she'd felt strong enough to do so. I read the words over until my mother noticed.

"What the hell's that?"

"Nothing," I answered, returning to the wallet with efficient-looking interest and slipping the quote into my pocket, where I had already hidden Gram's white plastic nurse pin and her silver sewing scissors shaped like a bird.

When we were done, we carried out the two boxes of things we were saving. One, which I would mail to myself, contained a footed bowl and some old jazz records; the other, which my mother was keeping, contained a family bible and photos and papers. "Someone has to keep them," she complained.

My mother's trunk was stuffed with a box of emergency repair tools her boyfriend must have given her. We attempted to place the boxes full of Gram's things on the maroon velour backseats of my mother's car, but they didn't scoot easily. She stood on one side and I stood on the other, each pushing and pulling with frustration.

"God*damn* that woman!" my mother muttered, as if her mother were trapped inside the box, pushing back. I climbed into the car and lifted the box. Finally it gave and my mother seemed to be satisfied with where things were. Crawling back out of the car, I hit my head on the metal doorframe. It felt like someone had brought a board down on my skull. I put my hand to my head. There was already a bump.

"Oh, honey! Let me see!" my mother cried, scurrying around to my side of the car.

"Leave me alone!" I yelled at the top of my lungs. I could swear it made the pain in my head feel better.

I had never yelled before. I was crying, like I always did, but this time I was also yelling.

"Stop! Don't say another word!" I shouted. "She's dead. She can't hurt you any more!"

She squinted at me in the glare, her beautiful skin flushed, her mouth and eyes drooping with years of disappointment. She gave me a look that said I'd gone way off a cliff and she was going to have to bring me back.

"Get in the car!" she whispered loudly between clenched teeth. "Right now."

But I didn't move. I looked up at the white February sky, empty but for a black bird crossing, flapping mightily to catch up with all the others. I could have slammed the door and stormed off, but I didn't. I drank in the milky sky and then ducked in beside her. We rode home in silence, because everything that needed to had been said.

Robin Bradford lives in Austin, Texas, where she writes a monthly column, "MotherLoad," for the web magazine *AustinMama.* She works as a fundraiser for a nonprofit that provides affordable housing, and she finds plenty to be angry about. Her essays and stories appear most recently in *It's a Boy: Women Writers on Raising Sons* (Seal Press), *Mother Knows: 24 Tales of Motherhood* (Washington Square Press), and *Three-Ring Circus: How Real Couples Balance Marriage, Work, and Family* (Seal Press).

portrait 4

Pinocchio

In March of 1998, I was wrapping up a two-month stay in Knoxville, where I'd gone to escape the remnants of my brief, disastrous marriage with Joe (and his consequential stalking). The two months had done Henry and me wonders. For one thing, I didn't spend every waking minute looking over my shoulder, terrified. I felt secure enough to return to Austin and try to reclaim my life.

Not long before we headed back to the Southwest, I took Henry to a Mardi Gras celebration held inside the magnificent Tennessee Theatre on Gay Street downtown. I'd lived in Knoxville in the '80s, my first job out of college was there, and I had a deep love for the town—especially its architecture and history, both embodied by this building. Among the various booths, I spotted a tarot reader and headed over. Tammie was her name, and I can still see her: tiny, blond, a real Southerner.

One card I pulled—the ten of swords (a guy, prone, with a bunch of blades in his back)—made Tammie very nervous. "Do you *have* to go back to Texas now?" she asked. I said we did. She cautioned me that a man there might try to hurt me. I assumed she meant my ex-husband, and I assured her that I was doing what I could to deal with the stalking.

It didn't occur to me that Tammie might be predicting a new hellish man on the horizon. I honestly didn't think life could get any more hellish than what I'd been through with Joe. Let me amend that—I guess life could've gotten worse if I lost Henry tragically, but the unadulterated terror my ex put me through left me with such a case of post-traumatic stress disorder that I now suffered from agoraphobia and jumped at the slightest noise. I slept with a phone nearby, anticipating the necessity of calling 911. How much more could someone wreck my life, right?

Wrong.

Meet George the Second (G2).

When I returned to Austin in mid-March, I was broke and needed a job. The good news was that the high-tech boom was on. If you could string three words together, you could potentially procure a six-figure job. I wasn't aiming that high—I just wanted something to tide me over. My friend Stephanie arranged for me to interview at her workplace. She also told me there was a cute guy there she wanted me to meet. I've never had a problem mixing business and pleasure, and being a slow learner, I've always refused to acknowledge what havoc this can wreak. New job *and* cute guy? Sign me up.

Being someone who typically dresses like a 1970s lesbian, I had some young thing at the Gap hook me up with a new outfit. I hoped it would help me look as if I knew what I was doing and, perhaps, give me a little external appeal as well. She did a decent job of it, and I arrived at the interview in a nice skirt/blouse combo.

Mary, a project manager, was interviewing me when an extremely tall guy with a pierced eyebrow and gigantic nose popped his head in to ask a question. Though it's atypical for me to be bothered by such things, I vividly recall a flash of irritation at this interruption. I think now it was the energy this guy was giving off, the first whiff of "Run now! *Run!*" which, as usual, I chose to ignore. (Or, worse, be drawn toward.)

I was surprised when, in my round of interviews with Important Employees, I was quizzed by this same guy—based on his appearance, I'd dismissed him as a low-level grunt worker. No—this was George, a programmer and Stephanie's friend, the one she was eager for me to meet. I would learn later that he'd added himself to the list of interviewers so he could check me out. I'd like to say I found this offensive, but I didn't, not really. I didn't give a rat's ass about the high-tech industry, but I would never stop caring too much about being desired.

Not twenty-four hours passed before G2 and I started emailing. When Mary wrote to tell me I wasn't a good fit for the job, I told her that was okay. It was. Because I'd gotten something I thought was better.

By then I was living in a little cottage in a nice neighborhood. I had a small slab porch out front that was a regular gathering spot for any friends who wanted to wind down the evening with a six-pack and a pack of smokes. G2 came by on a Friday, a couple of nights after our interview, and wound up staying until daybreak the next morning.

He wasted no time laying down a story about his tragic childhood, his dead baby sister, his disappearing mom, his stints in foster homes, his physically violent stepfather, and his cold, calculating biological father. By the time the story was finished, all I wanted to do was take care of him. Which is to say, he sunk his hooks in that first night.

In a cycle that repeated itself a humiliating number of times given our short stint together, G2 cheated on me. He was very open about it, and his lame excuse was that he'd *told* me we weren't monogamous, hadn't he? (This was the same man who would stop speaking to me and pout for days if I had lunch with a platonic male friend.) A month after we started sleeping together, G2 went on a trip, and cried upon his return as he confessed that he'd seen his old girlfriend and fucked her. He was so sorry. Could I ever forgive him?

I tried to be calm. Was this a new beginning with her, or a final farewell? I inquired. Final farewell, he assured me. Okay then, let's move on, I suggested. He agreed, but it seems clear now that he never had any intention of moving on. George lived for George. He loved the drama, the idea of two women fighting over him, the power it gave him.

He punished and rewarded me as he saw fit for anything he defined as an infraction. Typically his weapon of choice was sex (or the withholding of it). If I beat him at Scrabble, he'd refuse to have sex unless I'd agree to stay up for a postcoital rematch so he could win. He maintained and regularly discussed a mental spreadsheet listing all the women he'd slept with and how many times he'd slept with them. Sometimes, after sex, he'd say a number out loud, indicating I'd moved up on the chart.

Doesn't this make you cringe? Isn't it ridiculous? What kind of idiot was I?

I was damaged. From a lifetime of damage. From a bad marriage. From shitty self-esteem. From all that and more. That's not to say that I didn't fight back whenever I'd discover a new breach. For example, I discovered he was invited to a big company party but didn't tell me, because he didn't want me to come along. Humiliated—why did he want to hide me?—I'd start a fight. These blowouts were more frequent than any good times we had. We were locked in, a real bicker-and-fuck operation, hurting each other with angry words and emails, soothing each other with skin on skin.

And then: Once again, for the third time, he announced he was flying off and would see his ex. This was over Christmas, a holiday I already hated due to family associations and seasonal affective disorder. I didn't break up with him, though. I simply turned into a huge, drunken, insane mess of a human who woke up in the mornings to a bottle of wine and fell asleep drunk and crying at night, sometimes wishing I wouldn't wake up again. Ever. In the interim, I compulsively called G2's cell phone, which he typically wouldn't answer—but when he did, I turned into a screeching banshee.

I was deep in grief. *How could yet another man fuck me over so thoroughly? How could I allow this to happen?* I loved him so deeply. I had developed an intricate narrative in which he was just testing me to see if, like his mother, I would abandon him. I likened him to a Romanian orphan, deprived of touch and desperate (but unable) to connect. I felt that if I could just pass his ongoing tests, he would trust me: The golden gates would open, and pure love would flood through and envelop us. I couldn't envision any other scenario—like, say, *Here's a guy who's digging fucking two chicks whenever he feels like it, a pussy in every port and all that.*

By the time he got back from his trip, I was livid beyond livid. I had a few more episodes of manic, compulsive phone calling (which left me permanently turned off to using the phone). I called all afternoon at his office one day, only to receive regular online updates from him: "I'm here, but I'm not taking your call." I instant-messaged back: "Please, I can't bear this pain. Please pick up the phone. Help me." He refused.

But then, he couldn't have helped me. The only things that could help me, I would find out, would be nearly a decade spent without a man, the cessation of my substance abuse, some good therapy, and a shitload of self-analysis. I wasn't ready for that, though. I went back in for one more round, wanting him to soothe me, to block out some of the pain with more sex and false love.

It is February 1998. I have been drinking. I have been calling G2's house, repeatedly. He has four adult roommates. They all hear the phone ring. And ring. And ring. No one answers it.

There's a knock on my front door. It's my former roommate Genevieve, dropping in, unannounced, for a visit. In my drunkenness and grief I blurt out something about G2, and then Genevieve gives me the permission I don't need. "You want to go over there? Go over there!" she says.

And so I drive, drunk and blind with rage, six blocks to George's house. I knock on the door. His roommate, John, opens it a crack and says, "He doesn't want to see you," and shuts it. Then he loudly turns the lock.

The sound of that lock, shutting me out, is my final undoing. G2 has a key to my house. He can come and go. Supposedly I am equally welcome in his house, but he lives with a bunch of Trekkies who have spent the entire course of this disastrous relationship shunning me and doing everything they can to make me feel unwelcome during my rare visits. I have never felt right just walking in. Now I am physically shut out, cut off, wildly ripped open. I stand, fuming, on the doorstep.

Finally, he emerges. He stands there, all six foot five inches of him looking down on five-foot-five me. What am I saying to him? I'm trying to capture all the pain of the past ten months—of a lifetime, really—and deliver it to him in a way that he will finally, once and for all, get. But what is my goal? That we will, once again, fuck our way to a smooth spot, only this time it will stick? What do I want?

I want the same thing I've always wanted. I want some external source of love to provide me with inner calm. I am still in the naive place where I believe this is possible.

"I gave you everything I had!" I finally scream at him. *"Everything!"*

And here is where he slices me down. "You gave me all your anger!" he says.

He is, to an extent, echoing my ex-husband, who wanted me to read *The Dance of Anger,* which I sooner would've thrown at his head. Don't these assholes get it? They go out of their way to piss me off and then, when I get angry, which is the totally appropriate response under the circumstances, they complain that I'm . . . what? *Angry!*

Of course I'm fucking angry, you idiot! You rejected me! You made me angry! You lied to me! You cheated! You . . . you . . . you . . .

Me, me, me. You can see, as you take in this story, what I did wrong. I couldn't see it. I couldn't recognize that in staying, in fighting, in trying to make the clearly unworkable work, I was not, as I liked to think, demonstrating fierce and admirable dedication. I was banging my fucking head against a brick wall—no, wait; a masonry nail sticking out of a brick wall—until blood gushed over my face, filled my eyes, and blinded me to my own reality.

Hell yes, I was angry.

And then I was sad. Bereft. Horrified. Alone. Helpless. Another mess for my friends (oh, God bless my friends) to put back together.

I promised that this story would exemplify the upside of anger. And the upside was that while I did try calling G2 one more time—a couple of weeks later, to weakly wish him a happy birthday, a call he took reluctantly and dismissed cruelly—that was it. I finally broke the spell. Or he finally broke the spell. All ten swords were firmly planted in my back. It was time to try to pull them out, and come up with a new plan.

I had no idea that this would be my last relationship for seven years (and counting). I think if I could've known that, the thought would've distressed me. And sometimes, if I think about it too much—having missed sex for the entire second half of my thirties and going into my forties, these years said to be peak years, and me always someone who loved sex—well, I have a twinge of something like regret. But the regret is balanced by the knowledge that finally, after all these years, I have been still with myself long enough to recognize my anger, to see how I courted more anger, and—praise to the universe—to unearth some tools that have gone a long way toward calming that anger.

But I haven't forgotten that getting so angry led me away from anger. Anger is a genuine emotion. I can't believe it exists only as something to be overcome for the purpose of achieving enlightenment. Anger is a form of pain, and pain is how the body warns itself away from danger or lets itself know that immediate attention to a dire situation is required.

I think rationalization is to anger what Vicodin is to pain. Certainly there are moments of appropriate usage. Yes, you want painkillers after surgery. But if you grow dependent upon them, it screws up your whole life. For me, creating increasingly complex narratives that justified the things G2 was doing—things he knew were hurting me—was a way to stay in the game. I developed a heavy dependency on these theories.

Like a crack dealer, G2 recognized my dependency and provided fodder for the narratives. He did this during our first night together, telling me that long, complex, intimate, tragic tale of his childhood, which was sopped in neediness. I didn't think, *Whoa, this guy is telling me too much, too fast!* I thought, *Oh my God, I have to save him!!*

Pinocchio

107

Women do this all the time. A student at the high school where I teach was telling me about a peer who'd been in a terrible boating accident the preceding summer. He'd lost his leg. She detailed the steady stream of teenage girls who filled his hospital room during his rehab period. There was no end of girls wanting to care for him.

Women do this. We nurture. We worry. We're dominated by compassion—often, excessive compassion. This isn't to say all women are martyrs, or that no men are compassionate. But many women repeatedly set aside their primary feelings and needs and put their man (or child) first. Over and over, I took the anger I was feeling toward G2 and stuffed it, reminding myself what a hard time he'd been through, how it had shaped his life, how I needed to be more patient.

No. A bad childhood, a life of tragic occurrences—these are sad, to be sure, but they're never an excuse to behave like an asshole. A lot of unsavory things happened to me and they've fed my compassion, not cancelled it out.

I've had a chance to make these observations courtesy of my anger, and the way that anger catapulted me not just out of my nightmarish relationship with G2, but out of the whole dating game. And while I've been angry in all sorts of situations, romance has got to be the area in which I've been the most angry, the most often.

But it takes a certain specific boiling point for some (or maybe most) women to finally exit. Women often put up with far more than they should, exhibiting astounding thresholds for pain, before leaving. If they even do leave. And before leaving, they *(we)* voice an unhappiness that's often so great, the listener can't help but conclude that the partner is a total, loathsome idiot, and what the hell is the holdup—get out! But then, a proclamation is made: "It would be so much easier to leave if I hated him." *Well, honey, what else could he possibly do to foster the necessary hatred to liberate your ass?* thinks the listener.

Unfortunately, sometimes the answer is "A whole lot more." In worst-case scenarios, this "whole lot more" involves physical violence. And even this won't always prompt a woman to leave—or she'll leave, but then return to an abuser when things calm down for a stretch. Many of us have to be pushed three steps past what we think we can handle before we actually walk out that door. Often, cumulative anger is the empowering hand that does the pushing.

As I've noted, though, anger is a tricky thing, and hangovers from anger are to be expected. When you're furious, logic often flies out the window. The key is to go ahead and ride the initial wave of justified anger to get out of a bad situation (and this can be a relationship, a job, or an interaction with a customer service representative), but then distance yourself from the anger. Don't pick that scab. Be grateful for the burst that prompted you to make a change, and then figure out a way to defuse the bomb that leftover anger causes.

I didn't do this with G2. I let the anger he'd prompted grow for years after we parted ways. At one point, he started showing up at my son's school, and I realized why—he had moved in with a woman, another single mother, a taller, heavier version of me (same big hips, same long, straight brown hair—and in fact, I had once worked with this woman, had been her manager in a restaurant). He'd been so anti-monogamy with me, and he couldn't commit to my son, either. But here he was, Mr. Suddenly Domestic, in my face every day. I can't even find the words to describe the pain this evoked, but several *Sh*-words come to mind: *Shards. Shattered. Shit.*

I let my hatred for him fester. Even now, the best I can hope for is to not run into him—and given the age difference between my son and his girlfriend's daughter (he's in high school now, and she's still in elementary school), I think this hope might be achievable. Meanwhile, I learned a powerful lesson about lack of closure. I'd reached out and asked for help getting over the end-of-relationship hump. He'd said no—the man who cried as if he would break in half each time I tried to break up with him. Who begged and pleaded and said he would die without me, possibly by his own hand. When I asked for help, he said no.

How can we know who will or won't stick around to see things to the end, talk it through, move beyond? We can't. And I have no

Pinocchio

thoughtful techniques to help find closure when closure is elusive. I can only say it happens, it sucks, the anger is real, and if you wait long enough, time might not totally heal the wounds, but it will give you enough distance to be grateful for whatever final burst of anger got you out of the situation, and away from making it even worse.

audrianna gassiot

Forgiveness Is Not
a Requirement

Forgiveness is something I never required of myself. I wanted to be free to feel the pain of the terror, abandonment, and neglect I'd experienced, and the fire that roared in my belly whenever I thought about how much I'd been shat upon. And besides, *The Courage to Heal* had confirmed that I didn't need to forgive.

The book's message to incest survivors is that in order to really heal, each survivor goes through the same stages of recovery (in different orders), except for one—forgiveness. The authors write that forgiveness is optional and personal, and not a requirement for healing. This made sense to me and resonated with the stuff in my belly. After all, how can you get enraged and shoot fire like a dragon, or hiss like a venomous snake, at someone you love, when you bind up your energy with the notion that everything should end up sweet and resolved, with everyone forgiven?

My therapist told me years ago that my mother's physical, emotional, and intellectual neglect and abandonment of me had caused much more damage than the nightmarish terror I'd gone through when my dad had fulfilled his incestuous needs. I didn't know what she was talking about. I knew my mom had loved me and that I'd honored her. But, in the end, my mom went to her grave, never allowing me to tell her the story of what had happened to me on all of those dark and terrifying nights.

Yet, before she died, she'd told me about her own

experiences on those nights, how she had to have sex with my dad and suck his cock until he passed out, even when she could smell the scent of the whores who'd come before her. She said this was the only way she'd known to protect me. She said Dad had gone upstairs to my room every night, except for the nights she'd done this.

And in my lifetime, this has been my only confirmation from another person that these nightmarish years happened. No one else in our family has shared the stories.

My brothers have carried this silence forward, and by keeping the silence, they have denied me and denied what my life is about. My life has been dedicated to my healing process, because facing my past and healing from it was the only way I could stay alive. With each layer of the onion I've peeled away, I've healed, and then there has been another layer, and another. My older brother, a highly educated physician, says that the abuse didn't happen and I need to just get over it. My brothers don't want to know me, or acknowledge the many gifts I have that have come out of the pain of incest. They don't want to hear my story, because it would change their lives and their identities. They don't want to know the problems I face as I work to try and reclaim my sanity and health.

Today, I rarely see my brothers, and when I do, they control our time together. We have no empty moments. In empty moments, things bubble up from deep, dark, unknown places. My brothers can't be there if and when that happens.

When my mom died, I sat for three days alone on my porch. Every cell of me felt like a volcano. For those three days, I felt I would explode. My rage had the force of a rocket and sent me to the outer dimensions of my psyche. I was glad I was alone. No one deserves to experience that kind of emotion.

When my mom and brothers denied me, they cruci-fied me. The risk of hearing my story might have caused them more pain and guilt than they knew what to do with, so I was sacrificed. Over time, I'd adopted the belief that my existence was less important than theirs, and that they should be spared the pain of knowing me. There are many stories—many, many stories.

My anger turned into an unbearable sadness, and then a life-threatening disease. To stay alive, I turned to many healers and learned many methods of healing. I went to a nun, a healer who had survived the deep pain of living, as a young girl, in a Nazi concentration camp for several years and losing her entire family. She helped me see that my anger and pain were killing me. She advised me to distance myself from my brothers until they seemed able to hear my story. I followed her advice, and as a result, I healed partway.

Later, I realized that my parents and brothers had their stories, too. There were reasons for their limitations. They were also victims. This fact didn't excuse their actions, but understanding that each of us was unique and complicated gave me a better perspective. These realiza-tions were profound and took courage to accept. Following the acceptance, a natural and deeper current of forgiveness began to flow through me. I forgave my family for being limited, ignorant, and abusive, for not caring about me or respecting me. I began to accept the members of my fam-ily as they were. For the first time, I no longer needed them to change.

Years went by and we didn't see one another. My brothers and I were now middle-aged, and some of us had serious diseases. When I took a job in another country, I realized I might never see my brothers again. Because I understand how people can change and soften with age and heal over time, I called them to see if they wanted to hear my story. Miraculously (though not without resistance), one by one they committed to be present at our first family meeting. We are scheduled to meet next Sunday, five days from now, in my home. It will not surprise me if they cancel, but if they do, that's okay. I no longer need them to hear me, but if they do, my life and theirs could change. They also need to heal. I'm doing this for them as much as for me, and if they break down, I'll be there for them, because I've forgiven them.

Forgiveness has been a by-product of my lifetime of healing. I wouldn't suggest to anyone that forgiveness is required. If it comes, let it flow naturally—behind the natural process of healing, in its wake.

Audrianna Gassiot lives in Real de Catorce, Mexico. She is an artist, teacher, healer, mother, wife, and gardener who has spent a lifetime learning to heal herself.

Wayne Won't Budge

The anger I sometimes feel toward my partner, Wayne, can be more needling than mere irritation, but it's never strong enough to trigger the release of my middle finger and a well-timed "Cocksucker!" Normal Wayne anger instead begets meaningful sighs, passive-aggressive sock-collecting, and belittling digs at his fitness as a foot masseur.

So the unhinged rage I felt toward him when he matter-of-factly scoffed at the notion of a second child, after I matter-of-factly, and apparently naively, began talking about plans to get pregnant again, caught me totally off guard. His simple "No" triggered a seething and uncontrollable fury that I'd heretofore never felt toward him—an anger that had me slamming doors, collapsing to the floor moaning, and, honest to God, gnashing my teeth. Purposeful denial was all that kept the boiling anger from bubbling over every morning I woke up and saw his peacefully resting face. My burning desire for another child, not coincidentally, refused to cool as well.

Wayne's disinterest in adding another kid to the mix confused me almost as much as it pissed me off. Sure, we had unintentionally conceived our daughter, Beatrice, but we had managed to become competent and enthusiastic parents at some point between gestation and shortly after her birth. So smooth was our transition from working couple to traditional Cleaveresque household, I'd simply assumed I would at least be giving our Wally a Beav to make the family complete. There were other signs, too:

We both had siblings; we generalized about the narcissism of only children; and, well, two was an even number. We even lived in a four-bedroom house, for Christssake!

Adding insult to injury, Wayne, an academic, gladly espoused theories claiming that most human (and animal) attributes and actions are steps in the quest to perpetuate our genes. By wanting a baby, I was just being biological, I argued. He laughed, enjoying the incongruity between applied and theoretical studies. He still said no.

I channeled my anger into lists of reasons why I loved him, or of personal defects that brought me within a newborn's breath of hating him. Wayne did not budge on the baby issue, and my ire intensified. Periodically, I would broach the subject, thinking this time he would understand how deeply I felt about siblings for our daughter, or how excited I was at the thought of carrying and birthing another baby. He knew "No" set me off, so he quit saying anything at all. Instead, the corners of his mouth would turn up just enough to signal a patronizing *You know the answer already.* I stopped looking at him, and I couldn't take my eyes off expectant mothers or families of more than three. "Aren't they lucky?" I would quietly ask him through gritted teeth.

Getting pregnant again with someone you've already made a child with doesn't involve compromise. You can't have half a baby. You can't promise to parent the new one alone while you share parenting of the hypothetical baby's older sibling. Having another child is an all-or-nothing proposal—either you do it or you do not. Someone in this debate had to lose. I didn't want it to be me or my too-small family. I piled on the resentment. It was about more than just not getting my way; he seemed indifferent that he was altering my life's plan, and, by extension, me. His refusal put a new spin on my prochoice stance regarding reproduction.

The fact that Wayne showed no willingness to give in—say, by agreeing to just one more child—brought my festering rage frequently to the surface. The second-baby standoff continued for another year, and, among other aspects of our relationship, our sex life suffered considerably. I hated giving it up if this pleasurable little act didn't also get to be done, at some time, for its intended purpose. He held my ovaries hostage, and worst of all, I consented by choking back a little tab of hormones each night along with tears of frustration. I hated myself for being complicit. I hated myself for hooking up with him in the first place. I decided if I had to suffer, so did he. And we both did. We were just as miserable as we were resentful and angry at each other.

After leaving behind a miserable career, getting our first kid out of diapers and the terrible twos, and surviving a financially threatening lawsuit that required unprecedented mutual agreement and support, Wayne relented . . . kind of. He said another child would not be out of the question for him in the future.

The smoldering bucket of rage I'd kept ready to hurl at Wayne grew tepid. I knew he would keep his word. A year and a half later, he gave the green light, and nine months after that our family became just right.

Madeline Holler lives in Long Beach, California. A former beat journalist, a lapsed linguist, and a soap bead from the ruptured dot-com bubble, Madeline has finally found workplace satisfaction in the one job that holds her interest: mothering her two daughters.

With Friends
Like These

Kim, editor of *AustinMama,* a well-known online parenting magazine, had scheduled a big event and asked if I'd do the food. I'm not a half-bad cook, and, having grown up in an immediate family the size of a soccer team, I cook best in massive quantities.

I arrived at the venue—a little art boutique—weighed down with platters of food, and headed to the barn area in the backyard, where the music and spoken word performances were to take place. As I approached the welcome table, I spotted her. Anette.

I'd suspected, in a flash in the car on the way over, that this might happen. I'm a mom. She's a mom. We're both writers (I'd helped her first get published). We both contribute to Kim's website. But still, actually seeing her chilled me. Pretending not to see her, I whisked past her—which I would have to do a number of times, as I had several trips to make—and turned the corner to set up shop on the long tables facing the stage.

"Thanks for the warning," I said to Kim. Kim was aware of the problems between Anette and me, but she pointed out that at least she'd stationed Anette along one exterior wall and me along another, so we wouldn't have to look at each other throughout the evening.

To my surprise, after awhile, Anette, who is about six feet tall, approached me, looked down, and said, "It's still running."

"What?" I asked.

She offered a tentative smile. "The truck. Still running." That would be a reference to my 1967 Chevy pickup truck, which I'd given to Anette's husband before he was even Anette's husband. The truck had held a shitload of sentimental value for me—good and bad—but it was also a bear to drive, the linkage kept slipping, and I'd have to haul my ass (often in a miniskirt) up under the hood to adjust the engine. Besides, Ben really needed a truck to start his business, whereas I walked most places. So I gave it to him, thinking, among other thoughts, *At least I can visit the truck sometimes.* (Because I get very, very attached to my vehicles, this was not a minor consideration.)

I'd also made Anette and Ben's wedding cake. And when both of them were thrown in jail for bicycle traffic violations, I was the one each chose to call. I conveyed information from one to the other (they were in gender-separated cells), kept them as calm as I could, and picked them up when they were released.

To be fair, Anette had also done me at least a thousand good turns, helping me with Henry when he was little, taking him off my hands when I needed a break or wanted to write. She'd introduced me to some very good people when I started working at a restaurant with her—among them Elisabeth, an animated Parisian who would have a profound impact on my life.

And, to be more fair still, before I tell you why Anette pissed me off, let me tell you that all this happened back before she had kids and when we both still drank daily and heavily. It isn't an excuse, but I have to admit I'm a lot different than I was then, so maybe she is, too.

Still: One night, during a period when Henry's father and I were broken up (it took us a year of back-and-forth before our split became permanent), he and Anette went out drinking. Michael didn't show up to pick up the baby the next morning. As I walked down Elizabeth Street—Anette and I lived on the same block—

I spotted Michael's bicycle in her driveway, which gave off a whiff that would've been easily recognized in Denmark.

I marched up to the house and peered in the living room window. Michael was not on the couch. Anette's house couldn't have been more than four hundred square feet. Unless he'd slept standing up in her tiny bathroom, there was only one other place he could be.

Technically, Michael could sleep with whomever he wanted—we were broken up. It was Anette who infuriated me. Of all the men she could possibly pick, why the father of my child—a man she knew I was brokenhearted over, the corpse of our relationship not even cold yet? When I confronted her, Anette fed me this logic: "We were too drunk to fuck."

Why this consoled me, I can't tell you, except to say that I can be very good at denial (until I finally open my eyes, at which point all past ills fill my screen, like my own *Clockwork Orange* trigger). I wanted an excuse to get past the situation.

Years afterward, I found out that she actually *had* fucked Michael that night. Despite the passage of a great deal of time, learning that she'd lied to me on top of betraying me was too much. I can't think of anything I hate worse than being lied to. I put her on my permanent shit list, near the top, her name in indelible ink.

So when she stood there telling me, "It still runs," she could have just as easily been describing my vicious anger toward her. It still ran. And ran and ran.

I looked up at her, into those big blue eyes everyone loved so much, and I simply said, "I can't."

"You can't? You can't what? You can't talk to me?"

"You fucked Michael," I said, right to her face.

She took a step back. Trying to recover, she said, "That was so long ago," as if this would smooth away the pain.

Her sentiment echoed the words of a much earlier bad girlfriend, Melinda, I'd had in the '80s. Melinda had an affair with a married man. Though I'd introduced her to him, I didn't introduce them hoping they would partake in a sexual relationship. We were coworkers, all in one space at one time. I introduced them as in, *I know you and I know you, too, and you two don't know each other—let me introduce you.* Unfortunately, the situation instead shook down as if I had said, *Hey, I have an idea: Why don't you two start fucking on your lunch hour, and make his wife's life miserable, and make my life miserable when all three of you decide to blame me for the affair?* When it was over and numerous friendships had been destroyed, Melinda tried to refriend me, because she was lonely. And I let her. And then she proceeded to pursue and screw every guy I looked at sideways.

One in particular, Greg, was a guy I truly loved. We hung out together every single night. We were partners in crime. I confided to Melinda all of my deep secret feelings for Greg, bemoaning my shyness and inability to tell him about my love. She coached me on how to win him. Then she tagged along to a concert Greg and I were attending, and the two of them went home together. I felt so ill the following day I could barely move. Sensing I was upset, she left a mocking phone message—"Oh, come on! I just did it for *fun!*"

What is it with women who stab you in the back and then act like you're the big baby for not seeing that it was only in jest, no hard feelings? I mean, I still can't comprehend this—not nineteen years after Melinda's betrayal, and not thirteen years after Anette slept with Michael.

I bemoan the hurt I've experienced at the hands of men and romance. But it is a special kind of agony to be shit on by a girlfriend. Maybe this is because, despite whatever delusional early beliefs we have that Love Will Never Go Bad, in the back of our minds we all know romantic heartbreak exists. Most of us have experienced its particular pain more than once, and some of us have been through it countless times—so when it strikes, it sucks but it's not totally unfamiliar. Girlfriends are supposed to be truer. Girlfriends are our homeys. They validate us, cheer us on, console us. They do not, or should not, fuck our men.

One might argue that, as with romantic breakups, many of us have had experiences with traitorous girlfriends, so they shouldn't be any more surprising than a love affair's end. I could toss a little pop psychology into the mix and reply, *Okay then, maybe getting blind-sided by a girlfriend reopens the wounds I have from failed relation-ships with my sisters.* We could speculate all day, but I don't think a woman out there would disagree that when an alleged girlfriend steps in and sleeps with one's current boyfriend, or past love, a special kind of pain results.

Sadly, Melinda and Anette weren't the only two friends who've betrayed me. Claire watched me spend an entire wedding and reception flirting with the photographer, a fellow journalist, and then drunkenly tackled him at evening's end. (Did he have a choice to stay with me? He did. Did he choose to walk away? Yes. So was he complicit? Of course. But the behavior I'm examining here is when one girlfriend clearly sees a situation and inserts herself into it in a competitive way. Is there a female-gender-equivalent term for *cock blocking?*)

Similarly, Claire came by one night, unannounced, and acted as if she just wanted to say hi. But soon enough, her true motive became apparent. "You're not interested in Philip, are you?" she asked me, referring to the tall, dark, handsome lawyer I was regularly hanging out with. "No," I said. It was true: We weren't dating. He wasn't my type. "Good," Claire said. "Because I slept with him last night."

Maggie knew how much I loved Seth. I knew Seth would never be my partner. Well, I knew it on some level. But he and I also con-ducted ourselves in such a way—I had a room we referred to as mine at his house out in the country, and we attended events together constantly—that when one of us showed up without the other, people would ask where that other was. Maggie had an intimate knowledge of the Seth-feelings I wrestled with.

One day, after she'd moved away to California, she dropped an email bomb: Seth was coming to see her, she wrote, adding, "Long way for a booty call." You know, I could've done without that excess information—or her defensiveness when I told her she was being insensitive.

Am I an idiot to be so affronted by these infidelities? They felt less like infidelities to whatever relationship I was in (or hoping for) with guy X or guy Y and much more like a betrayal of another sort. I took these so-called friends into my confidence, telling them how much I loved guy X or Y—or, in Anette's case, not having to tell her, because she knew the guy when he and I lived together, and she knew he was my kid's father. If our situations were reversed, would I ever, ever have done the same thing—especially if doing it was all about the capture and kill, and not some *We can't help ourselves, this is true love* situation? No, I would not.

So I am no longer friends with Anette. Or Melinda. Or Claire. Or Maggie. Have I been able to forgive them? These days I mostly maintain an out-of-sight, out-of-mind policy. Not full-on forgiveness, to be sure. But at least I've given up actively directing fury and curses in their direction.

ruth gerson

I don't hold a grudge. I never have. I realized why a few
years ago. Growing up in my house, we learned to have
a sense of humor. Not just to be able to laugh shit off,
but also to have a deep sense of all people's humanity no
matter how mean they were, or how many times they hit
you—it was because they were angry in the moment, not
bad inside. The brother (I had three, older) who just kicked
my ass was the same brother I was playing spit with later
in the day. Ass-kicking forgotten. I had to sit down with
my dad—who'd just lashed me with his heavy brass buckle
a couple of hours beforehand—and eat dinner without
throwing it up. My mother taught me that my father only
beat us *because he loved us.* It showed how much he cared.

I'm five seven and a half, I weigh 125 pounds, and I
have a huge, loud, middle-aged-fat-man-smoking-a-cigar
laugh. I don't keep a lot bottled up inside. So when given
the task to describe a time I was really pissed off, I have
to stop and think hard. I can't remember. I'm trained to
clean-slate it to the point of complete blackout.

Fortunately, I'm spitting mad at this moment. It's
fresh in my mind, because the situation's still unraveling,
so I can tell you about my dear friend Paul Venezia. I love
him like a brother. We might not have picked each other
out in a crowd, but our four-year-old girls did, so now
we're best friends.

Paul Venezia (I often address him by his entire name
because I like the ring of it) just frickin' demolished his
kid at the public pool over on 10th between C and D. Em

(mine) and DD (his) were in the pool, and started playing rough. DD had Em around the neck and almost (but
didn't) hit Em's head against the cement. *Maybe* one of us
shoulda been a little closer, so we coulda just reached out
a hand and pulled them apart. Instead, we employed the
screaming-bloody-murder-from-across-the-pool tactic,
which—shockingly—went ignored. (It was my fault. I was
entrenched deeply in conversation with Paul, insisting that
being caught up in too much Internet porn means you have
issues with women to address, and that it probably isn't
doing wonders for your relationship with your spouse.
Du-uh—he's Cro-Magnon about the naked ladies.)

So, DD, being a four-year-old intensely involved
with the act of headlocking her best friend, doesn't hear
us as we yelp and wave frantically for her to stop. When
she finally looks up and discovers the lifeguard, her dad,
and her best friend's mom all careening down on her, she
bursts into tears, crying, "Mommy, Mommy, Mommy!"
That's often what four-year-olds do when they feel overwhelmed that three people, who together must equal ten
times their weight and size, are closing in on them like
goons. Completely lose their shit. Overstimulation.

She won't stop crying, and Paul Venezia's bullying
ensues. The yelling comes on, the insults, threats. And
when there's one breath—a moment where she might get a
grip, and you think it's over and she's going to be okay—
he revs up and starts again and she's in pieces again. She's
supposed to control herself, but he can't control himself. I
stay out of it—the "unspoken" but sometimes spoken rule
No interference. He's crushing her. It's not working, but
his own explosion has taken over and he can't let up. I've
got a brain ache and a heartache and I choose to break the
no-interference rule and run interference big time: "DD,
let's go wash our hands and face," I say, shielding her from

her over-the-line dad. We go, we wash, we breathe, we're happy. Back to the pool to play. Done.

Except. Paul Venezia's pissed at me now. He loves me, too, so he's desperately trying to wrap his head around the concept of not tearing me a new asshole. Pacing. Jumping in the pool. Swimming around like a hostile fish, trying to cool off. He's not gonna say what he would say to *anyone* else. If I were anyone else, he would tell me to mind my own fucking business, and then most likely come down on my shitty parenting skills. But I'm his pal, so he's taking deep breaths, telling himself, *Ruth means well, she means well.* Thinking, *All the things she does wrong, but I don't say dick. She should keep the hole in her head where the sounds come out—shut.* But he's not gonna tell me that.

I apologize. He forgives me. It's over. Kinda. But he thinks I'm wrong to intervene. And I let him think that, which is why I'm pissed. Because I don't just say, *No, Paul, it is my business. I'm standing here while you are damaging a child. I don't care if she's your child.* But I've broken the code. It's an ancient, male code: When a man is abusing his wife or his child, you don't intervene. And I just perpetuated it because I didn't say, *Your daughter does not have to learn by being bullied into submission by a male, even if that male is her daddy. It is my business when you make me and my daughter watch this shit. Should I just take my kid and walk away? That's not right either.*

I don't say any of that. I'm pissed, because I tremble in front of his anger. I'm shaking like a leaf in front of the big, mean man. I apologize instead and say, *I was wrong to intervene. I'm just an intervening ninny-woman.* I manipulate him, really. I'm not being honest. I don't want him angry with me, so I work around his anger, diffuse it. I'm pissed at myself, because I don't go with the truth.

The truth is, we're here to teach and instruct our

children, to help them learn and keep them from harm. The main point of them having parents is for them to be protected, so they can grow, be safe, and be happy. The main point is not *The parent is the boss and boy, you better cower before the king.* Teaching kids how to behave doesn't have to involve destroying the will or crushing the soul. You can't ignore gender, either—do you really, really want to teach your little girl to roll over and play dead for the man she's most afraid of? Do you want to teach her to bend her will toward yours because she's terrified? And later, toward some other guy's, because that's what she's trained to do?

A dad needs to be more patient with his daughter. Make her an unflinching woman, emotionally brave, instead of forcing her to stuff it until she gets numb or depressed or has an anxiety disorder. Whatever you have to do, make sure you keep the conversation open with her. If you shut her down and shut her down and shut her down, she'll stop talking to you forever and then you're fucked, Paul Venezia, because I know how much you love her.

I'll be pissed at myself forever, 'cause I was just a coward and perpetuated one of the oldest lies in the book. I don't hold a grudge, except against my stupid self.

Ruth Gerson is a singer, songwriter, and actor from New York City who has appeared on *Late Night with Conan O'Brien* and performed at the Newport Folk Festival. Gerson's latest album is titled *Wake to Echo.* Besides playing with her band in clubs at home and abroad, Gerson tours performing in living rooms, a.k.a. house concerts, across the United States. More on Gerson can be found at www.ruthgerson.com.

s. kirk walsh

For what felt like a long time, a very specific, yet vast, segment of the female population was the object of my anger—pregnant women and mothers of newborns. Complete strangers, intimate friends—it didn't matter. My acute anger and pain were triggered by the sight of a sleep-deprived mother pushing a stroller on a city side-walk, or a friend joyfully announcing that she was pregnant with her second kid.

As with any anger situation, context is everything, so let me provide some.

About four years ago my husband, Michael, and I embarked on the journey of conception. This was right after September 11, 2001. We lived on the island of Manhattan. Like everyone else, we were rattled, and the minutiae of our day-to-day lives were dwarfed by the smoldering mass of charred metal and unidentified remains that lay just a few miles south. *Why not have kids? we thought. That's what we're here for.* We stopped using birth control; we stowed the diaphragm and spermicidal gel under the bathroom sink. After a checkup with the ob-gyn, I started swallowing prescribed horse-pill-size prenatal vitamins loaded with iron and folic acid. I cut back on caffeine. We had sex, often. The first month in, my period didn't arrive on time. I felt passing moments of queasiness.

Could it be this easy?

For a good three or four days, I thought I was preg-nant, and I shared this exciting news with Michael. Then, one night, I abruptly woke to painful cramps and dry heaves that left me bent over the toilet. The next morning, my period began. Initially, Michael and I thought I'd experienced an early miscarriage—that something hadn't quite taken. Like any dedicated young couple, we tried again. And again. And again.

Six months later, Michael and I decided to consult the experts. *Suss things out. Run some tests. Ensure that all procreation systems are in check.* Most of the tests came back normal, until one day I received a panicked call from my gynecologist, a soft-spoken German man, about a sperm test Michael had recently undergone. Apparently, my husband's sperm weren't properly shaped; the heads weren't quite right. On the other hand, Michael had five times more of the little swimmers than most men. And they were active (as he'd proven during his youth, when he'd impregnated three different women). Michael visited a urologist, who assured him that sooner or later if we kept trying we would get pregnant. He claimed the sheer volume of sperm canceled out any problem that might arise because of their irregular shape. My gynecologist was less optimistic, and referred me to a nearby reproductive endocrinologist (RE, I later learned, is shorthand for *expert* in the infertility world).

On my first visit to the RE's office, I was nervous, but optimistic: *Just a little applied technology to get us going in the right direction,* I assured myself. I was certain that in a matter of months, the line on the pregnancy test stick would emerge that desired pale red. Instead, this referral— the RE's name and phone number barely legible on a prescription slip—sent Michael and I into three long years inside the hell of infertility treatments.

After several failed natural and hormone-induced inseminations, Michael and I agreed to try in vitro fertilization, or IVF. We tried three times, the number of times our insurance would cover a percentage of the cost. We came up with the money for additional expenses, and when all was said and done, we'd spent nearly $13,000. And let me tell you, beyond the cost, in vitro is a rough, rough experience. It involves three to four weeks of nightly injections. After the hormones produce a suitable number and size of ovarian follicles, the eggs are retrieved in an outpatient procedure calling for twilight anesthesia. If all goes according to plan with the embryonic cell division, a transfer (another outpatient procedure) follows.

At the height of my treatments, Michael injected me three times a night—twice in the thighs and once in the abdomen. And these were intramuscular shots (read: long needles), not subcutaneous shots (the short kind). We rotated sides of my thighs and stomach to avoid excessive bruising. Every other morning, along with fifty other hormone-addled women, I visited the crowded waiting room of Cornell's Center for Reproductive Medicine and Infertility for my blood and ultrasound checks. I cried, often.

One evening, Michael was tapping out the small bubbles in the syringe, and for one second I wished that the liquid bubbling at the tip were heroin rather than the powerful hormone meant to produce multiple follicles in my ovaries. The image of John Travolta dancing to Chuck Berry's "You Never Can Tell" in *Pulp Fiction* drifted through my head. Sitting in a chair, my pants to my ankles, my bare thigh tensed for the needle, I longed for a cozy, I-don't-care-about-anything heroin high. I'd never actually done heroin, but given my self-destructive track record with alcohol and drugs back in my youth (and a sustained abstinence of more than ten years), this fantasy, I knew, was not a good sign.

As with all chronic conditions, one procedure rapidly rolled into another, and one decision led to the next. As the drama unfolded, we began to understand that we had few options for a biological conception. And my anger toward pregnant women mounted. Most often, this anger was reserved for friends. Emails and phone calls often bore such lines as *I can't believe it. We weren't even trying.* The friend who sent this particular email was forty-two years old; I was thirty-seven, in the middle of my last in vitro cycle. Then another friend spoke to me about the essay she was going to write about her grief relating to her decision not to have any more children (after having given birth to two healthy girls). Another friend invited me to a farewell lunch because she was moving out of town—and I joined three mothers and their respective children, all under the age of two. Throughout the lunch, the women talked endlessly about the trials and tribulations of early mother-hood. At one point, one of them tried to sympathize with my situation, saying the first time she'd tried to get pregnant it had taken over a year—and I wanted to yell *Fuck you* as she brushed the hair out of her son's eyes. I became so sensitive that I began to look for the signs before the announcements: *Is that a small bump at her belt line? Are her breasts bigger?*

Anger is a two-way street. Had I been in a different space, I would have taken better care of myself, said something when I began to feel uncomfortable. I might have removed myself from loaded situations. Instead, I felt paralyzed by my anger and grief, and as the months passed, I became harder and harder on myself. *When are you going to get over this?* I thought. *What is your problem? You need to be less sensitive, more relaxed.* I felt like I was going to be crushed.

In between my second and third in vitro procedures, I joined a mind-body support group consisting of twelve women also undergoing IVF at the reproductive center. Every Tuesday we met with a psychologist in the hospital's conference room. One woman with blocked fallopian tubes had elected to go with an egg donor. Another woman was a single rabbi looking to get pregnant via a sperm donor. Another woman was part of a lesbian couple; during her first IVF cycle, she was overstimulated with meds and had to discontinue. Two of the women were under thirty; one was a cancer survivor. Several others were like me— in their mid-thirties, hoping to get pregnant. Each week, we talked about our struggles, and the psychologist offered simple breathing and meditation exercises to help us relax and cope. She guided us through visualizations. She encouraged us to call each other when we needed support.

Then, one evening, I brought up the subject of anger. My anger. My husband's sister had just sent news that she was pregnant. Again. I talked about my feelings, but soon a palpable discomfort descended upon the rectangular conference table. One woman erupted into tears. Slowly, the others began to share their stories—tales of insensitive friends, obtuse relatives, coworkers asking the question we all hated to face: *When are you going to have kids?*

This was the first step I'd taken to get closer to my anger. With therapy and guidance, as time passed I moved closer still, moving in on the anger's origins. After a while I began to identify other emotions fueling it, and I discovered that most of these emotions were deep-seated feelings of inadequacy and loss. I would never be a member of the club. I would forever be an outsider. I was too emotionally damaged to become a biological parent. The lies went on and on. As time passed, I believed them less and less.

The third IVF treatment was unsuccessful. For some unknown reason, the embryos wouldn't divide. Doctors couldn't explain it. *This is very rare,* my doctor said. *We don't see this, particularly in someone your age.* Soon after, Michael and I discontinued treatments. Physically and mentally, I didn't think I could go through it one more time.

And now?

This story has no end, but I know this much: After much grieving, I have let go of the notion of having a biological child. Michael and I talk about adoption, but we are not pursuing it at the moment. Last weekend my brother's wife telephoned to tell me she was pregnant with her second child. A boy. They will call him Isaiah. My sister-in-law is forty-one years old and HIV positive, making this a high-risk pregnancy that will require several months of bed rest. My brother, a film producer, will be away, working on location in another country, during her pregnancy. At the end of our conversation, I said to my sister-in-law, *I am here for you.*

And I meant it.

My anger and grief are not completely gone, but a shift has happened inside me, giving me room to feel other emotions, too—desire, joy, generosity. I'm able to see beyond this moment, able to feel a sense of possibility. And now, I fully understand that the only way out of the anger is to go through it.

S. Kirk Walsh is a writer living in Austin, Texas. Her essays and articles have been published in *The New York Times, The Christian Science Monitor,* and *Good Housekeeping.* She is currently at work on a novel.

portrait 6

Burning Bush

In April of 2004, the death count for U.S. soldiers in Iraq was fast approaching six hundred. I was pissed off. Really, really pissed off. I had been pissed off since Bush stole the election from Gore. Pissed off and sad.

Then there was the whole weapons-of-mass-destruction farce. Conservatives and jingoistic lunatics (and judging by bumper stickers, there was a glut of them) formed a posse mentality and the battle cry to blow shit up in Iraq gained immense force, even though nothing—not anything—linked Iraq to 9/11. But this was the claim the administration handed down to the people. Like advertisers selling sugar cereal to the kiddies on a Saturday morning, they delivered the message repeatedly until people bought it, until Congress bought it and designated $87 *billion* for a war game.

The thing about the death count was that in spring 2004 it was practically a secret. Certainly the numbers didn't trumpet forth from front-page headlines. You could hardly find them at all. *The New York Times* ran a little regular blurb called "Names of the Dead," but this was, pardon the pun, buried deep in the paper and you had to search for it. Which I did.

One day, I made a sign for my front yard. I put it together hastily, not thinking it would grow and turn into an ever-changing piece of political art. I wrote:

TODAY'S MATH LESSON

U.S. TROOPS KILLED	—	610
IRAQIS KILLED	—	UNKNOWN
WEAPONS OF MASS DESTRUCTION FOUND	—	ZERO
LIES TOLD BY THE BUSH ADMINISTRATION	—	COUNTLESS

It was a small sign, a political sign from a long-gone campaign that I'd simply turned inside out and pasted words to, which I then went over with laminate to protect from rain. A week or so later, I crossed out the 610 and put the new number beside it. I repeated this action every week, and pretty soon there was no more room on the sign for numbers. So I extended the numbers off the sign and stretched them to another wooden stake, and then another.

During this time, I read the AP wire and *The New York Times* headlines daily and listened to NPR almost nonstop. I attended war protests and proudly sported a FUCK BUSH T-shirt that my son made for me. Because I live in a liberal city—I call Austin "the blue polka dot on the red blanket"—and because at the time I lived in one of the more liberal neighborhoods in this city, I got plenty of support for my messages.

In fact, I had some support on a national level, too. In 2003, the University of Texas Press published a collection of my essays. The book's cover featured a picture of my then-vehicle, an old Subaru wagon covered in bumper stickers. Prominent among these, at the top center of the hatchback's window, was my favorite: BUSH IS A PUNK-ASS CHUMP.

However, UT Press had airbrushed this particular sticker out of the picture prior to publication without consulting me. Laura Bush happens to sit on the press's board, and you didn't have to be related to Einstein to put the pieces together. Hell, even George Bush could've figured out this puzzle. UT Press denied removing the sticker because it was anti-Bush and claimed they would've taken out any political statement. I doubt it.

Which is exactly what I told a reporter from the *Los Angeles Times* when she called to interview me about the missing bumper sticker. I ran my mouth about my First Amendment rights. I offered a bad extended metaphor about how UT Press was like an otherwise fantastic boyfriend with a terribly unsightly nose hair. I went on and on about the injustice.

When I was finished, or at least had paused, the reporter replied, "That's not what *they* said."

Let's have a moment of tangential pissed-offness here, shall we? As a reporter myself, I *never ever* try to trap people I'm interviewing. But this reporter, in revealing (after she got my quotes) that she'd already interviewed my editor, made me feel trapped. Not that I wanted to take back a single word I'd said—that's not my style even when I *should* eat my words. But I thought her approach was crummy, and in the resulting article she tried to pit me against my editor (who, to her credit, had a huge laugh over the whole thing and congratulated me, citing that old saying about the nonexistence of bad publicity).

Getting back to my lawn. As the death count for U.S. troops in Iraq approached one thousand, I got an idea. My signs now stretched halfway across my yard, and I wanted to make a bigger statement to mark this milestone number. I knew the small signs were having an impact, because I could look out my window and watch people stop, read them, and comment to each other.

The signs had an impact on me, too—not that I needed any more fuel to heat up my anti-Bush anger. By this point, I had already started learning forgiveness and working hard not to express hatred. For example, I felt that meditating while wearing my FUCK BUSH T-shirt probably constituted bad karma. But each time I put up a new number, I seethed at the idiot in the Oval Office.

A few nights before the death toll hit one thousand, I did a little shopping in my neighborhood, under the cover of darkness. I found a City of Austin roadblock by an alley, and—you know how when you're about to do something like make an illegal U-turn, you create a story in your head to tell a cop who isn't even there but *might* materialize?—I decided if anyone caught me "borrowing" this roadblock, I'd feign utter stupidity, point out that it was bulky trash collection week (it was), and innocently proclaim that I thought the roadblock was being put out for disposal. (Isn't my paranoia delightful and sort of stupid all at once? For the record, no one stopped me.)

Back at home, I spray-painted the roadblock black and affixed a poster to the front of it. GOT DEATH? I wrote, along with a huge number 1,000. Since the slogan I'd chosen was a play on the GOT MILK? ads, featuring celebrities with milk mustaches, I added one more flourish: a picture of Bush with a Hitler mustache.

I lived in a liberal neighborhood, but that didn't mean we could keep the conservatives away. I lived a stone's throw from five restaurants and cafes, many of them enticing to SUV-driving Republicans who loved to park in front of my house. They were easy to identify— my Republican radar is such that I can spot them a mile away. But also, just as I had my bumper sticker, they had theirs, typically featuring a big *W.*

As the Bush/Kerry contest got uglier, so did my temper. I was no fan of Kerry's, but he was a beacon compared to the fog of stupidity known as Bush. I was mad all the time. When Bush's weaselly voice came on the radio, I turned it off. (Back when I still drove the old Subaru, which had had the radio stolen from it, I carried a transistor with me to hear the news—and once, without thinking, I actually reached over and slapped the radio when I heard him.)

I got in verbal brawls with people who tried to tell me I was wrong to exercise my First Amendment right by displaying the PUNK-ASS CHUMP bumper sticker. One guy accosted me in the parking lot of my local grocery store. He told me I wasn't allowed to speak of the president "that way." I explained that Bush was not the president. The guy took umbrage. The argument escalated. As he got in his SUV to drive away, I hurled a clementine in his direction without thinking and found myself shocked, horrified, and rather delighted as I watched it run down his window. Not to be outdone, he got out, retrieved the pieces of citrus, and threw them back at me.

Later, my friend Sarah would assess the situation dryly. "Sounds like two people of equal maturity had a political discussion in the parking lot," she said. True. But my frustration was hardly unique, and there was so much distress around the 2000 and 2004 elections that people far more rational than me were feeling explosive.

How could so many people be so blind to what was happening? Besides countless young soldiers—so many of them underprivileged teenagers of color—being blown up for no good cause, thousands of Iraqi civilians were dying. And Bush just kept lying to the camera, acting all triumphant, suggesting evil was being put in its place— mission accomplished and that he was a modern-day hero. I was not proud to be an American. I was sad, mortified, and angry that the flag had been appropriated by warmongering office thieves.

Twice around the 2004 election—once right before and once right after—vandals destroyed my signs. The first time, I suspected the culprits were sorority girls, because whoever did the damage hardly knocked down the small garden stakes supporting the signs, and their attempt to smash my big Halloween pumpkin also failed— they managed to haul it to the street but apparently could not heft it high enough to produce the desired *splat* they seemed to have been contemplating. That time, I restored the signs and dragged the pumpkin back to my lawn.

The next time, I was less fortunate. I'd been at a friend's house, pet-sitting overnight, and returned to find my lawn bald of signs. It was a strange sight—at this point they'd been up for eight months and were part of my life. I stood there, feeling violated.

Don, my new next-door neighbor, asked if I wanted help with a more permanent sign. I told him I'd think about it. I didn't want to burden him. I then went inside and created a hasty message to the vandals. I scrawled: YOU CAN DESTROY THE SIGNS BUT YOU CANNOT DESTROY THE FACTS . . . I then repeated some statistics, hurled a little vitriol at the Bush administration, and planted the sign in the front lawn.

It was gone the next day.

Don approached again with his offer. This time I said yes and left to run some errands. I returned to see that Don had had a worker dig a trench, into which he'd poured concrete, into which he'd planted a thick, heavy fence post reinforced with steel pipes and rebar. To the front of the post, he'd affixed a huge, flat piece of lumber—even I was shocked (and awed, and delighted, and worried that the Republican landlady would evict me) at the size of it. They'd nailed my AMERICAN FOR PEACE sign to the top, but I still had plenty of room for my messages. I labeled it, at Don's suggestion, THE KILL-O-METER. Up one side, I drew a bar graph of U.S. military deaths to date; up the other, I made a similar graph of Iraqi civilian deaths. In the center I kept an ongoing count of dead troops, beneath which I placed a quote about how if the major export of Iraq had been palm dates, the United States never would have invaded.

So there. Fuck you! I thought. *Take that, you stupid fucking vandals!* They would've needed a jackhammer and a chainsaw to move that sign, and even then it would've been difficult (a point that was proven when I moved and had to hire someone to jackhammer the sign out).

This sign is the perfect example of what I'm talking about when I talk about justified anger. It astounded me how many people just sat back and watched the war unfold—or worse, averted their eyes altogether. Ultimately, I concluded that the bigger surprise was that I was even surprised at how people conducted themselves anymore. We'd all become so complacent, myself included. I'd gone from attending peace protests to sitting at home muttering about Bush. Yes, I had the sign, but I had stopped getting out there.

My signs provoked numerous responses. People would stop by, talk to me about the numbers, thank me for my work. The local weekly paper came by and took a picture, which was published back when the ranks of the dead "only" numbered in the seven hundreds. And when the signs were stolen, the neighbors rallied. I received a beautiful card—homemade and featuring a picture of one of my cats (who shared the yard with the signs)—thanking me for my efforts. I received a lovely picture of my house at night, illuminated by my year-round Christmas lights—my rainbow-striped silk peace flag from Italy backlit from the interior lights, and the signs in a soft glow at dusk. These tributes moved me. My neighbors were connecting with my anger, and feeling that anger themselves, and responding by offering me love and support in return.

The day of the actual election, November 2, 2004, I got up early and voted against Bush. I had very high hopes that day. I then went to the alternative high school where I teach literature and creative writing. This little school—there are about seventy students—is dominated by liberal kids (to put it mildly). However, the 2004–2005 school year had brought us Brandon. With his blond hair, perfect straight white teeth, bulging biceps, and jock wardrobe, he looked like he'd wandered over from central casting, looking for the set of *I Was a Hunky Teen Quarterback* but accidentally landing on the set of *Punk Rock High School.*

I was intrigued that a kid like this could wind up in a school like ours. Granted, we considered ourselves very open-minded, and all students were supposed to be welcome. But really, if I were Brandon, I'd have felt like a long-tailed cat in a roomful of rocking chairs. While I never thoroughly quizzed him on his anomalous presence, I wondered about it. And though he wasn't in any of my classes, I used the library as my classroom and Brandon spent a lot of time there. So we got to know each other. He'd tell me about hunting and raising steers, and I, non-meat-eater that I am, would listen, spellbound and borderline appalled but nonetheless fascinated.

I liked Brandon's impeccable manners, his soft accent, his willingness to put up with other kids' ribbing, and his unwillingness to change under peer pressure. I hated his politics—just as we spouted our liberal beliefs, he gladly shared his conservative ones—but I found in him a rare member of the opposing team whom I didn't feel blind rage toward.

And that's what the situation had come down to. An article I'd read somewhere made a valid point: The political climate had become so polarized that, unlike in eras past, it wasn't easy to keep mixed political friends. Did I have Republican friends besides Brandon? I had Republican *acquaintances,* and these were mostly parents of students I taught hailing from some of the city's tonier neighborhoods. Everyone was mad at everyone who didn't share similar beliefs. Tolerance was zero. Every time I saw a pro-Bush bumper sticker on a vehicle in front of me in traffic, I had a deep, serious urge to smash into it. I'm sure a lot of conservatives felt that way when they were stuck behind me in traffic, too.

So here was Brandon, and I couldn't dismiss him so easily. He's a good kid. He's not some anonymous member of a greater, hateable, generic *them.* He's an individual and a friend.

I walked into the library on Election Day and I said, "How many of y'all who are old enough voted?" And Brandon, eighteen, answered, "I'm going to the polls with my mom after school, ma'am."

Here's where I momentarily lost my mind—where my appropriateness filter blacked out, and where, without stopping to edit myself, I blurted out the first thing that popped into my head. "Wouldn't you rather . . . come have a drink with me?" I said. Crazy.

There was a moment of pure, white silence. Then the liberal kids in the room burst out laughing. Brandon left. I turned red and wondered if I'd just laid the groundwork to get fired. Had I been in a public school, I could've kissed my ass goodbye. Even in this tolerant institution, I wondered if I'd gone too far. Of course, I didn't really want to take him drinking, but that comment summed up my deepest sentiment: I would do almost anything I could to keep Bush from being reelected.

I left the library and walked down the hall until I found Brandon. I looked at the floor and apologized. He was very nice about it—he hadn't left the room angry, he'd just left to go to class. Then I went to Adam, our school director. Without putting too fine a point on it, I mentioned I'd said something I shouldn't have and if anyone came and suggested that to him, it was true. Adam, who is a living Buddha, was kind about the matter.

The next morning when I walked into the library, I was crying. Kerry had just conceded. I felt sick. Brandon sat at a computer. He didn't make a smug or triumphant face. I'm not sure I would've been as mature had Kerry won.

Fast-forward to May, school graduation. Before the ceremony, Brandon introduced me to his parents. By this time my friendship with Brandon had deepened, I'd been blown away by his senior presentation on being a cattle rancher, and we had an easy relationship. I gave him a big hug and told his parents that, despite our political differences, Brandon and I had had a great year together. "He's going to be a politician," I said. His mother agreed. I added, "And he's going to fund all my bleeding-heart liberal projects!"

We laughed and Brandon added the kicker, the part of the equation I hadn't thought of. "Yep," he said, putting his arm around my shoulders. "And she's going to vote Republican!"

That night, because our students graduated in alphabetical order by first name, Brandon was the first called to the podium. Each student could have up to three people say a few words about him or her. Brandon's mom, a tiny woman, stepped up to the microphone, and in an unwavering, proud voice, she told us a story I had never heard before. The family had moved from Ohio to Texas, she said, when Brandon was recruited to play high school basketball and football. As his appearance suggested, he had been a champion athlete.

A near-death car wreck changed all that: It shattered Brandon's hip, which eventually had to be replaced, and left him in chronic pain, which he never, ever mentioned to me or, as far as I know, anyone else in our small community.

I wept. I always weep at graduation because it's such a rite of passage, but I wept extra for Brandon's story. He wasn't ever going to get me to quit being angry with what I believe to be perhaps the most corrupt administration in this country's history. But by putting a gentle, thoughtful face on conservative beliefs, he was able to provide me with a reminder that while maybe we couldn't all totally get along, at least some of us could.

julia smillie

My mother and I had an understanding, or so I imagined. Starting in my teens, she would fail to understand me, and I would strike the match under my simmering anger and resentment toward her. I would spend my twenties fanning those flames, furious that she was not the mother I wanted her to be. My mother would admit no wrongdoing, and I would acknowledge no right-doing. It seemed inevitable that we would reach a point where she realized the error of her ways and came to me, repentant, begging to be forgiven.

At that point, I imagined, I would forgive and all would be well. Sort of. We would move forward, our relationship changed and both of us operating with the knowledge of how wrong she had been. Her love for me would be filled with regret and eagerness to make up for all her transgressions; my love would be gracious, slightly guarded, and forgiving—but not forgetting. This was how I planned to manage my resentment toward her over the course of our lives.

When I was thirty-two, however, my mother threw a wrench into my plans. On a chilly Sunday morning in October, suddenly and entirely unexpectedly, she suffered a massive heart attack and died. There had been no warning signs, no inkling at all that our family was about to change in the most drastic way possible. My mother left us reeling from a shock so great that the details of those days immediately following her death are a blur. My immediate reactions included the textbook mixture of disbelief, denial, guilt, and pain so strong and searing, it felt physical. What amazed me most, however, was what I felt within a few short months of her death. My anger at my mother returned to me, fresher and hotter than ever. I was furious.

As a confused and depressive teenager, I'd felt my mother was emotionally selfish, holding back from me the parts of her I needed most. Her death—induced, at least in part, by the smoking we'd all prayed she would give up—seemed like her last selfish act. She had abandoned us—abandoned my father to unspeakable loneliness after thirty-eight years of marriage, abandoned her children and grandchildren to a place of deep sadness and bewilderment. My anger was large and volatile, deeply penetrating, and I felt consumed by it. Thus, I found myself in a hunter green armchair in a grief counselor's office, acknowledging the six-month anniversary of my mother's death.

I was, of course, no stranger to anger or, more specifically, the seething resentment it leaves in its wake. Over the years, I had accumulated massive quantities of self-righteous bitterness. I resented my family for its genetic legacy of depression, obesity, nearsightedness, chronic sarcasm, alcoholism, and the overwhelming urge to correct other people's grammar. I resented my sister for being born first, my brother for being born last, and another brother for being so goddamn smart. I resented the exes who dared move on with their lives, and all the former teachers, employers, friends, and coworkers who had failed to acknowledge my greatness. I resented people for taking my parking spot, for having twelve items when the sign clearly stated no more than ten, for daring to procreate, and for raising children with bad manners.

I didn't just *have* these resentments, clustered at the bottom of my purse like loose change. I *lived* in them.

At some point over the years, resenting everything had become a full-time job—and not a particularly pleasant one. I wanted out. Through my therapist (and a twelve-step program with which I was already involved), I found the guidance I needed to dig out some of my anger and scrutinize it. I had to fully acknowledge that there was a difference between righteous and self-righteous anger, and that most of mine fit in the latter category. My anger wasn't just self-righteous, however. It was downright self-defeating. It was eating me up. Yes, some of my relationships had suffered as a result of my anger and resentment, but at the end of the day, *I* was the one with the bile building up inside. No one else.

I came to understand that what really angered me about my mother was that she wasn't the mother I needed or wanted her to be. In other words, her main transgression against me was that she was herself. My mother did the best she could, and it was no more her fault that we failed to reach an accord than it was mine. *I* was the one who couldn't accept her, who expected her to be someone different and then punished her with my anger when she didn't change. In fact, as I fanned out many of my resentments for inspection, I realized every single one of them existed because of my failure to accept. I was railing against people, circumstances, events, odds, and outcomes, all of which simply *were*. I discovered at thirty-four that I was still throwing the tantrums children throw when someone takes their ball away. I was angry at the person, the situation, and hell, even the ball.

What most motivated me to do something about these resentments was my increasing awareness that I simply didn't want to carry around all that weight anymore. I was tired of being angry, exhausted by grief, and unwilling to continue being a person of unreasonable expectations.

After all, as people around me pointed out, there wasn't much I could do about the things that angered me. Being angry at the person, the situation, the ball—none of it changed the outcome. In fact, it rarely changed the person, and it certainly didn't affect the ball. My anger was not the righteous sort inspiring nations to change for the good. No, it was selfish and indulgent, shortsighted and miserly—the very same things I had once thought of my mother.

As it happens, letting go of many of my resentments was not nearly as difficult as reaching a place of acceptance. In fact, once I arrived in such a place, I was surprised to find that certain resentments just petered out, robbed of fuel. Other resentments will require that I do more work, both in letting go and in making living amends to those I have harmed. But my mother is gone and I'm unable to tell her my regrets. I know now that she and I were at once very different and very similar. Had I reached this understanding while she lived, we still likely wouldn't have been close—but I doubt there would have been the animosity I breathed into our exchanges. That said, I can't afford to replace my anger with guilt, especially over circumstances I can't change. All I can do is change the relationships I have now—try to be a better daughter to my father, a better sister, granddaughter, aunt, friend, and wife.

None of this awareness and work has made me perfect—or even consistent—in the way in which I deal with anger and resentment in my life. An arrogant driver, rude waiter, or unreliable friend can still inspire anger that consumes me for hours. But I'm slowly learning that letting go of my resentments leaves me a lot more space. And in that space, I'm able to build a fuller, more peaceful life. Most of the time, anyway.

Julia Smillie is a writer living in St. Louis, Missouri. Her work has appeared in publications nationwide, and she is currently working on a collection of humorous essays about childhood. Current and past columns and essays can be found at www.readjulia.com.

marissa renee laham

Rant of an Angry Teenager

The appointment is for 5:00. The second hand on the steel gray wall clock hurtles around in circles. I wait.

Time, unrelenting, never yielding—I am helpless to its every whim. In the back of my mind, I can hear the incessant ticking of my littlest brother's cereal-box watch, resting lonely now against his bedroom wall. Time is everywhere: inescapable. Every minute of it.

I don't care about the time I have to spend in here. The time I have to spend waiting quietly, rolling my eyes or taking prolonged so-called emergency expeditions to the restrooms—I just want to get out of here.

This half-lit room, the stench of cheap cologne, and the subtle reek of decomposing mothballed clothes from thirty years ago—the ones only frail, elderly women still feel capable of unearthing from their shoeboxed closets. This half-lit room, with these impersonal olive suede couches, screams *prison*. Couches. Four of them. Identical, with the sole exception of the small imprint my ass will leave on this one medium-size cushion. When the five-foot-one, 160-pound ball-of-joy receptionist introduces me to the sweater-vest therapist to whom I am expected to spill my beating heart, and I stand to greet this newfound friend, my imprint will evaporate. Gone. Two minutes later, no one will know that I was even sitting here in the first place.

The woman on the couch to my right has dressed herself in floral patterns. Payless 100 percent leather sandals. Her peach skin thinning, her wavy brown hair frizzing.

She is a drained version of a once-great beauty. Mother. I don't even know her name anymore.

The walking Prozac capsule behind that IKEA front desk is staring at me from the corners of her eyes as she busily "types" away at her 1995 computer, and the doctor steps into the room. I eye him, observe his movements just as he will soon enough observe mine. He tells me his name and walks into the hallway. He coolly clutches his acrylic clipboard as if it were the shining keys to a red sports car, on both his way out and his way back inside.

Therapists. The honeybee ties. The cumbersome combovers. The squeaking black shoes. The everlasting monotony. The beeping pagers. The ringing phones.

Therapy. Glacial waiting room perimeters. Cream-colored Kleenex. Iceberg-size stacks of paper. Colorful emptiness hanging on whitewashed walls.

All I want to do is escape. Mother sits to my right. The chair next to mine. Nine pages. Nine pages of questions he asks me and her. Nine entire pages. It's policy. Mother sits to my right, in the carbon copy chair that for these three hours will embrace her, hold her tight, then spit her back out into the world.

She will be helpless. A newborn bird set to fly, stripped of feathers. Naked.

Mother sits to my right, and he asks *me*, sort of, these questions. These statistical questions:

Has she been arrested, Mom?

What does she like to eat, Mom?

Do you have nightmares?

Has she ever run into trouble with the law for drugs, Mom?

You can anticipate my next question: Have you ever done drugs?

When was the last time you thought about suicide?

Mom, are you taken aback by her responses?

The woman to my right is crying and grabbing at those hideous cream Kleenex.

I had no idea. I just had no idea it was like this. I mean, I just didn't know.

You're the one who drags me here, who harasses me about coming in because it will "help" and because I "need" this, and yet you have no clue that anything is wrong?

More bullshit.

I hate shrinks.

And I hate this woman I am forced to drag around to anything that affects my life in the slightest. She is no longer a part of me. She hasn't been a factor I choose to consider part of my life for quite some time.

I hate everyone, but of course this is only because I am a bitter teenager.

Oh, the bittersweet teenage years. And all because I am "just sixteen." Why am I doing this? Why do I act this way? Blame those fucking hormones.

If I answer your questions, your response will still be the same. I'm a teenager. My hormones are raging. I'm one big boiler. Don't come near. *Warning. Warning. Danger.* I am dynamite, but my emotions do not apply because they are identical to every other intangible teenager's. *Danger. Stay back.* I am hazardous waste for ten more years, until the moment when I become a vital and influential asset to society, serving my community and my world by establishing myself: by signing papers behind a desk, or teaching children in an underfunded public school room.

How beautiful. How precious.

Time. That cereal-box watch keeps ticking away, another second of my life passing by. *One more now.* Wait. Pause. *Two more.*

And I have been pulled into this office. I have sat and answered nine pages of personal questions for three hours, and now this doctor informs us that he can put my name on a waiting list if I'd like. He's kind enough to add my name to a list. His recommendation, however, is that I simply lean back and smile big as he scribbles a prescription for Prozac or Paxil or Zoloft or Effexor. I've spent thirty minutes of this time sporadically expressing my disbelief in the effectiveness of modern medicine and its haphazard distribution. We medicate everything in everyone.

I have finally caved in. I just want to get out of here. My white-hot anger tapping at the interior of my skull, screaming to be unleashed. All my frustrations. Write me a little prescription. I do not care. I tell both of them this. He excitedly comments on the way he must administer the pills little by little, so that I don't swallow them in an inadvisable fashion.

How do you think a doctor such as myself goes about diagnosing a patient such as yourself?

Well, I say, first we are brought in here by the lot. Then you sit here and ask us questions and draw conclusions from what you've learned in all your school and years of training and books and case studies, and you match A to B. Then, somewhere on your desk, there should be a little notepad. You grab your pen, grab your paper, and you scribble a prescription for a pill that will heroically make all of my pain go away, with the always-possible side effects. Then you hand it to my mother, who will insist we fill it right away, because of course this time will be different. Then we get home, and I refuse to swallow them.

He laughs.

Only this time will be different, the woman to my right says with a hopeful smile. Someone please tell

Rant of an Angry Teenager

153

her to shut up. *This time you're going to be so good about taking them, right?*

Right.

He talks to the woman on my right about which pill to prescribe. Then he scrawls a note about Zoloft. A new beginning. Apparently I have been showing "less interest in the things I once enjoyed." Every word I say, this psychotherapist reports, *sounds like something a clinically depressed person might say.*

Therapy. You spill your life story. You're shaking, you're honest and on the very edge in aching pain, and by the end of the session you are nothing more than the first letter of your last name. And your life story is now stored in millions of identical metal filing cabinets inside millions of identical therapists' offices.

You are a statistic. You are someone's dreaded work. But for that hour you are special. You are important. A beautiful and unique flower. And just like a prescription for a pretty pill that you pop to make everything painful disappear, you are only temporarily aiding yourself. Too afraid to open the doors inside yourself on your own, you have called upon the assistance of a perfect stranger. A perfect stranger, might I add, who you'll never be sure gave a flying fuck about you in the first place.

An avid hiker and aspiring novelist, **Marissa Renee Laham** spends the vast majority of her time exploring, reading, and writing. She attends high school and enjoys crocheting, painting, and observing the natural ebb and flow of life in her spare time.

portrait 7

The Shallow

Side of Men

Reggie's wife died suddenly in the spring of 2005, leaving him alone with their two young kids. I barely knew Reggie, but his brother and sister-in-law are like family to me, so he was family by extension. I insisted he let me help take care of the kids and cook for all three of them until he could get a system in place.

Numerous factors drove me to help, the main one being that my own son's father had split just before Henry turned two. I knew more than a little about the devastation of partner loss and about solo parenting, having raised a child on my own for a dozen years. I understood the initial chaos and panic that surfaces in the early stages of figuring out how the hell to proceed alone. Countless friends had stepped forward to help me in my grief. It was time for me to return the favor to the universe.

I had a light summer schedule and made myself available most days and at all hours. Many mornings I showed up before dawn to get the kids going. More than a few evenings, I read them books and put them to bed while Reggie went to work out and be alone with his thoughts. I took the kids swimming and to the library and out to eat and on long day trips. We painted and sang and danced. The extra baby seat was installed rather permanently in my car.

Bliss filled me when I was with those children, and the attachment and joy I felt surprised me. If someone had told me a year before that, after raising a child to young adulthood and independence, I would find contentment shuttling two little kids around, listening to the grating Clifford the Big Red Dog CD, and splashing around in the kiddie pool, I would've laughed dismissively—I had big plans for the alone adult time I saw on my immediate horizon. But I felt an immediate and ferocious love that was as sweeping as it was inexplicable. I never got tired of being with them.

Unfortunately, I developed a ferocious love for Reggie, too. There was never any question that I found him attractive—I can't imagine who wouldn't. He's good-looking, with deep blue eyes so intense that, like some seventh grader, I could hardly look at him before having to look away again. I felt simultaneously shy and comforted in his presence. In our conversations and emails he displayed a brilliant mind, dazzling wit, and the most incredible grace under the most intense pressure I've ever witnessed. He was gentle with the kids and appreciative of me—we went out often, as a twosome or foursome, and he celebrated me in ways I was unaccustomed to and entirely bowled over by. If you had seen us out, you'd have thought we'd known each other about ten minutes shy of forever.

I kept my mouth shut about my growing feelings for as long as I could. Reggie's wife's death was fresh, and I knew from my own experience that he was going to need mountains of healing time before he could be genuinely involved with anyone again. Even if the attraction was mutual, I'd been the rebound girl before, and I never wanted to play that role again. A decade earlier I'd spent six months of my life soothing Divorcing Man, not realizing until he dumped me unceremoniously that I'd just been a warm body to distract him from memories of his wife. I didn't want to revisit the devastating feelings that epiphany left me with.

But increasingly, I feel like a protagonist in an Olivia Newton-John song—you know: *If we both were born/In another place and time/This moment might be ending in a kiss . . .* which is not really the best way for a forty-one-year-old woman to conduct herself. And so, when the elephant had grown to take up the entire living room and spill over into the kitchen, I decided to usher it to the door. I came clean with Reggie. I explained that I didn't want a relationship, that I only wanted to speak my feelings, clear the air, put it out there, and switch my mental juke-box to something a little more soothing, like Nick Lowe's "(What's So Funny 'Bout) Peace, Love and Understanding."

Reggie's response was harsh—he abruptly shoved the elephant out back and shot it in the head, letting me know bluntly that, for a number of reasons, under no circumstances would he ever consider me partner material. I was too similar to his wife in negative ways, he pointed out, and furthermore I was too old for him (I'm two years and 364 days older than Reggie). Ouch. Later, when I called him on his callousness, he apologized. The apology moved Reggie up another rung in my esteem. Rare were men I'd found willing to talk through a situation, back down, work it out, and admit mistakes.

We got past that bump and continued spending an inordinate amount of time together. Being around Reggie made me rethink being single (which I'd been for nearly seven years) and contemplate finding a partner. I decided to open myself up to dating again. I knew he was contemplating doing the same. Knowing that dating others meant our dynamic was bound to change, I requested that we be gentle and display consideration for each other and the kids as we brought other adults into our lives.

Reggie defined "gentle" differently than I did. When I found his online personal ad, in which he described wanting a woman exactly like me—only younger—it stung. (The ad was titled "Must Love Johnny Cash," and when I pointed out to Reggie that June Carter was three years older than Johnny, he shot back that Johnny had outlived June, and being a widower once was enough for him.)

Then he sent an instant message to me while I was on vacation, informing me that he had a new, younger, wonderful girlfriend, and that they were happy together. I thought this lacked the consideration I'd requested. I felt punched and gutted. I had a strong Pavlovian urge to do as I'd done in past times of hurt—I wanted to fly into a rage.

I fired off a couple of angry emails, attacking Reggie for being horribly insensitive and suggesting he'd used me as a romantic surrogate so that he could get his dating sea legs and find a younger woman. Reggie insisted he hadn't been gloating, as I saw it, but had delivered the information because he worried someone else would tell me first. In his mind, he *was* being sensitive.

Decades of old wounds tore open. I hydroplaned on my tears from one bad memory to the next. How many men had misunderstood me? How many had I misunderstood? How many had accused me of being unfairly angry, overreactive, and too goddamned sensitive, while I felt my anger and sensitivity was justified, a legitimate response to their pure tactlessness? How loudly had I protested, and what had those protests netted me other than accusations that I was out of control?

For once in my life, I stopped myself, forcing myself to not argue the point any further with Reggie. This was not the same as letting it go. Reggie had tumbled in my mind, fallen far and hard off the pedestal I'd built beneath his feet. When he said he understood I couldn't hang out with him anymore because, in his words, being "just friends" with someone you're attracted to is "unnatural," my urge to scream at him resurfaced with a vengeance. I explained that my desire to see less of him had nothing to do with the attraction, and that he could take a place way in the back of the line of men I'd been attracted to who hadn't shared my dream of romantic love.

No, what pissed me off most was being misunderstood. The feeling that Reggie was being a real dick to me compounded that anger. Making matters worse, my new desire to rejoin the dating world—and Reggie was the catalyst for this—came with the horrible realization that, apparently, some stereotypes are true. For instance, a whole hell of a lot of guys are ageist pigs.

Now hold on. That last sentence was over the top for a reason.

I've spent a good quarter century as a feminist, an idealist, and a romantic. I've convinced myself that equality can be a real thing, that there are sensitive men, and that somewhere, a good partner for me exists. My knee-jerk response to Reggie's meanness was to go fishing for a date online—and if you ever want to reinforce the notion that all men look for younger women who must never weigh more than two sacks of potting soil, reading online personal ads is the way to do it.

I was forced to face a truth I hadn't anticipated: Even men in their forties are often not interested in women past their thirties. God, that pissed me off. When I was thirty-two, I weighed 125, I didn't have much gray hair, and I was wrinkle free. Which is to say I looked pretty good, by society's standards. I also drank (usually heavily) every day, smoked like a chimney, had a mountain of debt, and suffered intense bouts of depression. At forty-one, I might not be Audrey Hepburn, but I work out every day, I'm sober, I'm sane, I'm successful, and I'm independent. My depression has been at bay for a long time, thanks to lifestyle changes. I'm *together,* I'm *ripe,* and I should be the *most desirable* I've ever been, right?

Apparently not. "What's the first lesson?" asked my friend Shaun when I called to cry on his shoulder about Reggie. Shaun is an Olympic gold medalist swimmer and a former womanizer. He taught me, at age thirty-eight, to overcome my water phobia and learn how to swim. I figured he might also help me overcome my dating phobia and teach me to understand men.

"I forgot the first lesson!" I cried.

"The first lesson is that men are stupid," he said.

"I don't want to believe that," I said.

"Believe it," he said.

Shaun has worked to convince me that men, unlike women, are not sitting around going over every detail of every conversation, wondering if some woman likes them or figuring out what that dangling participle in the third-to-last sentence of that last email meant. The flip side of this, he explains, is that men also aren't, as I've often suspected, sitting in their lairs and maliciously plotting to make my life hell. They're just doing what they need to do to meet their needs. *Let go,* Shaun tells me.

Well, I can't let go. Now that the idea of dating is in my head again, I'm applying my goal-oriented side to acquire a partner. I know some folks would preach against that: *Just forget about it—it will take care of itself, when you least expect it.*

No—I forgot about it for seven years, and it didn't take care of itself. I told Shaun I thought it was a little creepy and totally nonorganic to go actively shopping for a mate. He answered that it wasn't creepy at all. You need clothes, he told me, you go to the mall.

But whenever I run into cliché behavior in personal ads posted by men *(must be twenty-seven to thirty-five; must want to perform fellatio around the cock . . . er, clock; must be independent, beautiful, sexy, accomplished, and tolerant of cats . . .)*, I get mad. And when I speculate who these ad writers are *(probably out of shape, underemployed, delusional jackasses, and deadbeat dads to boot)*, I get more mad. And when I'm mad, I'm not exactly attractive.

This unattractiveness showed in the personal ad I composed about a half hour after Reggie's rotten "I have a girlfriend!" instant message punched me in the stomach. Under Type of Man I Desire, I wrote, simply (and bitterly), "a non-asshole who can read and spell." And then I responded to an ad for a guy who seemed like he might be compatible, but I opened up by telling him his picture looked like the Shroud of Turin. I know, I know—totally charming of me and without a hint at the anger simmering beneath the surface, right? (In my defense, his picture did look like the Shroud of Turin. In my limited experience, guys seem more likely to post pictures of themselves that feature only an elbow, or a face smashed up against a fisheye lens, or something else designed to either be arty or disguise some pretty horrific physical flaws.)

I still see Reggie once or twice a week. We don't hang out, but I do get the kids—that was my request—so there's the hand-off interaction. Plus I'm now friends with his entire family (a result of all that intense daily time I initially spent with the kids), so there's bound to be some overlap between us. I have a temptation to sustain the anger his insensitivity provoked, but I fight that urge using the Geraniums Must Live method, which I developed as a tool to help me fend off creeping seething sensations.

In the mornings, when I get the dogs fresh water, I pour their old water on the potted geraniums on the front stoop. This takes a few extra steps, and it would be easier to pour that water down the drain. But in redirecting it, I help keep something living. I think about those geraniums when I think about what to do with what I'm feeling about Reggie, and when I think about transitioning back to the place where my relationship with him and his kids started: love for the sake of love, and not in hope of something in return.

I recall the one word I thought of when I offered to help him in the first place: *compassion*. I recognize the error of having fallen for him, but I cut myself slack because it was impossible not to fall in such a situation: rapid intimacy brought on by highly emotional circumstances, and constant closeness with an attractive man. Above all, I think about the joy of being with those kids. You know, I'm taking fury and making fury-ade, smoothing the hot reds into something blue and soothing.

diane fleming

I was the *good* one, and he was the furious, sociopathic, battering addict. It had taken me five years to divorce him. I anguished over the effects of divorce on my children, ignoring the effects that his daily abuse had on them. But after I started taking antidepressants, there was no way I could continue living with him. After we separated (he refused to leave our apartment when I asked for a divorce), he became violent. Someone called the police on him once at a drugstore because he had shaken our oldest son, spit at him. He grabbed and screamed at the kids, punched holes in walls, destroyed telephones, screamed "Bitch! Cunt!" at me in front of the kids, and refused to work.

My ex-husband inspired me to fantasize about murder. I dreamed of breaking into his bedroom in the middle of the night, injecting him with an undetectable poison. I didn't want him to suffer, just to die. But when I thought of my children and how they might suffer if they lost him, my daydreams stopped.

I moved across the country from Florida to Austin. He followed me. He came to the house and took the kids when I wasn't there. He came into the house without my permission, going through my things. We arranged a visitation schedule, but he didn't feed the kids on the weekends when he had them. My therapist said I had to go to court, ask for supervised visits. I resisted. I'd already obtained sequential temporary restraining orders, and no judge would make these orders permanent. One judge's logic: Though he'd threatened to kill me, he didn't actually have a gun. In court, I felt like a hysteric.

I finally went back to court. He was ordered supervised visits, at my expense. But he immediately broke the rules, showing up at the exchange location early, with the intention of running into me so he'd be able to scream at me in the street. The judge canceled his visits after that. She asked me how I'd explained their father's behavior to our children. I said I'd told them that their father raged, which was not okay, and that if someone else, a teacher perhaps, had done the same, it would not be acceptable.

The judge threatened to put my kids in foster care. I was wrong to speak badly about their father. I explained that at the battered women's center, the counselors had told me to speak plainly and clearly to my kids about their father's rage—to identify it as inappropriate, unacceptable.

I was the *good one*. I'd removed my kids from their father to protect them (though I'd taken too long to do it). I'd gone to counseling, taken them to counseling. I went to the battered women's center. I went to court. I paid for supervised visits. I insisted on sanity. But I'd done something wrong by speaking the truth.

I hated my ex-husband, hated the fact that I'd ever met him. My anger consumed me, inhabiting me like a foreign body. I didn't want it. And even when it overcame me, my anger was barely perceptible against the backdrop of his.

I felt like Ebenezer Scrooge, but rather than being obsessed with penny-pinching, I was obsessed with my own rage. I was haunted by my own ghosts of past, present, and future. Ghost of the past: My rage always turns to self-loathing. Why had I married him? Why hadn't I run away when I learned I was pregnant, never to involve him in my unborn child's life? What if I'd never divorced him? Would he have suppressed his rage? Ghost of the present: I am just like him. Ghost of the future: I will become a lifetime collector of grievances, imprisoned by the act of keeping a running tally of his outbursts.

Unlike Scrooge, though, the error of my ways wasn't my lack of benevolence, but my abundance of it. My own epiphany was unpleasant, but true: I couldn't change anything until I felt my rage, became ugly with it.

Diane Fleming is a technical writer living in Austin, Texas. She has published short stories and poetry and is currently working on an MFA degree at the University of British Columbia.

elena eidelberg

Just My Type

While doing our usual day-after-the-party postmortem on the phone one day, my good friend said, "You liked *him?* I don't get it. I just can't get a fix on your type!"

I knew what she meant. If you considered only physical features or jobs (or lack of jobs), you would think I had no preferred type, but unfortunately, I do. The men I fall for slam the doors of their cars too hard when they get in or out; they deny they are ever angry about anything over which they might have some degree of control; they *will* admit to being angry over things like politics—and about *those* things they are very, very angry. They consider themselves above anger, or they long ago decided not to get mad about things, having had a role model who couldn't make that claim. They often drink too much. They are usually brilliant and hyperverbal, but they don't have a clue about themselves. They think I ask them too-personal questions; they aren't curious about me, though I would love to tell them anything they asked. They brood. Oh, how they brood. One literally didn't leave his house for a week once but denied he was depressed. They have a hard time getting things done but it's never their fault—the one thing they're really good at just doesn't bring in any money. Their skin is hot at night—every single one of the men I've really loved had burning-hot skin. They immediately think the worst about people they meet, and even of their own friends. They are what you might call negative, usually in a funny way.

I am trying to recover from my attraction to these angry guys. It's so trite, so high school. I'm a grownup—or want to be—with grown-up desires, a kid, a plan. I don't want to be around the anger anymore, and yet I choose guys like these. Thanks, I already know why. Anyone who's watched Oprah or Dr. Phil even one time knows. This is how people behaved in my "family of origin"—a phrase that always makes me recall a particular drawing of a caveman walking in profile, not yet upright, his head sticking forward like a turtle's from its shell.

In many ways, the way these guys behave is how I behaved before I started going to therapy and learned (1) that it's human to get angry, (2) that I can just *tell* someone I'm angry instead of mentally disemboweling them, and (3) that just because I'm angry it doesn't mean anything is going to change (which makes me angry—see [1] and [2]).

In addition to my strong sexual attraction to this type, they bring out my desire to "help." With these guys I get to be the good witch: "He's really very nice," I say. "You just have to get to know him." I get to be the therapist: "It's okay, you can get mad, I can take it. I'm real and I'm strong. You can be angry, as long as you aren't abusive, and I won't go away." I get to be the cheerleader: "You can get that job—I believe in you!" I also get to be frustrated with people other than myself. I get to affectionately (or not so affectionately) complain about them to my girl-friends in a way that is probably irritating to those listening. *Why,* I'm sure my friends wonder, *doesn't she pick a different type of guy for a change?*

I ask my friend on the phone if she wishes I would pick a different kind of guy. I explain this stuff about my "type."

"Wow, you really *don't* have a type," she says. "You just described all the men I know."

Elena Eidelberg is a writer and tile maker who lives in Austin with her fifteen-year-old son, Curtis.

portrait 8

Random Acts of Anger

and Senseless Fury

Here's where, if this were a movie rather than a nonfiction book, I'd hit you with a montage of images of me traversing the spectrum of anger, from mildly irritated to hopping mad to *If I were you I'd get the hell out of here right this minute* furious. There would be no dialogue, just snapshots of me rolling my eyes or yelling, perhaps crying or making pained faces, and maybe a few shots of me lying wide awake in my bed, subtitles revealing the contents of the furious missives forming in my mind. As this pugilistic PowerPoint presentation is projected onto the screen, dramatic, swelling, and wholly unnecessary-to-convey-the-message music (deafening timpani drums, anyone?) would further drive home the point: I am *pissed off.*

I could carry on in the fashion I've begun here for another five hundred pages (at least), offering detail after painful detail of moments when I totally lost it. But I want to switch gears and look at life on the other side—this search for the land of forgiveness—because that's so much more who I am now, or at least who I'm working hard to be. Writing what I've written so far fills me with something that fluctuates between embarrassment and sorrow. I've wasted so much time being pissed off, and finally, finally, I feel like I'm in the beginning stages of comprehending what not being constantly prepared for pissed-offness feels like.

To repeat: Not all anger is bad. And many instances of anger are genuinely justified, or at least provide us the catalyst we need to exit a bad situation. I will always be grateful to those moments of anger that rescued me from hell, or at least pointed me in the right direction. The Buddhist monk Thich Nhat Hanh, in his book, *Anger: Wisdom for Cooling the Flames* (a book I love very much), writes about the importance not of eradicating anger, but of recognizing it, acknowledging it, and treating it like a baby:

"Just like our organs, our anger is part of us," he writes. "When we are angry, we have to go back to ourselves and take good care of our anger. We cannot say, 'Go away anger, you have to go away. I don't want you.' When you have a stomachache, you don't say, 'I don't want you stomach, go away.' No, you take care of it. In the same way, we have to embrace and take good care of our anger."

For me, the first step in taking care of my anger is recognizing it as it's happening, before I open my mouth and give a gateway to the (usually expletive-laden) thoughts running through my head. It's not always easy. Recently, a woman pissed me off badly. A lot of things flashed through my mind: *Throttle her, rip her a new asshole, put her in her place, scare the shit out of her by going totally apeshit bonkers and screaming at the top of your lungs.*

We were at the downtown YMCA in Austin, my least favorite branch, a place where I'd already had unpleasant exchanges with the staff, a place that also reminded me of my ex-husband. I was at this location only because it was a rainy day, I'd promised Reggie's kids earlier in the week that we could go swimming, and this branch had an indoor pool.

I hadn't thought ahead and put the kids in their swimsuits, the way we do before swimming at an outdoor public pool. So I took them into the locker room with me, and as I did so, I remembered the rule: No opposite-gender kids older than five in the adult locker rooms. Reggie's son Jack is ten, but he has a brain injury from a stroke he suffered at the age of four. So Jack, a wonderful, articulate child, operates below what is considered typical for his age. I couldn't send him alone into the men's locker room.

On the way in, there were no other people. No problem. I got them dressed, we played in the pool, they had a great time. On the way back into the locker room, I stopped to rinse the chlorine from my hair. Here's where trouble started. One woman said to another, loud enough for me to hear, "He's too old to be in here."

I compounded the problem by saying, "He's five." I said this only because I knew five was the cutoff age and I wanted the woman to shut up. Jack, however, was not amused by my remark. "I'm not *five*," he said, and I realized I'd insulted him.

At this point, my adrenaline was on the *very* side of high. I made myself walk away from the woman. I hustled the kids to the locker aisle to change them. Tears stung my eyes, in part because I knew I was wrong for having brought him in, but much more so because this woman was being a compassionless bitch. As we walked away, I heard her announce that she was going to report me to the staff.

That did it.

I told the kids to stay put and I returned to the showers. "He's had a stroke!" I hissed at her. "He can't shower unattended." I also wanted to say, *"And his mother died a month ago and he's had more to bear in his little life than you'll ever have to bear, so why don't you just shut the fuck up, bitch!!"*

But I didn't say that last part. I didn't say it because I didn't want to scare the kids. And I didn't want Reggie to be mad (though of course, I would have to tell him what happened because surely the kids would offer some version). And I really worried that if I flipped out and Reggie heard about it, he wouldn't let me see the kids anymore because he'd worry that I was too emotional around them.

So I shut my mouth. But the woman did not, going on about how there were attendants for this sort of thing and blah blah blah. I walked away. I fought back tears. I fought back the urge to wish for a falling anvil to hit her as she left the building. *Walk away, walk away, walk away*, I told myself.

Walking away was hard, but I had some experience at it. Years before, I'd learned about removing myself when I studied martial arts (I have a red belt in tae kwon do, which is just beneath a black belt). While I did learn how to defend myself and while I could (at least at one point) quite literally kill someone with my hands and feet, the most repeated lesson was about combining vigilance and evasion: *Pay attention. Don't go after the fight. Go away from the fight.*

That interaction, in which I allowed a stranger's meanness to anger me, was hardly the first time something like that had happened. It surely won't be the last. I don't care how many self-help books, therapists, or Oprah experts tell us not to let other people's shit ruin our day—just letting it go is nearly impossible when you feel attacked by another human. If that woman were telling her side of the story, she'd probably try to make it an open-and-shut case by saying I brought the kid in, it was against the rules, I was wrong, end of story.

Feeling wrong (and I did feel wrong breaking the rules, but the kids were freezing and wanted dry clothes) exacerbated the feeling her bitchiness fostered. There was guilt on top of my defensiveness. For every action there's an equal and opposite reaction, and all that. Of course we're going to let other people get to us, even if we've never seen them before and won't see them again—even if we can make ourselves believe some other something is making these mean people miserable. In the moment, all that falls aside. Someone is mean, it hurts, we get mad.

Here are some more stories of anger—and while some of the situations I describe may not be universal, I think most of us have faced the same feelings.

Airlines

It is entirely possible that I've written more words of hatred toward American Airlines than I have words of love to all the men I've loved combined—which is saying a lot, since I started writing love letters when I was around eight. Back before 9/11, when you could still complain without risking imprisonment in Cuba for potentially being a terrorist, I chronicled every American Airlines infraction against me, mailed them all in, and was often compensated with discount coupons worth hundreds.

But if you think I did it for the money, you're wrong. I did it because time after goddamned time, those fucking idiots fucked up my trips and my son's trips. Once they left us stuck on the runway in Los Angeles for three hours, and then, when the weather finally cleared, they realized there was an engine problem so we had to wait some more. I'd been stuck across the aisle from a drunk guy who reeked and would not shut the hell up. I was losing an entire day of an already too-short vacation to San Francisco. This was back when I still smoked, and I hadn't had a cigarette in a very long time. Why the hell hadn't they inspected the engine during all those hours we were on the ground, instead of waiting until it was time to leave?

Finally on the ground in San Francisco, I waited in a long line for a chance to demand the airline extend my trip and/or pay for a night of my hotel lodging. When it was my turn, I didn't mince words. The "customer service" rep was a very talk-to-the-hand caricature of a gay man, and he wasn't budging. In fact, at one point, he said, "I'm done with you now."

Well, I wasn't done with him. I got increasingly angry and raised my voice. Since I already talk at about a ten in anger-free situations, you can imagine I was calling some attention to myself. My son, beside me, was getting anxious. Finally, a service representative from the next station walked over, smiled a fake smile at me, and said, "I can help." For a split second I thought she meant it. Then she said, "Call security!"

There I stood, having suffered sundry injustices all day, and now they were going to have me arrested. Terrified at the thought that they'd cuff me, haul me off, and turn my kid over to Child Protective Services, I stormed away. I still want to call these people pigfuckers for the way they treated me, so I guess that's another example you can chalk up in the As Yet Unforgiven file.

Editors

Freelance writing is a phenomenal exercise in masochism. Having been a freelancer since I was nineteen, you can see where I fall on the spectrum of favoring constant self-inflicted pain. Just yesterday I got an email from an editor asking me to rearrange this, that, and the other thing in a piece I'd turned in. She wanted more substance, more references, and more quotes. The note she sent was 354 words long. The article was supposed to be 350 words.

This has been the case forever. Editors—too many of them frustrated writers, as far as I'm concerned—want so badly to put their distinctive mark on the work they aren't actually writing. There's an old joke about this, which I originally heard involving a screenwriter and a producer, but have changed to feature a writer and an editor:

> A plane crashes in the desert and the only survivors are a writer and an editor. They crawl around for days, nearly perishing, until at last, on the very brink of death, they happen upon an oasis. The writer, overjoyed, plunges her head in the water, laps it up thirstily, and is just starting to feel better when she looks over and sees that the editor has dragged himself to his feet, pulled down his zipper, and is pissing in the water. "What are you doing?!" she yells. "I'm making it better!" he says.

That joke still makes me laugh because it has felt true for me on so many occasions. I still remember, nearly twenty years ago, getting hired to write a piece on children and depression. The piece was returned to me with a request: Couldn't I make it more "fun," like the samples of writing I had sent in to get the job? *More fun? It's about children and depression!!* I wanted to scream. I still remember that editor's name. She's a writer now, and I cringe when I see her byline.

I think, though, that just about all of us get angry in the course of our work sometimes, even if we have jobs we love (and, all kvetching aside for a moment, there are many things I love about my job). Or maybe we just get mad at the fact that we have to work at all. Not to suggest we're lazy—but the daily grind can be, well, grinding.

Back before the big Internet bust in 2000, Austin was a high-tech mecca. Young, often arrogant twentysomethings were trading out one six-figure job for another, as if changing underwear. At the time I was doing all right myself, cranking out web content, making money hand over fist. At one point, I published a piece about quitting one's job to follow one's dream.

When this essay ran on MSN.com, it ranked somewhere in the all-time top five hits for articles, suggesting to me that even twenty-somethings making more money in a month than the GNP of some small nations, kids whose offices featured Ping-Pong tables and pin-ball machines and gourmet meals delivered several times a week, had something to be frustrated and angry over in the workplace.

I haven't totally solved this puzzle yet, except to say that perhaps the very thing that can give you a Zen peace of mind can also drive you mad: repetition. Most work is repetitious. Plus I've found, having been both managed and a manager, that any work situation involving more than one person (and that would be all work situations, because even if you work alone, as I often do, your work is received and judged by oth-ers) is going to generate friction. No matter how much you love your boss or underlings, if you're in a crappy mood one day (for whatever reason), you're likely to take it out on your coworkers, in part because you probably spend an inordinate amount of time with them.

And just as justified anger exists in other parts of our lives, more than a little justified anger occurs in the workplace. Backstabbing, petty gossip, mean-spirited delegation, missing-but-earned promotions, and passive-aggressive competition (to name but a small handful of the hell we find at work) can naturally drive us to anger. Unfortunately, it can also put us in a tight enough spot between a rock and a hard place that our mental and physical health is gravely affected.

Case in point: I had a newspaper column in college, and when I lost that column due to a fallout with the editor (who many, many years later emailed to apologize), I thought, *Fine, fuck you, I'll just go get another column somewhere else.* I was young and naive, and I didn't know the difficulty behind my proclamation. But after a very long time—around thirteen years—I managed to score a column with *The Dallas Morning News,* one of the largest papers in the country. It was a contract position and I wasn't allowed to call myself an employee, but I didn't care. Once a month, my words, accompanied by my picture, ran in the paper. I was overjoyed.

The reader response to my writing was overwhelming. I was told repeatedly that no other columnist had ever evoked the quantity or intensity of letters that I had. But—can you say *high school?*—the more popular I became, the more certain staffers, including my immediate supervisor, began to resent me. One reporter falsely informed a top editor that I had misrepresented myself at a conference. I was called on this and had to explain why the accusation was wrong. I was bothered that this reporter, whose name was never revealed to me, had gone so far out of her way to make my life hell. Why?

When the paper cut my fee in half (blaming it on hard financial times), I protested. Then, my pieces started getting deemed too edgy (like one about battered women). I knew I had to walk. I hated it. I was grief-stricken giving up what had been my dream job. But more than one employee confirmed (off the record, of course) that some people had it out for me.

I wrote to the head of the paper, a man who had once sent me a heartfelt fan letter. I outlined my grievances. Still naive after all these years, I thought he'd feel the pain behind my words and rectify the situation. Instead, I was shown the cold wall of corporate America. My complaints were deconstructed and dismissed as inaccurate. My career at *The Dallas Morning News* was over. Sadly, in real life, Davy rarely beats Goliath.

These days, when an editor asks me for changes, I've developed a routine, along the lines of walking away, in hopes that my heart will follow. I read the criticizing email with one eye shut, or read every other word. I discern that—surprise—the first draft wasn't perfect. I feel a pang, every single time, of rejection. I feel a desire to write back a letter of defensive protest. Then I get up, walk away, and go swimming, or do some knitting, or listen to some music. Later I come back, and I always say the same thing: "Sure, I can make those changes." Because I know that even if I think the changes are stupid, I won't get paid unless I make them, and I won't get assigned more work if I'm a dick, even if I feel justified in acting dicky. If there is a point I strongly wish to argue, I force myself to assume a gentle tone and lay out my thoughts in a "How about this?" manner, rather than saying, "Fuck no, there's *no way* in hell I'm changing that."

Does this method work? Usually, but only to a degree. Obviously, if I'm still writing about editors' remarks as a source of anger, I still haven't reached that Let Go place yet. But I'm moving in that direction. I've also diversified: I got so burned-out freelancing, and dealing with so many inane remarks from so many women's-magazine editors, that I took on other work, like teaching, to decrease how much hack writing I would have to do. Trim the hack, reduce the anger. It works.

Road Rage

Based on my incredibly informal survey of friends as I wrote this book, I'd estimate that road rage runs neck and neck with romantic conflict when it comes to things that piss us off. I'm convinced that if cars disappeared tomorrow, once everyone got over the change we'd all love each other a whole lot more. Really. Carry a sticky note with you some day, and affix it to the dashboard. Every time you yell at, scream at, flip off, or even think a mean thought about another driver (or pedestrian), put a mark on the paper (carefully—you're driving). You'll be surprised and probably—hopefully—appalled at the amount of anger inside your head when you're behind the wheel.

One day, I picked up Henry's friend after school. This was during the period I was being stalked, and my life felt very out of my hands. I was suffering, pretty severely, a symptom of PTSD known as exaggerated startle response—any unexpected noise could make me jump and even start crying. We were on a residential road, one with speed humps and no passing lane. I was following the very slow speed limit when a guy in a huge truck came up behind me, honked hard, and passed on my right, driving up on the curb.

This scared the crap out of me, and I wanted to punish the guy. I didn't slow down and remind myself that he was a lunatic, maybe even a dangerous lunatic. I was completely and totally out of patience with everyone and everything in my life. Incredibly sick of having my life run by a guy who was stalking me, I attached all of my anger at the stalker to the truck's driver. And I did what no human should do—certainly not a human with a child in the car. I went after the guy.

What felt like a long car-chase scene from a movie probably only lasted four blocks, and Henry's friend did not seem aware of my angry pursuit. I eventually lost sight of the maniac truck—but not before my adrenaline had risen to heart attack levels.

On a much more subtle but also much more regular note, I very often have kept (and sometimes still keep) a running commentary while driving. I don't flip anyone off. I only really *yell* if someone has just jeopardized my life, and even then I'm yelling within the confines of my car, with the windows up, and typically with the radio on, so whomever I'm screaming at has no idea. The commentary might go a little something like this:

You jackass! Where'd you get your license? Pep Boys?
What the hell was that? Hang up and drive. Oh, what?
Did the Lexus not come with turn signals, you poor thing?
What the hell are you? The Random Brake family?

Such a regular part of my life have these running commentaries been—like sports announcers droning on during the Super Bowl, compelled to say something, anything, at all times—that I've mostly stopped noticing I'm even talking at all. But once, during a visit, Henry's father could no longer stand it. I was freaking him out. What I viewed as an exercise in catharsis and (hopefully) clever sarcasm, he viewed as spleen venting that was hard on everyone in the car. My bad will was contagious.

These days I attempt to reserve the expletives for times when I'm truly scared shitless (and having had two not-my-fault collisions inside of seven weeks in 2004, I can say these things do happen). When I honk, I try to only tap the horn in a way that says, "Excuse me, could you please wake up?" unless leaning on the horn means saving lives. And I work more to focus on those who do me a good turn out there on the road—letting me cut in, waving for me to go first at a four-way stop, et cetera. I always wave and grin wildly.

Jogger

For over twelve years, with very rare exception, I walked at least four miles a day, sometimes ten or more. Few things in my life have been as centering or rewarding as long walks.

My thirteenth year into this routine, the walks were becoming shorter and less frequent. I blamed an overly heavy work schedule and bad weather because I wasn't yet ready to admit the truth to myself, which was that the arthritis in my right foot was growing exponentially worse, to the point of crippling me. Days I did get to walk, I moved more slowly than I had at the height of my walking days, when I could easily clock four miles inside of an hour.

By then, walking had taken on a new face for me. It was no longer about losing weight (the fifty pounds I'd lost when I first started walking had found me again over time). It was about meditation, contemplation, and bonding with my three dogs.

Every day I left the house, the three of them eager to accompany me, and we walked, at whatever pace my lame foot would allow, a mile through the neighborhood to a little park with a one-kilometer walking path. There I did three laps and then headed back home. Typically I'd have my iPod on, listening to a book or some music.

During one of these outings it was damp out after a rain, and as I approached a narrow wooden footbridge on the little path, I slipped. I didn't fall, but my pace, slow as it was, was broken and the dogs were startled. Meanwhile, unbeknownst to me, a stealthy jogger was coming up behind us, all long legs and gazelle gait.

She was—at least to my way of thinking—full of the sense of entitlement I witness in so many runners, especially when they're passing walkers. She didn't call out that she was behind me, or on my right. She just came charging up, passed us, and then cut in front of me. Too closely. My big dog, Satch, hoping to protect me, lunged at her, nipped, and got her leg in his teeth.

Satch is a sensitive, extremely overprotective dog. I got him when I was first being stalked, and my own fear passed on to him. I've had him trained, and he listens to me most times. When we walk, he always wears one of those pinch collars some people find cruel. All this is to say, I control him. But if you run up behind me, then cut into my space, Satch is going to do what he is hardwired to do—he's going to defend the pack, especially the alpha.

I did not feel good about this—or proud, or smug. I felt totally horrified and I burst out crying. And though I could hear all of my lawyer friends saying, *Don't apologize! That means you're liable!* I apologized. It felt like the right thing to do. I was profuse and sincere. For even though I felt it was her sense of entitlement that got her into this jam, ultimately I think it's my duty as the human with the dog to take responsibility for that dog's actions.

I offered her my contact information and she declined, saying she was fine. I insisted. "You'll want it later," I said. By now we had determined Satch had broken her skin. "You'll want to see his papers to know he's had his shots." She said she didn't have a pen. I told her my website address, very easy to remember, and noted that my email address could be found there. She said, repeatedly, that she was fine. I still felt awful.

Later that day, I got an email from her telling me not to worry, she wasn't the type to call the dog pound or file a lawsuit. Two seconds after that, the City of Austin contacted me and said she'd reported me.

This is where the story turns around. She'd said she wouldn't report me. She reported me. My defenses went up. I found out a little while later that if you go to the hospital for a dog bite (which she did), it's mandatory to report the dog. But the city now wanted to punish Satch. I explained to them that the incident wasn't his fault, that the runner had barreled straight into our path. I pointed out that she'd described the dog totally wrong (she had), and that if my dog were to be put in the pound for two weeks he would die of anxiety. Finally, I got them to put Satch under house arrest, where he remained for two weeks, totally depressed when he missed his morning walk.

Sometime after this—after I'd forgotten about the incident, when we were back to our regular walks, the four of us—we were out one day on the path and (ironically, as it would turn out) I was listening on my iPod to a Buddhist monk talking about love and forgiveness. From a distance I heard someone call out, and I pulled one of my earbuds out and turned to wave and smile. I had walked that path probably a few thousand times, and I knew all sorts of regulars as a result. I figured whoever was calling out knew me.

Well, that much was true. It took a few moments for my brain to register what was being said, and the tone in which it was being said, and then, finally, to recognize who was saying it. It was the jogger, resurfaced. She was a good distance away, and she was screaming at me—how dare I have that dog out without a muzzle, and what kind of irresponsible person was I?

I pointed out that I was within my rights to be walking my dogs. Understand that, as this was all going down, my dogs were heeling perfectly, the big ones on their choke chains, the little one in her harness. They were not barking or growling or threatening in any way.

And we were at least thirty feet away from the jogger. Still, she managed to ruin my walk, to tap into my lifelong fear that no matter what I do, I'll be yelled at.

As I walked home, a debate raged within. I had her email address. To attack her or not to attack her, that was the question. I knew what I wanted to do. But in the interest of trying to change my behavior (note aforementioned Buddhist audio on headphones), first I emailed my lawyer friend Lenny and asked for his calm advice. Then I emailed my friend Dan and asked for his advice. These guys give me really good advice. Once in a while, I even take it. Not surprisingly, both counseled that I drop the matter.

So I did. For about six hours. And then, though I am a crappy liar, I composed an email that included a large piece of fiction. Was it wrong of me? Possibly. But I wanted this woman to shut up and leave me alone. I had Googled her name and was pretty sure she was a law student. And so, preying on this, the story I composed centered on the law. I told her that after she'd accosted me, I'd called the cops and asked what to do should it occur in the future.

I went on to say that I'd been instructed to call 911 and report her, and then to file a restraining order, which would be a public record. I said I understood that her fear was causing her to yell at me. I added that some of her problem was that she felt embarrassed because she'd been so stupid, running in front of a dog like that. I wrote that the city had found her entirely at fault and that she was the one who should have been impounded for two weeks. And I pointed out that my dogs were all completely under control when she was screaming at me. Then I told her that under no circumstances was she ever to approach me again—or else.

This worked. I never saw or heard from her again. But it only worked to a certain extent, because I had to admit that I didn't feel so hot about lying like that and jumping her case. Here, then, is where the table turns. Yelling at people and being aggressive back (or even initiating aggressiveness) so often left me with intense mixed feelings of triumph and defeat. Like I'd won the battle and lost the war.

Full consciousness of the sick side of "winning" was only gaining a real foothold for me at this point in my life. There I was, forty years old, on a walking path supposedly to calm my mind, listening to a Buddhist monk telling me to let shit go, and what am I doing? I'm fully engaging with a perfect stranger, spewing venom at her for spewing venom at me. Pity our mommies weren't there to drag us away by the wrists and sit us both down for a time-out, maybe threaten to take our Barbies away if we didn't apologize to each other.

But I had only me to drag me away. And imposing time-outs on myself has become one of the best, and one of the hardest, tricks I've learned as I have begun—sometimes seemingly rather by accident—to move toward forgiveness.

amy friedman

My Mother's Glass

There are tears in the nature of things.

That's Virgil. A quotation my brother sent me ten years ago.

Back then I was living on the banks of the Saint Lawrence River, in my early forties, and unaccustomed to loss.

One day in early May, just as the last snow was melting, my dad phoned to say he and Mom were coming to visit.

"We arrive Thursday," he said. Then he pointedly added, "Mother's Day."

"Dad," I sighed, "it's a conspiracy. A holiday designed to send kids and dads en masse out to buy things nobody needs."

"Which is great," my dad enthused.

Classic Dad.

Ever since the day, more than sixty years ago, when my father was released from a German prison camp, he has celebrated life. Every morsel Dad tastes, every sight he sees, every walk he walks, every conversation, every meal, every song, every person he loves, and even those he barely knows—except die-hard Republicans—is, in his words, "the greatest." And my mom? She is incomparable. The smartest, sexiest, most extraordinary person in the world.

No, it's bigger than that.

In the universe.

"Your mom's phenomenal," he'd say as she served pot roast for the third night in a row. "Not just a beauty, but an ace chef." Then he would touch her cheek or fingertips.

I'd scowl. "We've eaten the same thing for days," I'd remind him.

Undaunted, he would cast me a look. "And it's better every day."

I always used to tell my dad—before the visit that year—that he had spawned an army of cynical children. In the face of parents who celebrated life and love so heartily, how could we be anything but? I'd ask him.

That is, I asked him that until that Mother's Day visit.

Before they arrived I steeled myself, as I always had, to shun Dad's corn. I had often amused myself on Mother's Days past by ticking off names of rotten mothers, citing some of my favorites, like Peep, of the Heaven's Gate cult, the woman who had once seduced a stream of faithful followers into flying with her to the spaceship in the big, black beyond. That year, like every other year, I brought up all the Mommie Dearests, every Medea of literature and life. I talked about how we'd been brainwashed to believe that once a woman had given birth, she automatically became a saint.

"Settle down," my dad said, as he always did—as did my sisters, as did friends. And okay, I knew my wrath was over the top, especially since never in all the forty-two years I'd lived till then had my mom demanded or even hinted at her desire for a card or flowers or perfume on Mother's Day. She hadn't asked for anything from me, in fact, on that day or any other.

But wrath I spewed. I blamed my mom for the guilt I felt about how accepting she was. I blamed her for my insecurity, my temper, my moods. I accused her, usually silently, of playing me, trying to bend me to her will by never insisting I be or do anything but what I wanted to be or do.

Had my mom been the intrusive sort—a woman more like so many of my friends' mothers, who continually wormed their way into their daughters' most intimate corners, choosing their wardrobes, their jobs, their lovers, their cars—I'd have blamed her for being smothering. But because she wasn't that, I called her cold.

Then I blamed her for being beautiful, for wowing my boyfriends, for turning heads in crowds, for looking equally good in jeans and gowns. Had she been unbeautiful, I'd have blamed her for being an embarrassment, for every flaw of mine.

I blamed my mom for being too loved, for being confident, for encouraging me to make my own choices. This freedom, I reasoned, had caused my mistakes. It was my mom's fault I was booted out of AP English class—she hadn't grounded me for not reading the books. And if only she'd chosen my boyfriend, I wouldn't have dated a cad. If she'd insisted I wear the clothes she loved, I'd have attracted a different sort of guy. If she had picked my career, I'd be successful. If she had insisted I not move up to Canada, I'd never be homesick.

I was relentless.

So my dad asked, "You'll remember? Mother's Day?"

I figured he'd forgotten who he was talking to. "I don't celebrate it, Dad."

"That's cold," he said.

I silently blamed my mom for the coldness that crept over me on such sweet holidays.

Of course, long before that Mother's Day visit I'd begun to recognize this blaming child-me in others' daughters. That year it was seventeen-year-old Erin, who could find nothing to admire in her mother, my oh-so-admirable friend Diane. When Diane was caught up in her work or in her private—separate from children—life, Erin accused her of neglect and carelessness. When Diane nursed Erin through cramps and heartbreak, Erin complained her mother was overbearing.

I carefully suppressed any urge to defend my friend.

I told myself I respected Erin's need for rebellion when, truthfully, I was as critical of mothers, even my friends, as any teenager around.

But then, the day my folks were to arrive, Erin came to visit me, and as she began an unreasonable rant, I felt something shift inside me. I must have sensed what was coming; I can't be sure, but I know I took Erin's hand and held it for a long, long time, and then I silently willed her to feel some empathy for her mother.

That day the river was cloaked in fog, and I'd begun to visualize my aging parents driving over the long suspension bridge, crossing the border, traveling five hundred miles out of their way to see how we were up here where the weather—"great," my dad would say—was rainy and difficult.

Then they were there.

My mother stepped out of the car.

She was smaller, frailer, and her once bright blue eyes were glazed.

She smiled at me. Her smile spread across her face the way it always had, and I felt myself relax, a little. She was clutching a packet of photographs in her hands, and when I saw her usually flawless nails hadn't been clipped, I stiffened.

"Here," she said, thrusting the package toward me, proud that she'd remembered to bring along pictures of my nieces and nephews.

Her memory was slipping away. The long descent had begun four years before, but suddenly I understood—I saw—my mother wasn't suffering ordinary forgetfulness. My mother, still in her sixties then, was gravely ill.

I took the photographs from her and raved over her grandkids' growth.

Then I stepped forward to hug her, embarrassed as I

always had been at public displays of affection, for which embarrassment, naturally, I'd blamed my mom.

She lunged forward and hugged me more tightly than she ever had. She could no longer concentrate on playing the sports she'd always loved, and I could feel the muscles in her back melting away.

For minutes we held each other. I breathed in her scent, until it stirred so many memories of all the ways she'd loved me that I had to pull back.

Harder still than public displays of affection are public displays of longing.

Those glassy eyes looked at me, startled, and so I reached for her hand, an apology for letting go.

For ever letting go.

Again she moved close. She took my face between her hands. "Darling," she said, astonished, "you're so beautiful."

She'd forgotten my face.

"You too," I whispered, and that's when, for the first time, I wished I could relive those forty-two years, begin again. I wished I had long ago chosen corniness over cynical chic.

Two days later, when my parents left to drive back to Ohio, I collapsed, sobbing as I thought of all the ways my mother was leaving us, every way but physically.

I phoned my brother and cried, and that's when he sent me Virgil's quotation, hoping to soothe me by reminding me that such is life. There are tears in the nature of things.

Now, all these years later, my mom remains with us physically, but every year she grows more lost.

Last year, after our annual family gathering on the beach in Montauk, we sat in a circle in the sand and agreed it was time for Mom to have more constant care. Time for Dad to have a break.

And so, at that time of year when days are growing shorter, nights cooler, leaves beginning to die, we moved my mom into a nursing home.

She no longer speaks. She has no memory of any of us—though sometimes I imagine I see a shiver of joy in her when my dad touches her face or holds her close. He visits her every day, and every day relives the heartbreak of a farewell without end.

That first day when we dropped her off, after we walked away, we sat around together and wept, and we admitted that we were among the lucky few; we had found Mom a good place to live, a place that would give her some comfort. And Dad could afford it.

And there was more. Each of us admitted Mom had been one extraordinary dame.

Then my brother did what he does best. He had found the perfect quotation to nail down feelings I could not describe. He handed me Shakespeare's Sonnet III.

Thou art thy mother's glass, and she in thee
Calls back the lovely April of her prime.

I am my mother's glass, and she is mine. I know that now. She is my glass, and every time I look at her she calls back the November of my discontent and blame.

Amy Friedman writes for magazines and newspapers in the United States and Canada, has published two memoirs, and writes an internationally syndicated column of stories for children, "Tell Me A Story." She teaches writing both at UCLA Extension and through her course, From Page to Stage.

My Mother's Glass

katherine tanney

In dreams, my mother and I were pitted against each other in hand-to-hand combat inside of a house. We were practically naked, like sumo wrestlers, as we tumbled from room to room, beating the living crap out of each other. We were very violent, but like certain types of movie violence, our fighting went on and on without either party getting hurt enough to stop. No injury was beyond a quick recovery. I must have snapped her neck to the breaking point dozens of times. I impaled her skull on a fireplace poker once, right before waking up.

These were the worst dreams I ever had. They left me deeply depressed and mentally exhausted. In them, there was no possibility of victory. We were matched, muscle for muscle, spit for spit. We fought to the death but could never get there, I think, because death would have been some kind of resolution. The joy and horror of these dreams was in sinking my fists into her flesh—turning my rage into brutal blows that knocked the wind out of her and took her down to the ground.

She'd whacked me around a good bit when I was small, and later, too. She was a big, strong woman, seething with rage toward her parents. She broke a lot of objects during her many tantrums, said a lot of insanely cruel things. So it's not surprising that I grew up with a bellyful of violent rage toward her.

The dreams finally stopped when I initiated a period of zero contact with my mother. Already I'd found a therapist to help me begin to separate, emotionally, from her, but it wasn't until I put an end to actual interactions between us that I stopped having those kill-or-be-killed dreams. In time, we resumed communication, but she was never able to get under my skin again, the way she had before I'd sought therapy.

She died almost a year ago, following a heart attack and prolonged stay in the hospital that left her small and weak and utterly pathetic. I cannot forget that final version of my mother. It stands like a commentary on all the other versions.

Nowadays, I use my breath to cope with feelings of rage that come up unexpectedly. If possible, I give myself private space and a time-out for breathing in and out. I reflect on the situation at hand and what it means to me on a deeper level before losing control and upsetting others. That's not always possible, of course. With boyfriends, I've found play wrestling to be a great form of release. It's also good exercise and, some of the time, very effective foreplay.

Katherine Tanney's essays on love have appeared in *The New York Times.* She has published a novel, poetry, short fiction, and several reviews.

elizabeth topp

Let's start with my golden rule: *Do what you say you are going to do.* Other iterations of this rule include, *Don't be a fucking asshole to your girlfriend.*

I developed this rule on my seventh lap around a colorful block in San Francisco, six months ago, as I raged at Adam on my mobile phone. We were stuck in the fog between friendship and romance. He'd agreed to pick me up in San Francisco and take me back down to Los Angeles with him. But at the last minute, we'd gotten into a big fight and he'd blown me off. I was left to rent a car with money I didn't have, drive it to Los Angeles, and tell him that if he wasn't going to do what he said he was going to do, then I couldn't count on him—and if I couldn't count on him, then as far as I was concerned, our relationship was a nonstarter.

So he said I could count on him.

Six weeks later he moved in with me in New York.

Perhaps it was hubris to think that as long as we had the very basics down (love and commitment), the rest (cooking, garbage, dirty toilet bowls, laziness, strife, excess, extreme closeness, and the pressure of everyone we know looking at us as if to say, *You two are fucking nuts)* would take care of itself.

Sure, there were bound to be tough times. I expected some fighting and "space issues." Adam wondered about the effects of giving up surfing and sun.

In the end, those "tough times" were so much worse than we could have imagined. Forget tests and speeches— this was tough like standing out in the pouring rain with a howling wind, dressed in your skankiest undies, ankle deep in mud, with a team of the people who matter most to you in the whole world screaming in your face that you suck. And if you're rightly wondering what in God's name could make something like that worthwhile, that's how good it is when we aren't screaming at each other.

The silence between us tonight is the eye of the storm. Today is Thursday, September 8, 2005. This weekend my oldest friend, Joanna, is getting married in San Francisco. I am a bridesmaid, which is an expensive honor. So here we are, on the plane, enjoying an unofficial détente on our way back to cheery San Franfuckingcisco.

The beginning of great anger can be tragically minor. In this case, it started with one of those things that had bugged me consistently, if not that much—one of those inevitable shortcomings that the gracious girlfriend lets slide. Like, he leaves empty glasses all over the house, or the shower faucet just the slightest hair loose so that the *drip drip drip*ping only becomes apparent as you flip the lights off at night.

Some saints can spend their lives like this, silently collecting empty glasses and shutting off leaky faucets. Some will grow more and more frustrated until they one day erupt, throwing glasses and banging bathroom fixtures with hammers so that they cannot be budged. Instead, I waited for a day of exceeding good will between Adam and myself, where it seemed a surety that we'd tie ourselves into pretzels just to please each other.

Adam likes to start cycles on major appliances— like the dishwasher and the laundry machine—but he rarely completes these tasks. I'll happen upon a tub of damp laundry two days after the fact, a few dry-clean-only items hanging like skins on the rim of our laundry basket. So last Saturday, I asked Adam to do the laundry, and he agreed. Nice. Encouraged, I let drop that doing the laundry included the whole soup-to-nuts operation, not just an abortive first pass.

On Wednesday, I skipped into the laundry room to find the you-guessed-it laundry in midprocess, hanging all over the place. It was extraordinarily generous of me to finish the chore, and only then mention it to Adam. In passing.

And there's the rub: There's this whole other person there who's got his own crappy job, long day, and small resentments building. And these innocuous components combine to create a chemical reaction that trips along to a dangerous explosion:

"You said you were going to do it."

"It doesn't matter."

That was the upshot, here on this plane, in these crappy JetBlue seats that he loves. Adam threw 50 percent of the foundation of our relationship under a bus. I know he doesn't mean it. He knows I know that he doesn't mean it, but it's still sacrilege and a lot of unfinished laundry.

I am in the middle row of a cross-country flight, sandwiched between a smelly woman, whose watery eyes beg for conversation, and the most vile and loathsome person on earth, my boyfriend. I'm typing. He knows I'm writing about him, and he's fuming. We're hurtling forward, through the dark, thousands of feet above the ground. It's quiet all around, but between us, there's a perfect storm.

Elizabeth Topp is the coauthor of *Vaginas: An Owner's Manual* (Thunder's Mouth Press), which she wrote with her ob-gyn mother. Presently, Liz is making a film in conjunction with InCite Pictures. Her work can be found at: www.SearchingForG.com.

part three

The Upside of Anger

chapter 3

Fear and Anger

In the movie *The Upside of Anger*, the main character, played by Joan Allen, is so pissed off so much of the time that even I wanted to slap her on occasion. Me, who recognizes anger as a tool and catalyst. Me, who would be hurling a car-sized boulder at a fragile, handblown glass house if I judged that character.

Mostly, I empathized. Of course she was angry. Much of her anger seemed of the justified variety—everything was out of her control, the people she loved were hurting her, she'd suffered the huge trauma of sudden spouse loss, and all she could do was drink to distance herself from what was pissing her off. (Aside: I requested an interview with the guy who wrote the screenplay and played a key role in the film, and he declined—and I admit this momentarily angered me. Ha.)

Though this movie was merely a ninety-minute escape into someone else's fictional world, and not designed to rival, say, a Bergman film, *Upside* certainly had its moments. And I watched it at a time in my life when I was contemplating my own lifetime of anger and thinking about ways of overcoming something that seemed as much a part of who I was as my brown eyes.

The simple truth—about the characters Joan Allen's character had to deal with, and the real-life people I've had to deal with—is that, yes, others are bound to piss us off. That sounds like a very *No duh* observation, and on one level it is pretty simplistic. But it's also an important reality to keep in mind when dealing with the complexities of conflict. But my tendency to view the world as black and white has been a real problem over the years. Someone would piss me off. I'd yell. Then I'd feel remorseful. I'd think, *Why did they do that? What's wrong with them?* Or I'd think, *Why did I do that? What's wrong with me?*

I've come to believe now that the problem is much more a matter of what's wrong with all of us. And what's wrong, I'm convinced, is one thing: We all spend a lot of time feeling entirely misunderstood, or unheard, or ignored. We want people to get us, to understand what we're saying—whether we're requesting that someone pass the butter or entertain our latest JFK conspiracy theory. And if the butter doesn't get passed or the theory gets dismissed, here comes trouble. Response: anger.

My friend Marty told me a great story once, and I never forgot it. As a kid he was riding on the subway in New York with his mom. There was a crazy guy in the car who was yelling and freaking out the other passengers. Marty's mom, Trudy, a no-nonsense New Yorker and Jewish mother, didn't avert her gaze as the other commuters had. Instead, she looked the guy right in the eyes, and with sincerity in her voice, said to him, "I understand." And the guy calmed down.

Had Trudy, in one sentence, cured the guy of a lifetime of mental illness? Doubtful. But in a few breaths, she'd comforted him, if only temporarily.

Recently, I was talking to my friend Kat about teaching knitting. I've been teaching knitting for awhile now, and Kat, who is always looking for ways to do less office work and find more flexible gigs so she can stay home with her baby, was about to start teaching some knitting classes of her own.

I told her the biggest thing I'd learned while teaching anything (besides knitting, writing, and literature, I've also taught martial arts) is that everyone just wants to feel heard, to be genuinely understood. And, I suggested, when students come to her frustrated—which all students but especially beginning knitters are bound to do—the best thing to ask is, "How do you think we can resolve this problem?" If the problem is obviously beyond the solving skills of a novice, I said, she could at least offer this reassurance: "Oh, I can show you how to fix that." (Under no circumstances should you say, upon observing an error, what a phlebotomist once loudly muttered when she shoved a needle *through* my vein: "Oh, shit!")

Allowing students to feel included in the solution process gives them room to exhale and suggests that, ultimately, they'll be the ones in charge. Too many teachers (and I fall into this category often enough, because I suffer regular bouts of teacher amnesia during which I forget all my own good advice) want to just reach in and take over, because they can, or because it seems easier in the moment.

Frustration, the seed of anger, is highly contagious, so it's extremely easy to respond to a new knitter's exasperation with your own. But you cannot—absolutely cannot—simultaneously successfully teach knitting and be impatient. You can't. You'll fail. I admit there are times when, sitting down to teach yet another kid how to knit, I first tense up and then sigh. *Oh god, not this again,* I think. *How am I going to get this kid from here to there?*

Here's the good part about knitting, though—what probably keeps me teaching it. In an overwhelming number of cases, it only takes twenty minutes, tops, for the knitting lightbulb to go on. When this happens, *bam*—the kids (and also the adults) get it and take off knitting. Granted, most of them make piles of mistakes and turn up for the next class with something that has grown into an odd shape and appears heavily moth-eaten. But they understand the general concept.

I attribute some of my success to a "method" I developed at least as much to protect my own sanity as to protect that of the new students. "You must be a fearless knitter!" I insist (partly so they won't bug me every two seconds with a problem). "You must keep going through the mistakes! You mustn't worry about loops and holes. This is about muscle memory and repetition! Don't think too hard, or you'll get analysis paralysis. Just knit, knit, knit!"

Telling them this reduces the fear and anxiety most new knitters have about "failing." The thing is, most people fail at their first knitting attempt, if by *fail* we mean "do not come up with a perfectly knitted, mistake-free angora sweater with complex cable patterns." That sense of failure pisses them off. Remove that sense of failure and you remove at least some of the potential for frustration and anger. Better, the new knitters have a sense of fun. It's very hard to be angry when you're having fun.

Coming to understand how intertwined anger and fear are has taken me forever. I suppose it should have been obvious to me early on. My father enraged me, and also scared the shit out of me. I realize now that his anger must have had some basis in fear, too. I don't know what fears he had as a child that might've influenced his becoming an angry adult—he never told us about his childhood.

I know one major source of fear he had as an adult: He was afraid his nine kids would go out in the world and fuck up, or become fucked-up at the hands of others. Some of this fear came from the scary newspaper headlines and melodramatic TV news reports he constantly assaulted his senses with—they fed him horrific tales of everything in the world that was going wrong. Besides fearing for our well-being, I think, he had a fear of losing control of us.

I didn't come to the conclusion *Anger = fear* on my own. I've been working with an amazing healer/therapist, Luisa, for some time now. She has given me a series of metaphors and visualizations that have helped me reorganize how I approach the stumbling blocks that appear regularly in my life, seemingly popping up out of nowhere. Let me give an example.

In April of 2005, I was about to buy a house. This was an incredibly big deal. I'd been living in dorms, apartments, and rental houses since I was eighteen. I had flushed probably a couple of hundred thousand dollars in rent money down the toilet. I'd overcome bad credit and qualified for a mortgage. There I was, at forty-one, about to take a big leap into adulthood and major fiscal responsibility.

I'd heard the process would get hairy at points, and I'd been told to expect an emotional roller coaster. I didn't discard this advice, but initially I couldn't see a place to use it. In fact, the process seemed to go very easily. I found the house I wanted on the first day I looked, in the first hour—it was the third house I walked into with my realtor friend Andy. I'd found a mortgage company that showed me, step by step, how to clean up my credit record. The mortgage agents had held my hand, at least in the beginning, through every minor detail.

Henry liked the house I'd picked—and of course I wanted to have his okay. Like me, he was pleased that the garage had been converted into a bedroom. We called that the teenage wing of the house, a place he could sleep and make music, two concrete walls between his electric guitar and my need for quiet while I write.

Things were moving along at a nice clip, and I started wondering why people bemoan the house-purchasing process. Hell, this was easy.

Then, as you can guess, the shit hit the fan. It wasn't that the process was easy, I discovered. It was that the mortgage company forgot to call me and tell me a few things until the last minute—such as the fact that the closing had been postponed, meaning that I had to cancel the fifteen friends I'd scheduled to help me move. Meaning that instead of moving on a weekend, I'd be moving on a Monday, with hardly any help at all. Meaning that my stress, which had built as I packed up the old house, went into overdrive. I started crying. And I cried for five days straight.

Meanwhile, something happened with Henry. He was fourteen, and going through an abrupt personality change. It was as if I'd walked in the house one day and my precious, spoiled, loved-beyond-compare lapdog, Princess Bubbles, had leapt up and sunk her teeth into my calf. I reacted to Henry as I would've to Bubbles: I cried out, surprised and hurt.

We exchanged heated, ugly, loud words. I was overcome with

deep sorrow, masked by my screaming rage, that he had—at least this is what I suspected—burst through the door of angry adolescence, suddenly and without warning. *So this is the teenage stuff I heard about and thought I was immune to,* I thought. *God, this sucks.*

Our mutual and simultaneous outbursts seemed to be a nonstop string of child-parent hatred. I found myself channeling my father, threatening Henry with Catholic school. I threatened him further, telling him he could move to Saint Louis and live with his father. (In retrospect, I deeply regret brandishing time with his father as a possible punishment. What I'd been thinking in this threat was not *This is the worst possible thing, living with your father,* but rather, *You will so regret being sent away from your friends.* But he couldn't discern that—not the way I was yelling.)

He yelled back. It was horrifying how masterful he was at slicing me down, going for the jugular, making precise hit after precise hit with his vitriolic spew. And where had he learned such skillful, wicked techniques? From the master. And where had I learned it? From the grand master. I was no better than my old man.

I sent Henry away to Ross's for a few days. I called him a little shit. I said I hated him and never wanted to see him again. I couldn't understand how I could live with him for another four years. I grieved the loss of the little boy and young man who'd been so delightful and polite for so long.

And then we moved.

Actually, I moved. Henry, in a dramatic moment, slung his backpack over his shoulder, grabbed his guitar, and announced, "I'm not moving." I sat and watched him walk out, thinking, *I can either go after him or I can keep moving.* I kept moving, knowing Ross would pick up Henry and take care of him, knowing I was too worn out, from the stress of the preceding days of packing and paper signing and air traffic controlling a logistical nightmare, to effectively deal with my son.

What I didn't know is that Henry would stay gone for days.

I tried to put up a good front. I got all of our stuff moved from point A to point B. I unpacked the vast majority of the boxes (or shoved them into closets) inside of forty-eight hours. I had a box garden built. I had my room painted Honolulu Blue. But at night, when I lay down to sleep, Henry's absence was a forceful presence.

There was no doubt he would return. Still, I was having a hard time figuring out how we would patch things up. Ross was starting to get irked with me again (as noted, this was a real rarity—the only other time he'd been mad at me was when my screaming induced the major panic attack that put Henry in the ER the preceding summer). I would call Henry at Ross's, vow to be calm as I punched the number, fantasize about him loving the house, about this anger just dissipating. Then I would hear his voice, one of us would revisit a bone of contention, and we'd be at each other's throats again. No matter how hard I tried, I couldn't keep myself from dropping to his level. And he couldn't keep from sinking cruel barbs into my heart.

Ultimately, I said, *That's it—you're moving home.* And he did. And in a remarkably short time, he calmed down. What I had thought was a hellish start to angry adolescence proved to be fear of moving. While I'd known the transition might prompt some nervousness, I was surprised to learn that it had been the primary source of Henry's pain, since he'd had a say in buying the house, and he seemed to love it as much as I did when I showed it to him.

What I hadn't thought about was how, despite loving the new house, he might miss the old one. That house had been sanctuary when we fled from my horrible marriage. We took every first-day-of-school photo from first grade through eighth grade there. In our old neighborhood, he could easily walk around to all his friends' houses—and we weren't yet clear if this would be true of the new neighborhood. Though just two miles away, it was on the other side of a busy highway.

During all the yelling and crying, Luisa gave me one of the best visualizations I've ever used in a crisis. She asked me to imagine what would happen if I walked into an ER with my arm hanging off and the doctors and nurses who came out and saw me began screaming in horror. Of course, we agreed, this would amp up whatever panic I was already suffering.

Henry's yelling at me during the move was a form of fear and panic, she explained. Moving from a place he loved was an amputation. His anger was just how the fear of this loss had manifested. By yelling back at him I was doing a very shitty job of triage, to put it mildly. I was the ER doctor. I was supposed to be calm and observant and soothing. Instead, I was pointing at his wounds and shrieking.

This was truly a lesson learned. Henry and I have had our moments since that rough period, but so far I've been able to revisit Luisa's imagery whenever I'm tempted to yell back. It's a method I'm testing in other areas as well, though I'll probably need at least eighty more lifetimes of working on it before I really am able to view someone's mean or rude remarks, when directed at me, as rooted in a place that has nothing to do with me.

This is something Trudy understood on the subway. It's something I hope to come to one day, so that remaining calm becomes second nature for me. I know if and when I achieve this goal, I will stop greeting anger with anger. Meanwhile, I am revisiting some of my past hurts, looking for the fear at the root (the fear that caused others to say or do something I took as a slight, and the fear that made me react in anger). Again, it's slow going, but at least I'm moving in the right direction.

chapter 4

Punting the Pope

In the fall of 2004, my old friend Hillari, then an editor at *Natural Health* magazine, asked me if I would write a story about forgiveness. When I told my friend Sarah about the assignment, so strong was my reputation as a sufferer of Irish Alzheimer's (someone who forgets everything except grudges) that she nearly spit her teeth out laughing. What could I possibly have to say about forgiveness? she wondered. I defended myself, pointing out that I was capable of forgiveness. But the truth was I'd taken the assignment primarily for the money and I, too, wondered how, exactly, I would tackle the topic in a sincere way.

When contemplating where to begin the piece, my mind immediately conjured Thubten Chodron, a Buddhist monk and the author of *Working with Anger*. I'd met her just once, and only briefly, years before, but her presence and message so impacted me then that not only had I not forgotten her, I'd also started exploring Buddhism as a possible spiritual path as a result of our encounter.

I'd been in Saint Louis taking Henry to see his dad. It was May, and I happened upon an article in the *St. Louis Post-Dispatch* about a Buddhist celebration—Vesak Day—taking place in a small town outside of the city at a monastery. Henry and Michael both pooh-poohed my suggestion that they join me. Undaunted, I set out on my own, down country roads, to locate the event.

Though I'm someone who makes a fair number of public appearances, and though I can be what is known as a "situational extrovert," I will never stop feeling shy and awkward in my heart whenever I find myself in the midst of strangers. Typically, when in such a situation, I'll find an excuse to leave as quickly as is politely possible. But on this day, I felt no such discomfort. The grounds of the monastery were beautiful, everyone gathered for the day seemed content and serene, there was a stunning spread of food, and the weather was perfect. I settled in to observe, participate, and, hopefully, learn.

After leading us in a meditation session, Thubten Chodron told the story of her life, talking about how she was drawn to Buddhism as a young woman, and where it had taken her. Chodron sat still and straight, her shaved head setting off her beautiful face, her voice soft and lifting at the end of each sentence, almost as if she were asking a series of questions.

I was in touch with Chodron once or twice after that first visit, hopeful that I might interview her for a story. Opportunities slipped away, though, until Hillari gave me the perfect excuse to call. Chodron agreed to give me her take on forgiveness, and I was surprised at what she had to say. In a brief conversation she was able to get me to rethink a lifetime's perspective on what forgiveness is.

My whole life, I had tied forgiveness in with religion. When I fled the Catholic Church at nineteen, disgruntled and dismayed, I rejected much of what I'd learned there. While I didn't reject the idea of forgiveness out of hand, I certainly associated forgiveness with Catholicism, thus tainting the concept. Worse, forgiveness was tied in with confession and penance, which had an element of punishment to it that I loathed. I always hated confession as a kid—there was something very creepy about telling all your "badness" to a strange man behind a screen.

As I grew older, I wrestled with the idea of forgiveness. I heard over and over that when we forgive, we don't do it for the other guy, we do it for ourselves. I had also heard that forgiving someone brings an overwhelming sense of joy and peace.

That was all fine and good in theory, but I encountered many obstacles when I contemplated application. For starters, forgiveness isn't like starting the car or throwing in a batch of laundry. You can't just say, "I'm going to do this now," and then snap your fingers and it's done. Even if I had wanted to forgive certain people, I didn't know how. There was no button to push, no series of steps I knew of. And, like saying "I love you" when you don't, saying I forgave someone when I didn't seemed pointless. And I certainly did not forgive the people who had hurt me the most.

My perception of what forgiveness entailed—specifically, what a relationship was supposed to resemble postforgiveness—caused another problem. Over the years, many people had urged me to forgive my father. But I had a video clip stuck on a loop in my head, showing what I thought other people thought it would look like if I did forgive him. What they wanted, I believed, was some happy movie-of-the-week ending, a resolution that would find my father and me embracing, setting aside our differences, and revisiting the strong relationship we'd built when I was young but stubbornly abandoned due to our many conflicts.

But there was no loving relationship to return to. My father never liked me to begin with. Despite the fact he had nine of them, my father had little patience for children. He had the least patience for me, something none of my siblings would deny and even my father has come to admit in his old age. People not raised by a parent who can't stand children never, *ever* understand this. They think I'm full of shit, misinterpreting, that surely my father loved me. But ample evidence and numerous witnesses confirm that my father was no fan of mine, going back as early as my infancy.

I began to wonder: *What if I could forgive him? What if I understood the concept and application of this thing that supposedly brings peace? Then what? What relationship is it that we'd revisit, exactly?*

We only knew how to hate each other, and we had demonstrated it continuously and zealously over many years.

Then, when I was around thirty, I had a major breakthrough in my life. I was in the earliest stages of confronting—for the purposes of healing from—what my father had done to me. In fact, I was in such an early stage I didn't know it was a stage at all until much later. I wasn't ready for therapy yet. I was still incredibly angry and hurt. I was still drinking regularly and still suffering from depression, which I was not yet ready to admit was linked to the drinking.

A friend had given me a copy of Alice Miller's *Banished Knowledge,* in which Miller suggests that we need *not* forgive people who've abused us. She theorizes that a lot of us are in deep pain because we feel tremendous pressure to overlook or get beyond parental abuse—a pressure literally of biblical proportions, since it ties in with one of the Ten Commandments, the one about honoring one's mother and father.

Why should we forgive abusers? she asks. This rang a huge bell for me. *To hell with my father and the pressure to forgive him,* I thought. Why must I bear all the weight of what he'd done? Why did it fall to me to forgive him *or else?*

Though I'm not fully in line with Miller's theory anymore, at the moment that I read it, it worked. The revelation I felt upon completing *Banished Knowledge* empowered me. I'd needed a catalyst to fling me into another mind-set—away from the depression and guilt I felt about my relationship with my father, and into a helpful angry place where I could, as I analyzed my childhood, stand up for myself and recognize what happened to me was not okay.

Allowing myself to be openly enraged at my father (which some people, my siblings in particular, might say I never had a hard time with, but I'm talking about being both openly enraged and okay with it) unleashed something in me. I cried a lot. I was furious.

When I detailed my relationship with my father in my first book, I chose this Elvis Costello quote as an epigraph: *Don't ask me to apologize/I won't ask you to forgive me/If I'm gonna go down/*

You're gonna come with me. I loved the bitterness of that remark, the *Screw you for screwing me* implication.

My memoir was, in large part, about cataloguing all sorts of pain from my first thirty-three years, putting the pieces of the puzzle in some order so that I could begin to see the old picture of me and watch as some vague new picture floated to the surface—sort of like those posters where, if you stare long enough, an image of a dinosaur or Jesus or Washington crossing the Delaware pops up out of nowhere.

Miller's book got mine rolling. In a way, *Banished Knowledge* offered me permission to write the memoir. And as I began to increasingly think about things in a psychoanalytical fashion, I took baby steps toward accepting the idea of therapy, which I'd known was a good and helpful thing *for others* but which I'd hesitated in seeking for myself, courtesy of the stigma attached to it in my childhood home (we were threatened with therapy if we didn't "shape up") and my very stubborn I-don't-need-anyone's-help streak. (I eventually dipped my toes into and out of therapy before diving in deeply in my forties.)

Between reading Miller and fully embracing therapy, I encountered Chodron. When I interviewed her for the magazine story I experienced another big epiphany, one that would shove me forward ten steps on the path toward understanding this forgiveness stuff. Chodron laughed a little—softly, not unkindly—when I asked her if forgiveness always had a religious component. Not at all, she said.

"I think forgiveness is something totally different than religion," Chodron told me. "It has nothing to do with God or Buddha or anything. It doesn't matter if you believe in creation or not. If you want to live a happy life and live in harmony with others, forgiveness is common sense."

Once again, in an instant, Chodron had influenced me deeply, dismantling my lifelong (negative) intertwining of religion and forgiveness. It reminded me of the umbrella story, another example of how I spent many, many years misperceiving a reality.

One rainy day when I was in kindergarten, I tromped to school proudly toting my new umbrella. It was clear plastic, with red STOP signs and green Go signs printed on it. I was so proud of that umbrella. It couldn't have cost very much, but to me it was priceless. Growing up with eight siblings on my father's truck-driver salary meant hand-me-downs and very few extras. This umbrella was mine and mine alone, brand-new, and I loved it.

Arriving at school, we kids parked our boots and rain jackets and umbrellas in the mudroom, then commenced our happy, busy kindergarten day. *Until* . . . Until a big dog got into the mudroom and chewed up all our possessions, my beloved umbrella among the lost.

I spent much of my life since then afraid of umbrellas, avoiding them with rare exception, until a few years ago. I was explaining my phobia (which I now suppose was a fear of loss) for the ten thousandth time to a friend who found my aversion odd. This friend, unsuccessfully suppressing a grin, informed me faux-somberly that I was "blaming the victim," the victim being the umbrella, when really I should fear dogs. (Which I don't—in fact, I'm obsessed with them.)

Similarly, I'd assigned forgiveness unsavory characteristics, throwing out the baby with the bathwater because, for one, I had a fear that if I went around forgiving people, I'd somehow be affiliated with Christianity. Not that Christians have cornered the forgiveness market—I mean, even before Chodron separated forgiveness and religion for me, I knew it was more than a Christian thing—but I strongly associated the two. (And for the record, I think Jesus sounds like a swell dude and a fine role model. But the things people say and do in the name of Christ—well, hell, that's not something I ever want to be tied to again.)

So what *is* forgiveness, if not some religious command that we let people stomp on us as we smile politely and allow them to do it? What does forgiveness look like and smell like? Must it take the form of a movie-of-the-week finale, as I always wincingly presumed? Again, Chodron corrected me. She didn't tell me I was wrong—she simply shared her idea of what forgiveness was, and it made good sense. And inside her model, I actually felt like maybe, without realizing it, I was already on the road to forgiving a number of people.

"The way I define [forgiveness] is to stop being angry, to stop holding a grudge and holding on to resentment," she told me. "It doesn't mean saying that what the other person did was okay. You can still be quite clear that their behavior was harmful and inappropriate. But that doesn't mean that we need to be angry about it and hold onto the resentment about it. They often say 'Forgive and forget.' Some things should be forgotten, other things shouldn't be forgotten. For example, something like the Holocaust—you can forgive the people who perpetrated it. But as a thing of inhumanity it needs to be remembered so we don't do it again. You need to look at [situations] case by case."

How can it be that I spent a lifetime angry and unforgiving and then, inside of a moment, felt something like an epiphany? I mean, I didn't walk away from Chodron's interview suddenly feeling that I could issue blanket forgiveness. But listening to this magnificent, calm woman, I felt a decided shift in my attitude. If forgiveness meant letting go of some of the anger, then okay, maybe I could do that.

In the article I eventually wrote, I likened releasing my anger to those old cartoons where someone is hanging on to the side of a cliff, tenuously gripping one long protruding branch. Letting go in these cartoon situations isn't born of a desire to let go, but from pure exhaustion. Like Wile E. Coyote, I quit holding on simply because I couldn't hold on anymore. Life wasn't worth living if life was all about holding onto the lone branch of anger. Perhaps that's a dramatic metaphor, but there's real truth in it.

Focusing on being angry at my father for what he'd done to me, and for how his awful behavior continued to pop up in my life in so many negative ways (in how I acted toward others, in how I allowed others to treat me, in how I treated myself), wasn't helping me. And finally—finally!—I was reaching a place where I could not only acknowledge this fact (which had occurred to me intermittently over the years) but also do something about it.

We all know some miserable old person who can't let go of something that happened fifty or sixty or seventy years ago. My heart hurts for those people, and now I can finally see that my father is one of them. I don't know what made him so angry so long ago, but I'm done letting his anger rule my life—which in turn alleviates the lion's share of my own anger—and I feel bad for him for whatever it was that took him down, that he was never able to shake.

More than this, I'm grateful that I'm removing myself from that same misanthropic path. I could just as easily have kept charging along it, blaming the hurt my father and others inflicted on me for whatever pain I was feeling. But with Chodron's advice that I could work on forgiving without necessarily forgetting, I'm able to feel some healing that, in turn, has opened my eyes to some unexpected gifts my father gave me, which I'll reveal shortly.

chapter 5

Reframing Past Anger

Looking back on each of my past bad relationships, I have to admit there was always a time in the beginning (typically the very beginning, before I had any idea of who the guy was) when I would proclaim I was "in love." And, of course, after the bitter end, there was always a time when I thought, *No, I couldn't have really been in love.* I wanted to deny the truth of my original proclamation, to myself and others. Loudly.

So, to ask the corny question that's the stuff of pop tunes and Lifetime Movie Network dramas, what exactly *is* "in love"? You can't define love concretely, and you can't perform a blood test to prove that it's real. Similarly, what is forgiveness? If you say you forgive someone, does that make it true?

Of course not. But even before Thubten Chodron helped me rethink what forgiveness equaled, I had my moments of trying to forgive others. Besides disliking what I saw as the religious aspect of forgiveness, I also feared that saying "I forgive you" might actually come off as condescending. I mean, who the hell was I to forgive? I couldn't move away from the idea that forgiveness involved some sort of power play where the forgiver deigns to absolve the forgivee, who is then forever beholden to the forgiver.

And yet, I don't think I was going for the power play (at least not primarily) when I told myself—as I did nearly from the moment he left—that I'd forgiven Henry's father for leaving us. No, with Michael I engaged in a different psychological process altogether.

Now, I *was* in love with Michael. And no, I can't fully define how that felt or what that meant—but it's been over seventeen years since we initially connected, and I can still remember our first afternoon together. I remember sharing early awkward kisses in the months we moved toward coupledom, and once even breaking one of my biggest rules against major public displays of affection. (We just couldn't unwrap ourselves from each other in the Saint Louis airport that day.)

When Michael first left us, initially to move down the street, it was 1992. Within a year, he'd moved back in and then out again. He was suffering from severe alcoholism and having grand mal seizures as a result. I couldn't care for both him and Henry, and I couldn't deal with the pain of watching him fall apart. I asked him to move back to Saint Louis so his family could help him. He did.

I'm not going to say that I issued a grand forgiveness and marched on with my life after he left. Now that a dozen years have passed, I think I have a clearer vision of what truly happened. For a very long time, Michael was in and out of rehab, on the cusp of death, and living on the edge of homelessness, so I squelched whatever anger I had toward him best as I could. Or I displayed my anger in passive-aggressive ways. Or I explored it late at night, lying in bed—sometimes in the form of missing him, of being angry that he had left me when I loved him so much, sometimes imagining what a lifesaving windfall I'd receive if he miraculously sent me all the back child support he'd never been able to afford to send.

Mostly, I tried to not be upset with him. I knew, despite his obvious and deep love for Henry, that he had not been ready for fatherhood. When I was pregnant with Henry, pending parenthood scared the hell out of Michael. Because I could choose to terminate the pregnancy, I extended to Michael a chance to also "not be pregnant"—to walk away if he felt he needed to. As a pro-choice feminist, I only felt right giving him the chance to opt out, too.

I still think life would've been less complicated for all of us if he'd chosen to exit while I was pregnant, rather than two years after Henry was born. The messiness, the grief, the intense pain of having him leave after the three of us had bonded—it was overwhelming. But he had to go. He couldn't function, and I couldn't function with him around. My heart was breaking, and when he was within sight I did feel angry. My own drinking accelerated when I was around his drinking (partly to numb my pain and partly because when I compared myself to him, I seemed like a social drinker).

When he was nearly a thousand miles away from us, life became easier in a sense. Or at least it became easier for me to create a tolerable myth about Michael. Yes, I might cry sometimes at the loss of him, but I cried nobly, like a martyr. I could tell myself that his drinking was a disease, that he hadn't really chosen booze over us, that he'd been swept away by something over which he was powerless, and that I had no choice but to bravely soldier on and raise our son.

When I took Henry to visit Michael in Saint Louis, or had Michael come for a visit, Michael would typically attempt to quit drinking, if only temporarily. His body—at this point needing the alcohol—would respond with grand mal seizures, and we'd wind up in the hospital. It was an ugly cycle, and I'm sure some people questioned the intelligence of exposing Henry to his father in such a condition.

But the way I saw it was, Michael was probably going to die before he turned thirty-five. I didn't want Henry's only memory of his father to be of a funeral.

I was passive-aggressive all the years Michael was sick. Only when he finally got sober, when Henry was ten, did my real anger surface. My fury seemed to arrive from nowhere. I mean, he was *sober,* for God's sake—finally where I'd wished he'd been all those years. There was no more denial or condescension in his voice when he talked about support groups. Something had changed in him, something that made him want to change himself. He was humble and stable and doing the work he needed to do to get healthy.

I voiced my anger—and my surprise at feeling anger—to one of my sisters, who made this astute observation: "All those years you wanted desperately for him to live. Now that you know he's going to, you want to kill him."

It was true. Here's what drove me to drop my forgiveness stance and embrace the anger: All those years of thinking each time I saw him would be the last, I couldn't allow myself any sustained outward, high-level signs of anger. You can't be angry at the dying. *That's just not right,* I thought. I didn't want to find out that he'd dropped over dead from a seizure and then spend the rest of my life reflecting on how pissed off I'd been at him, with no way to work through it since he was gone.

I'd merely stuffed all that pissed-offness, over a decade's worth, and now here it came to grab me by the throat. Of course I was angry with him. He'd left me. He'd left Henry. How dare he? And now he was going to be healthy, and have his life and no responsibility. How fucking dare he?

The above logic is a primary example of my infamous black-and-white thinking. Of course I know now, and knew then (even if I acted otherwise), that life was far more complex than *Michael is drunk and miserable—I should be kind* vs. *Michael is sober now and off the parenting hook, irresponsible and free, and I hate him for that.*

To get past those oversimplified thoughts, particularly the latter, I needed to think the situation all the way through. A friend of mine who does AA told me about this thing they talk about in meetings called euphoric recall. Euphoric recall happens when you're sober and you're longing for the alleged good old days. Let's say you remember some great time you had in a bar one night with your buddies. You miss that. Missing it makes you miss the whole lifestyle. You want to go back and drink again and live the good times.

The key, in this situation, is to think through the entire memory. *And then what happened?* you ask yourself—at which point your memory, if it's truly serving you, will remind you: *And then you got drunk, and then you said or did something stupid, and then you went home with a stranger, drove drunk, had bad unsafe sex you can't remember, and woke up puking with a hangover.*

I could sit in Austin and resent Michael all I wanted. I could resent that his family continued to rally around him with emotional and financial support while they offered neither to Henry and me. I could resent that Michael was working toward getting a job and making money that he could and would spend on himself first.

Or I could stop and reframe the picture. I've gotten very good at reframing things— I can even consider other people's perspectives now, sometimes even when those people are pissing me off. (Contemplating the viewpoint of someone you're angry at can be difficult, to be sure, but it can be done.) If I thought hard enough, I could understand that resenting Michael wasn't getting me anywhere. He had missed out on every single milestone in our son's life, from toddlerhood on. He had missed out on his own life, having spent years in a stupor. Why would I want harm to befall him, even the small harm of the angry vibes I shot at him?

I'd like to say that was that—that I thought the situation through and became logical and forgave him again, for real this time, and moved on. But that was hardly the case. I'm still working on forgiving him. I think I've gotten pretty good at it. There have been backslides.

In 2004, when he came for a visit—and he always stays with us when he visits, to save money—I fell into one of my *Michael's visiting* patterns. I got bossier with Henry (perhaps to demonstrate I was the parent in charge), I got agitated over their activity choices, and I seemed to exhibit a lot more road rage. My irritation with other drivers, an especially sore spot for Michael, ratcheted up his anxiety until suddenly we were on the front porch and he was leaving early for the airport. I was crying and begging him not to. Major scene.

When he left, I screamed at him in my head. *Fuck you! Fuck you for all the good things that you haven't done, and for all the stupid stuff you have!* I fell apart. I cried until I shook. At that point, every ounce of rage I'd ever let myself feel toward Michael, all the rage I'd suppressed, shot out of me. I was a human volcano.

Michael called the next day from Saint Louis, apologizing profusely. We'd both succumbed to temporary insanity, and he was faster to regain his footing. Me? I couldn't shake my anger. But, in what was progress for me, if only limited progress, I was able to tell him something very, very clearly.

"Michael," I said, in the calmest voice I could muster, "I know my own self very well now. I know how I am and how I need to be. You have upset me completely. I do not forgive you. I can't. Not yet. I need time to heal. I need time for this to go away. It could take me a year. I don't know how long it will take. But for now, I want you to leave me alone. Don't call me, don't email me. Just shut up. You have Henry's cell phone number—you know how to reach him. You can be in charge of contacting him. I'm done leading you down the parenting path. And I'm done with visits for now."

Harsh? Absolutely. But a step forward, another example of how anger worked as a catalyst for me. If I could have said those things sans anger, I think now that I would have. But I couldn't. I was a huge pool of emotions. I was fully acknowledging how abandoned I felt. The moment on the porch when he walked away symbolized the bigger departure, when Henry was a baby. Even if I hadn't learned how to deal with my anger yet, at least I was acknowledging its existence, not making excuses for it, and demonstrating that I understood my own patterns and needs.

I didn't speak to Michael for months, but something both trivial and crucial in both of our lives helped us move to a better place. I was out at a restaurant with some friends and a song came on. I swore it was the '80s band Split Enz, and my friend Tim swore it was some other band. Tim and I both fancy ourselves music experts, so the five-dollar bet was on. Michael is one of the few people I know who has retained even more stupid music facts than me, so I called him to settle the bet.

I got his voicemail and left him a message asking for the correct answer. He called back soon afterward. It was a baby step, two people on beloved, neutral territory.

We slowly advanced (though we still had, in our future, the specter of his sister's wedding and her Bridezilla behavior, developments that would slide us backward some). In less than a year—the time I'd predicted it would take me to settle down—I allowed Michael to visit us. By then he had demonstrated constant, responsible interest in Henry. He'd sent me money each month. He'd called Henry a few times each week. He'd straightened himself out.

I calmed down. I also think I rose to the occasion of Michael's newly demonstrated responsibility. I remembered the goal I had tried so hard never to lose sight of: to above all else raise a physically and mentally healthy child, no matter what. Fulfilling this goal entails not filling Henry with conflict over his parents' relationship. That's not the same as having a false friendship with Michael. But I wanted Henry to know I didn't hate his dad. I also wanted him to know that anger is a real, inevitable feeling.

And I wanted him to know that anger can be worked through.

As I write this, Henry is asleep in the other room. In less than an hour, I'll wake him up and take him to the airport, and he'll fly to see Michael and his family. I'm not going this time. I won't be there to be passive-aggressive or let myself feel regret and irritation over what might have been. Henry will be spoiled and adored and appreciated. It won't be a perfect happy ending, but it will be another step toward Michael and I acknowledging not only our failures, but our mutual desire to move on, for our son, and for ourselves.

chapter 6

Teachers

(Positive and Negative)

Let's get back to religion for a moment. I figure several million people, without batting an eye, would say if queried that Jesus is the best practitioner of forgiveness they can come up with. I've already pointed out how the religion stuff has bogged me down. And while I like the idea of Jesus and Buddha as great masters of letting stuff go, I admit that more immediate, contemporary role models come to mind when I'm looking for inspiration to make the practice of forgiveness a regular part of my own life.

Several years ago, my friend Hank Stuever, who is now an editor for *The Washington Post* but who for a long time was a reporter, wrote a piece about a guy I refer to as Bud the Forgiver. Emmett "Budd" Welch lives in Oklahoma City, as did his twenty-three-year-old daughter, Julie, until she died in the Oklahoma City bombing—when Timothy McVeigh blew up the Alfred P. Murrah Federal Building in 1995.

Hank wrote his piece about Bud not long before McVeigh was scheduled to be executed. At that point, a whole lot of people were eager to watch him die—some of them wanted to literally witness life leave his body.

Bud was not one of those people. Though he described himself to Hank as politically rather conservative, he said that at some point he just sort of let go of his anger toward McVeigh. Bud called this a mercy he himself didn't fully comprehend. But forgiveness was what he'd decided on (or what had come to him). As a result, Bud became involved in the anti-death-penalty movement, a choice that brought him a lot of media attention, given his circumstances.

Bud's stance and the ensuing attention it brought him were very polarizing for the people of Oklahoma City. Some viewed Bud as a saint, and others despised him for opposing the death penalty and for being such a media magnet. Let's face it: A guy who wants to forgive and let live the brutal killer of his own daughter and over a hundred other people (including little children) might be considered certifiably nuts, especially by those who believe in eradicating evil through any means necessary.

Here's a quote from Hank's piece:

"I didn't say I was going to forget what Tim did. I said forgive, but a lot of people just don't get it," Bud says.

He understands why they don't. He also wanted Tim to fry, once.

"I'll tell you, if between now and May 16, Tim would ask for forgiveness, my life would get a whole lot simpler. I'd forgive him," Bud says. "But he hasn't asked. So I guess I forgive him anyway."

McVeigh never did show remorse before his execution, and didn't really help his reputation when he gave that steely last look of hatred and defiance to the camera mounted in his death chamber.

This next excerpt makes me cry every time I read it:

In the summer of 1998, a nun in Upstate New York arranged a secret meeting at a house with a garden out front. Two men in their late fifties, with only their Catholic

Pissed Off

upbringings and an insistent grief in common, had agreed
to meet, with no media, no specific thing to talk about. Bud
Welch went up and knocked on the door of Bill McVeigh.

Never mind the media attention. Bud did something very private, a true testament to forgiveness. He reached out to the father of his daughter's murderer. And he made friends with a man who, no doubt, must have felt an overwhelming grief. Thinking about that story makes me want to go back and apologize to everyone I ever did anything shitty to. It makes me want to let go of all the petty crap I ever held on to. It makes me want to flush all grudges. It makes me want to rise to Bud's example and try to walk in the shadow of his compassion.

Obviously, these are not desires I've sustained or fully acted on. Some grudges remain. And even if I'd started apologizing ten years ago to those I've slighted, I'd still be sending flowers and soothing words a hundred and fifty years from now (at least). But sometimes I think about Bud, and how he found this thing, which I guess can most aptly be described as grace, and it blows me away and makes me want to be a better person. A much, much better person.

I've been equally moved by the actions of the parents of Amy Biehl, who was a Fulbright scholar and humanitarian worker. In her twenties, Amy traveled to South Africa to fight apartheid. A few days before she was slated to return to the United States, Amy, who was white, was stoned with bricks and stabbed to death by four black youths. These young men, originally sentenced to eighteen years in prison, later applied for amnesty under a program established by Nelson Mandela to help ease the country's past political strife and pain.

Amy's parents supported the amnesty request and shook hands with Amy's killers at their amnesty hearing. They also established the Amy Biehl Foundation, which works to prevent violence in South Africa. (Amy's father has since died, but her mother carries on the work.)

I don't know about you, but if my kid were murdered, I'm not entirely sure I could keep from wanting to murder the murderer.

Sitting here in a safe place, typing quietly, contemplating these big acts of forgiveness, I like to think I, too, could forgive anything. But reflecting on the reality of who I am—well, I'm not so sure I could.

But each of those stories, though I first heard them long ago, have stuck with me and called out to me. Surely if Amy's parents and Bud can do what they've done, then I can at least keep myself from screaming obscenities at the guy who cuts me off in traffic. (Okay, I can't always do this, but I'm working on it.)

Perhaps the very best teachers for me have not been the forgivers, but people in whom I've seen my father's anger and my own anger reflected back. These reflections have caused me to at first recoil, then gingerly examine and process that anger and draw conclusions about it that I surely couldn't have reached in the past, before I started working toward change in my own life. Two very big examples come to mind.

Once upon a time Henry and I lived in a house next door to a house in which resided a family: Mom, Dad, and kids. On the surface, this family seemed a little eccentric but overall well-meaning and enthusiastic. Mom and Dad were big-time school volunteers, constantly working on extracurricular projects with their kids, who always appeared cheerful and well behaved.

Being next-door neighbors, we couldn't help but sometimes know more about one another than was comfortable. For instance, once the dad came to me and said, sarcastically, "I want you to know I can't hear anything that goes on in your bedroom." I suppose he'd heard me having sex—my bedroom window was practically up against his kitchen window. I could've said, "I hope you enjoyed it," or "Yeah? Well, I heard you washing dishes," but I bit my tongue.

My loud sex was nothing compared to what they did loudly. I knew something that many of this family's mere acquaintances did not: that both the mom and the dad had mean streaks and awful tempers. I think we've established by now that I recognize that parental anger happens. And yes, this kettle is calling that pot black. But their parenting anger, unlike mine, was persistent.

Eventually, I recognized something in the family that struck a very deep, very old chord. The kids' good behavior, I decided, was not about the importance of manners. It was based in fear. I could relate to this fear. The kids were terrified of setting their parents off. Henry and I would be in our rooms at night, trying to sleep, and we would hear the father screaming, telling his son what a loser the son was, how stupid and awful. Henry would come to me and we'd try to think of what to do.

I fantasized. I have friends all around the world. I wanted to ask them to mail anonymous letters from exotic locales, addressed to the father, telling him to lay off his kids. I wanted to confront him and tell him to fuck himself. I had confronted him once, when he said something that upset Henry so much he couldn't eat. I said, "Henry feels like you yelled at him."

The neighbor looked at me and, without a whiff of humor or irony, yelled, "I did not yell at him. All I said was, *'You sit down and shut up!'*"

He reminded me so much of my own father, Mr. Tell the Kids How Shitty They Are. His kids were reliving my childhood before my eyes. I wanted so much to rescue them, because I was having traumatic flashbacks and I wanted someone to travel back in time to rescue *me*.

But I couldn't rescue them. I had no idea how. I would invite them over when I could—they were kept on a short leash, and even when they were allowed to visit the visits were timed and controlled by their father. When I got them in my clutches, I'd offer them piles of ice cream and other sweets, praise them, laugh with them, all in hopes of bringing them a little respite. Savior-complexy of me? Yes. But I was also reaching back to my young self, telling myself, *See, you weren't awful—you were a good kid with an angry parent who told you you were bad, but you weren't bad, not really.*

Dealing with these folks (which I did for years) was complex and brought forth tricky emotions. One minute I'd want to pound on the door and tell them to quit yelling. The next minute the dad would be mowing my lawn for me, without my asking for his help. I took so many lessons from this experience. I had final proof of what I'd suspected for a long time—that my father was inexcusably wrong to scream at me when I was young. I wasn't at fault, regardless of how many times my father had told me otherwise and added that I was going to hell.

I also finally understood something that I never had been able to grasp before. As an adult, I'd sometimes wondered why some neighbor hadn't intervened on my behalf when my father was behaving so horribly. His temper was no secret in the neighborhood—we had neighbors he cut off for good and didn't speak to for decades. Why didn't someone just knock on the door and say, "Look, fucker, quit riding your kids so hard"?

Now I knew. As much as I wanted to confront my neighbor, I simply couldn't. I knew it would compound the problem. I knew trying to defend the neighbor kids would bring the wrath of their parents down on my head—they would cut me off, and then I wouldn't even have the rare chance to have the kids over for games and sweets. I also suspected that if I pulled the kids aside and told them no one deserved to be yelled at like that, ever, I would make them uncomfortable and tear a huge hole in the fabric of their fear-based parental allegiance. I did not confront.

The second example of negative teaching involves a former friend of mine whom I'll call Cranky, because this is the trait that most readily defines her. Cranky is a filmmaker who used one of my articles as the basis for a documentary. I was featured in this work, and I also narrated it. The piece turned out well and aired on PBS. Consequently, when I decided to make my own documentary, I asked Cranky to be my director of photography.

At preshoot meetings Cranky would dominate, which I accepted since she understood the process of filmmaking whereas I was an idea person. The documentary, a look at the curious culture of quilters, was to be based on a book I'd spent two years researching and writing. I fed Cranky an overview of the topic, and she came back with thoughts on how to best capture the essence of this topic.

When I came into the tiniest sum of money, I decided we should use it to get the project started. This entailed an eight-hundred-mile road trip to a quilting retreat in Colorado. The retreat was led by a celebrity quilter, and attended by a dozen or so women who were more than a little passionate about their art. I knew the celebrity quilter—I'd interviewed him for my book and a magazine article, and I'd seen him at several International Quilt Festivals—and I counted him as a friend.

Cranky complained about everything on our drive west. Most famously, she bitched about a boyfriend, declaring that his flabby ass, flat feet, overbite, and lack of ejaculatory force discounted him as a permanent mate. She also kvetched constantly about genetically altered food—it was the focus of another documentary she was working on. I thought my ears would bleed if she didn't shut up. But she didn't.

Cranky was also incredibly defiant. A hundred or so miles into the trip, I noticed a light flashing on my dashboard. I looked closer. The flashing light indicated someone was not wearing a seatbelt. "Cranky," I said, "you forgot to buckle your seatbelt."

"It makes me claustrophobic," she replied.

When I'm on the open road, I drive around eighty-five miles per hour. I wanted to say, *You're going to feel a lot more claustrophobic if we get in an accident and your head becomes lodged in the windshield.* No matter how I asked, though, Cranky wouldn't yield to my request that she obey the law and click it.

Once we got where we were going, Cranky realized she had forgotten the camera's battery charger. When Cranky started flipping out about her oversight—it wasn't like we could go down to Main Street and rent another charger—I actually responded with great calm.

"Look, don't worry about it," I said. "If I have to drive to Colorado Springs tomorrow and rent one, I will." I meant this. I was tired from driving so far. I was glad to be here, about to embark on this new creative project. I was doubling up my time here as a minivacation. And I was dropping several thousand very hard-earned dollars, so I was determined to have some fun. Getting mad over something I couldn't change—or at least couldn't change at that moment—was not my idea of vacation. Fortunately, Cranky had a friend coming down from Denver to do sound for us, and a phone call secured the promise that he would track down the necessary charger and bring it with him.

Though the shoot took only three days, it is a blur of psychobabble in my memory—as if Cranky had taken a bad hit of therapy cut with way too much speed. She was determined at every moment to stop and bombard me with how she *felt* about the situation, and how we needed to *process* this, that, or the other thing.

Let me make a sexist statement here: When I'm working, I operate much like a guy. There's plenty of time later to process, emote, get in touch with my feelings, and perform other cathartic exercises often more strongly associated with the female gender. But if I'm on a journalism assignment or a documentary shoot, I don't have time to fuck around. I like to get in, get what I need, and get out.

Not Cranky. She was compelled to pull me aside at regular intervals, accuse me of not listening to her, and insist we talk still *more* about our feelings. She got stuck in moments of utter frustration during which nothing I could say or do soothed her. She grew furious with my cell phone for not working (she didn't want to try her cell phone because she was freakish about using up her minutes). She screamed at my phone. I calmly responded, "Cranky? I'm going to buy you a phone card, and you can use the land line at the hotel."

"No!! That won't work! Don't you understand?"

I had to take a lot of walks around the block, breathing deeply and setting aside murderous thoughts. While I was away on one of these walks, Cranky whipped out her camera and began interviewing a quilter—an ob-gyn who showed Cranky a quilt she'd made. It was covered in appliquéd vaginas, which the ob-gyn had made for a production of *The Vagina Monologues* she'd been in. Cranky asked the woman, "So, do you make penis quilts, too?"

Now, these women were not prudes. But I heard about this

exchange later from the retreat leader, who was visibly pissed off. Cranky did nothing to appease him when, the next day, she insisted he change his shirt before we filmed him and she tried to demand that he close his art gallery, where we were shooting, to reduce the risk of background noise.

Worst was the fight she incited at dinner one night. A wonderful fiftysomething hippie named Pat and her partner, Randy, cooked each of our meals. Pat had helped start a number of communes in the area back in the day, and she and Randy had no shortage of colorful tales to share. Pat's cooking was so mouthwatering it could make you weep. Everyone was high on quilting and the panoramic mountain view and the pure air and the shared stories. So it was really, really difficult to imagine the collective euphoric mood being spoiled by anyone or anything. Well, except for Cranky.

I made the grave error of telling Cranky, who happened to be seated beside me at this particular dinner, that the nice woman across from us was a retired professor of nutrition. Without pause, Cranky began to interrogate the professor on her views regarding genetically modified food, a subject on which, as noted earlier, Cranky was basically a Nazi. The professor's opinions differed from Cranky's, leading Cranky to rip into her and also to go on and on about slovenly Americans and the disgusting nature of obesity. As it happened, a very overweight quilter was sitting next to the professor, well within earshot. (Cranky, of course, didn't have an ounce of fat on her body.)

On the interminable drive home, Cranky revisited her argument with the food professor. Now, we'd been having our own arguments the entire drive, but I feigned Stockholm syndrome as best as I could, praying that the powers that be wouldn't let me give in to my true desire to push her out of the vehicle. But when she brought up the topic of arguing with the quilters, I couldn't help but take the bait. "Don't they teach you in film school not to attack the people you're supposed to put at ease because you're filming them?" I asked.

Cranky emitted an audible hiss, then waxed vitriolic. She launched into how she was well aware that she had given her obesity-is-evil schpiel in front of the very overweight woman. I interjected: "As some-one who is considered overweight by society's standards . . . " I got a few more words out about how I thought sensitivity was a priority, and then Cranky let me have it.

"You people with weight problems are *so* defensive!" she shouted.

I was wounded. "I don't really consider my weight to be a prob-lem," I countered. "You know, I gained weight when I quit drinking and I gained more when I quit smoking, but I'm glad I did both of those things, and each prolonged my life."

Cranky didn't want to hear it. She continued to fill the car with anger the whole way home, a drive that was made longer because we had to detour to return the charger, adding a couple of hundred extra miles, and many hours, to our trip. Though we'd talked in the car of how we would continue working together, that was just part of my please-don't-kill-me hostage routine. I knew I needed to fire her when we got back, and I did.

You might think that I hated Cranky after this. Mostly, I pitied her. What made her so fucking miserable? God, it was horrible. Noth-ing, not one single person or thing, she observed or interacted with seemed to bring her any joy.

Being with Cranky made me sad for her, but it made me sadder for myself. How much of my life had I wasted—completely wasted, never to have back again—being angry at one person or situation or another? I didn't want to do the math on that one. Cranky was reflect-ing back the very worst in me, and I hated what I saw.

Alice Miller—the author of *Banished Knowledge*, and the woman who first introduced me to the idea of nonforgiveness—coined an expression that has sustained me for some time. And while I've come to stray from some of her theories, I still like this expression: *Con-tempt is the weapon of the weak and a defense against one's own despised and unwanted feelings.*

That was how being with Cranky left me feeling: Like I was watching myself at my very worst. I felt bad for both of us.

And so I have taken from Bud the Forgiver and from Amy Biehl's parents the idea that we can forgive those who have hurt us the most. Or we can try. And if we accomplish a letting-go, then it won't just feel good, it might produce a greater good. And I learned from my next-door neighbor why, when I was a child, other adults did not come to my defense. And I learned from Cranky that I really, truly did not want to be like her ever again.

On my trip out to Colorado, I was already working toward being more consciously kind and letting go of my sarcasm. Cranky's behavior reinforced for me what I wanted in my life—or, more precisely, what I didn't want. Now, when I open my mouth to bitch and be angry, I can choose to conjure an image of her face, twisted in anger at a dead cell phone or some other circumstance she cannot change, and I can ask myself, *Do I really want to be like that?*

I know the answer before I get to the end of the question.

chapter 7

The Big Forgive

How I came to forgive my father—or to begin to forgive him—isn't entirely clear to me. If you had told me twenty, or ten, or even two years ago that I would ever let go of all the awful things he'd done to me I would've laughed in your face, in part because at those points I still held on to the idea of forgiveness as something linked with a church I hated, something hinged on yielding Lifetime Movie Network–like results.

My lack of relationship with my father, I've come to understand, has quite possibly been the biggest relationship in my life. I got a clue that this was the case in the early '90s, when I visited my then-roommate's psychiatrist. It was my first attempt at therapy, and I entered the office feeling some resistance. Intellectually I knew, or claimed to know, that therapy was a good thing. But I'd been raised believing that only crazy people seek help.

Though I felt bad being there, I also felt a door open up. I remember the calming gray carpet and a desire to lie down on it, curl in a fetal position at the doctor's feet and just let it rip. Wylie, the therapist, was more of a prescribe-meds kind of guy—which I wasn't interested in—but he gave me some talk therapy I never forgot.

"If your father tells you, 'Under no circumstances may you go to San Antonio,' and you don't go, you are listening to him," said Wylie. "But if you go simply because he told you not to, in order to defy him, then you are still listening to him. You have to make your decision whether or not to go to San Antonio on your own."

While his words registered and made sense, they weren't a cure-all. I continued, as I had my entire life, responding to my father's voice in my head. Typically the response was of the defiant variety. *Fuck you—I will too do that,* I'd think. *Do that* might mean anything from *write a tell-all memoir about him* to *drive on a dark road, alone at night, faster than fifty-five miles per hour, in the left-hand lane.*

Here is a picture of my father and me. It is 1988, and I live in Knoxville. I have driven several hundred miles up to New Jersey to spend Christmas with the family, even though I hate Christmas and have a hard time with the family. I arrive, exhausted from the long drive, and am not in my parents' house ten minutes before my father comes barreling in. He's seen a bumper sticker of mine he hates, and he gives me an ultimatum. I can remove the sticker, or I can leave. I want to punch him in the face. I pick up my bags. I leave.

I drive south, about sixty miles, to Atlantic City, where my friend Jonathan resides. I come in, all drama, and proceed to drink my way through the next several days. At some point, one of my siblings tracks me down. It's nighttime. I'm wasted. And I'm screaming into the phone that I will dance on my father's grave. *Dance on it,* that fucker.

That was a critical mass moment for me. But even after it passed, I never stopped having low-level anxiety about my father, and a background head-buzz of anger.

When I was researching the article on forgiveness for my friend Hillari, and when I heard Thubten Chodron describe her idea of forgiveness, something changed in me. Could it be true that forgiveness didn't involve some ritualistic moment that ended with a group hug and an attempt at a long, loving relationship? Could it really be about letting go, period?

Because I *was* letting go. I had held on to my anger for nearly forty years. I had hated my father and I had clung to that hatred, and I didn't even realize how exhausted it was making me until cumulative exhaustion took a toll. When I let go, it was more about lacking the energy to keep holding on than about desiring to do the "right" thing. The low-level anger was always there, barely below the surface, ready to rear its head at any time: when someone cut me off in traffic, when I perceived some slight from a customer service rep, or when anyone else pissed me off (for real or imagined offenses). I was tired of it.

Something else affected my decision to start letting go. Sometime in the past couple of years, my father developed Alzheimer's. My joke is that not only can't my father remember he hates me now, he simply has no idea who I am. It's a little hard to sustain a grudge against someone who is completely absent.

Though my father has intense memory problems, my mother informs me that he sometimes announces that it's his fault I don't live near them anymore, that he drove me away. Well, you know, that statement is entirely accurate. He *had* driven me away. And I'd resented him for it all my life. But I was starting to see the coin's other side.

I was listening to a series of tapes called *Your Sacred Quest,* by the spiritual lecturer Joan Borysenko. At one point, Borysenko talks about how our enemies can sometimes be our greatest teachers. The word *enemies* immediately brought to mind my father. I couldn't think of another person who had so consistently worked against me, from the time I was very little. *What could I possibly learn from him?* I wondered.

Then the answer came to me. I already knew that my father's mean streak had made me compassionate. I'd so hated the way he'd yelled at me and told me I was stupid, I'd been so incredibly aware of the pain he'd inflicted on me as a child—pain that had informed my low self-esteem and so many of my poor choices—that I'd vowed to be the opposite of him. I was hardly successful 100 percent of the time, a statement that probably goes without saying. But when people complimented my parenting or asked me why I was so patient, I would say, or think to myself, "I just do the opposite of my father."

At the workshops and writing camps that I teach, the high-maintenance kids sometimes irritate the hell out of me. But I stop myself when I start feeling irked with a particular kid, and I tell myself it's entirely possible that he's demanding more attention because he's having some bumpy situation in his home life. That's not necessarily always the case, but I bear in mind the possibility, and doing this helps me to be patient.

Something else occurred to me as I listened to Borysenko talk about enemies as teachers. I considered my father's declaration that he'd driven me away, and imagined what my life would've been like had he not driven me away. It's entirely possible, I concluded, that I would've remained stuck in South Jersey—undereducated, married, with a bunch of kids, maybe teaching high school English.

There's nothing tragically wrong with any of those components (I mean, I am, among other things, a parent and an English teacher), or even the combination, if those things are what you want. But they weren't what I wanted. I wasn't even sure what I wanted when I left at eighteen. But getting out of that place was one of the best things I ever did. Because I left, because he drove me away, I have managed to travel extensively, make friends around the world, and come to know things that were so far beyond my South Jersey scope that even a glimpse of them was unavailable to me as a child.

Would I trade my experiences in if I could go back and have a loving relationship with my father, the sort of relationship I've witnessed between many of my friends and their fathers? Is it awful that my answer is *I'm not sure?* Or maybe it's *Hell, no!* Because, after forty years of flailing, I'm pretty good with who I am, pleased with the culmination.

The next question, then, is *Must I be grateful to him for being so hard on me?* My sixth grade teacher once wrote me a letter, about twenty-eight years after sixth grade, upon finishing reading my memoir, in which I did not spare my father. She had a theory that maybe he was trying, in his own way, to protect me. Others had offered variations on this theme, to which I'd always responded, "Talk to the hand." When Mrs. Brzuska entertained the possibility, I still didn't want to hear it, but my utter respect for her caused me to at least file the concept under Revisit in the Future.

I'm not ready to send my father a gold engraved thank-you card for driving me far away, into a world that I love and that loves me back. Similarly, I'm pretty sure that I will never, ever extend gratitude to my ex-husband for stalking me. And yet that stalking drove me to take martial arts, and the martial arts training instilled confidence, helped me overcome agoraphobia, increased my limited physical coordination, and showed me that I could kill people with my bare hands—while teaching me it was far, far better to walk away. Martial arts also led me to yoga and daily meditation practice, which ushered me to Buddhist teachings and, ultimately, a desire to learn forgiveness.

I don't want to make too big of a stretch here, but I find it interesting that the Borysenko tapes were among the last things I listened to before I was forced to stop taking my long walks. My walking ritual had begun back in 1993, when I was substantially overweight. My French friend, Elisabeth, actually dragged me out walking, kicking and screaming, until I was totally hooked. Then she left me to my own devices.

I lost fifty pounds and gained, to my surprise, some mental clarity and balance. I became reliant on my daily walk to the point of superstition. Days when depression revisited me, I'd walk ten miles or more. People saw me walking with my dogs so often they would stop and inquire about it—was I a professional dog walker? Walking was my passion—the place I worked things out, wrote rough drafts in my head, found solace.

In early 2005 I noticed I was walking less frequently. I'd stumbled into some soul-sucking textbook-writing contracts that, silver lining, would help me qualify for home ownership. But in addition to being agonizing to write, these books required, often enough, that I work seven days a week, for over eight hours per day. I was miserable.

During this miserable time—and by now I'd gained back the fifty pounds thanks in part to quitting drinking and smoking, habits I'd replaced with food and more food—I told myself, *If only I could take long walks again, my life would be better!* or *Once I start walking again, the weight will come off!* Walking had been a magic cure for me on more than one occasion, and I looked toward resuming my regimen as a way to improve my life some more.

When I could, I continued to walk, but for fewer miles, and not every day. I kept trying to avoid admitting there was another factor keeping me from my routine.

I suppose it'd been 2002 when my right foot had first started hurting. I remember saying to my friend Jeff, "I probably have toe cancer," and his logical response was, "Think about it. Do they run marathons to find a cure for toe cancer? They don't. Toe cancer is rare. You're fine."

So I ignored the pain. Which got worse. And I continued to ignore it because, in part, I had no insurance. Then it got bad enough that I applied for a medical assistance card from the city, which scored me cheap healthcare at municipal clinics and x-rays at the city hospital, where it was determined that my self-diagnosis was incorrect and I did not have a stress fracture.

During this time, I was twice misdiagnosed as having gout, a disease associated with overweight middle-aged men who eat piles of red meat and animal organs and drink red wine—not sober women who haven't touched red meat in twenty-four years. When gout was eventually ruled out, a nurse practitioner at one clinic ultimately deemed my ailment "joint pain," a diagnosis even my least smart dog could've given me.

The pain got worse. My right big toe was swollen two to three times bigger than my left big toe. But I refused to give up walking. Or I refused to give up the idea of walking. The truth was, I just wasn't walking much at all anymore. I guess we call this denial.

Then—talk about being thankful for negative things—my son accidentally ran over my bad foot with a shopping cart one day. In my experience, when your child does something that causes you physical pain—say, slams your fingers in a door or bites down hard during breastfeeding—it is important not to scream really loud, lest you freak out the child. In this case, I couldn't help myself. I fell to the sidewalk and cried and cried. The pain was unbearable. My foot was already starting to swell even more, and turn black. I figured it was broken.

I went to a specialist. He did new x-rays and, being a specialist, readily gave me a proper diagnosis. I had advanced degenerative arthritis, there was no cartilage left in my big toe joint, I would never have mobility in the foot again, and the best I could probably hope for would be to have the bones fused together to prevent the bone-on-bone rubbing that was causing so much of the pain. Well, if I had seven thousand dollars.

I didn't. Nor was I sure I wanted such radical surgery. After crying for two weeks, grieving over my foot, and acknowledging, finally, that a crucial ritual in my life was gone, I began to swim daily. I also got a cane and a disabled parking permit.

Two interesting things strike me about my final walks. First of all, I typically listen to audio programs on my iPod. But since the Borysenko program was on audiotapes, I'd gone out and bought a little cassette player with headphones. I bought one for my dad, too, for his birthday, possibly the first gift I'd given him since I was ten years old. I did this largely in hopes that it would bring my mother some relief. She was taking care of my father 24/7, which was beyond taxing. I thought maybe if he would retreat with his headphones, she would get a break. I knew, too, that sending him something—anything at all—brought her another sort of relief. She had watched us, two people she loved, hate each other for decades. It was a curious olive branch.

I called my father on his birthday, as well. And then again on Father's Day. Again, I did this in great part to comfort my mother. But I also heard something like happiness in my father's voice when we spoke. I don't know if these calls would've taken place had I not listened to the tapes, and I doubt I would've thought to buy him a cassette player.

The other observation worth noting about those last outings—because I do so like applying Greater Meaning to things—is that ending my long walks with those tapes was, in retrospect, quite fitting. How many times during those walks had I thought about, cried about, and tried to figure out my relationship/nonrelationship with my dad, and attempted to decipher how it affected my other relationships? It was as if my feet had been allotted fifteen or twenty thousand miles in which I could mull this great puzzle and then, *bam,* it was all over. More than once I'd literally walked until my feet bled, trying to get through a situation that was haunting me—Michael's alcoholism, my sister's proselytizing, problems with one lover or another.

Finally, I reached a place that looked something like steady peace—just as I had to finally acknowledge there would be no more walking to contemplate it. Ironically, it was also as if what had long felt like an emotional limp had, after all those years, manifested as a physical limp. And yet, with this manifestation, much of the emotional limp seemed to dissipate.

Which is hardly to say I'm done thinking about it, or that the forgiveness is complete, or that I have a desire to race to New Jersey and hold my father and will him, if only for one of his rare moments of lucidity, to work with me to find a place of love. I just feel like I can see now how his weaknesses contributed to my strengths. And I'm sure that dancing on his grave would only serve the purpose of hurting my foot.

appendix

What I Think About
When I Think
About Forgiveness

Honestly, I think all the best advice in the world makes a pretty short list and that the list has been around for a very long time. In fact, the shortest version of the list is two words: the Buddhist tenet *Be mindful.*

But in the interest of making a short story long, here's my version of things to contemplate and steps to take to move from anger toward forgiveness.

Remember that Anger Is Effective

When one person is angry, other people usually respond. They might not respond the way the angry person hopes, but still, they respond. That's because anger is an effective attention grabber. Anger is a siren. But there are other effective ways to get people's attention. The key—and here's why I think everyone should take at least ten years of martial arts training, starting preferably at age two—is to try very hard to use something besides anger, especially in the first attempt to achieve a goal.

Let the knowledge that you can tear off someone's head with your swift and biting tongue be like the knowledge a black belt has that she can floor someone with a single roundhouse kick. That is, let this knowledge be satisfaction in itself, and then either walk away from upsetting situations or force yourself to not yell. Sounds utterly impossible (and I still succumb with some regularity when the voices tell me to yell). But the more you practice not yelling, the easier it becomes.

Sober Up

I have no idea if I might've sobered up sooner than I did had my friends done an intervention on me. I imagine I would've become enraged and stopped speaking to these friends, and found new ones down at the bar to support me in my habit. I can remember my friend Coury, back in the '80s, getting on my case for drinking. I was furious with him. Then, for show, one or two nights when I went out I drank orange juice, but before too long I resumed with the booze and spent less time with Coury.

I loved booze. Loved it. What I loved about it probably only lasted a half hour each day. That half hour would typically occur on my old house's little porch, around six or seven in the evening. In those moments after the second or third beer was consumed and before the third or fourth beer was finished, something like relaxation would sweep over me—me, the one who worried all the time about everything, who never sat still, finally gaining respite, throwing back some cold ones, smoking end-to-end ciggies, and laughing with my friends, who were also drinking and smoking. I still, in an odd way, miss those moments, though I wouldn't actually want to relive them.

The catch was, of course, that all the other moments that went along with that half hour of chemically induced joy added up to significantly more than a half hour—the moments when I passed that euphoric buzz and I was actually drunk; the moments I had to get up and stumble through the house to pee in the middle of the night; the moments, also in the middle of the night, when I would wake wide up even though I still needed more sleep, because the booze had worn off. And then there were the mornings (and by this I mean most mornings) when I would wake up so hungover, my first thought was, *When can I take a nap?* I put up a good front, and people didn't know I was hungover unless I said so—I ran the house, raised the baby, worked hard (sometimes at two or three jobs), and got shit done. But inside I felt incredibly sick.

And the booze fed my anger. One of my most embarrassing booze-related moments (and this is saying something) came when I went out one night with my then-roommate, Paula, to see a local yodeler, Don Walser, play at a punk club, Emo's. Henry was very little then, and I didn't get out much without him—and at home I could better measure my alcohol intake, or at least lie down once I'd overindulged.

Here at the club, I lost control. I drank too much too fast, and quickly became very drunk. Which is when Paula pointed to a young woman across the room and announced that this woman had been to the restaurant where we both worked and had left an unacceptably small tip. At this point, I'd probably waited on tables a dozen years. I indulged my drunken, self-righteous inner bitch, the one sick of serving people, the one tired of shitty tips. I brought this inner bitch out and walked her over to this woman, who had no idea who the hell I was, and proceeded to blast her for her terrible tipping ways.

She yelled at me and said she couldn't afford to tip, that she was on state assistance. To which I responded that she then shouldn't wear an expensive leather coat and order mixed cocktails in bars (both of which she was doing). Can you even imagine this? Picture a three-hundred-pound cowboy onstage yodeling while one drunk woman lectures another on restaurant etiquette. Maybe you're laughing, but I'm certainly not.

There's no way around it. I'm going to sound like the nondrinker I've become when I say that booze is fuel on the fire of anger and depression. Some of us just can't drink, and that's that. We can split hairs over whether we're alcoholics versus problem drinkers (a distinction eloquently outlined in Caroline Knapp's brilliant memoir *Drinking: A Love Story*). We can tell ourselves that we'll only drink once a week, or two drinks every other night. But those of us who need to quit usually know we need to quit, and until we do quit our anger is going to grow and our ability to forgive is going to remain at bay.

So if you're feeling hungover a lot, pissed off with the world, and miserable with yourself, quit the chemical substances. Don't slow down. Don't invent elaborate psychological games in which you're only drinking every other hour, or drinking a glass of water for every beer, or drinking on a full stomach to lessen the impact. Quit. Stop drinking or using whatever your preferred poison is. Stop. Period. It's much easier said than done, but it can be done.

Use Righteous Anger as a Catalyst

I said anger was a siren, and it is. Sometimes sirens are good things. They let you know you need to get out of the way, pull over to the side of the road, and maybe even think a good thought for the person at the receiving end of the sirens racing past you.

If it's your anger, it's your siren. You pull over and you wonder why the emergency vehicle is on its way to you. What is causing you to scream in anger? Is it a shitty partner? A bad job? An abusive parent who berates you into your twenties and thirties and beyond?

Look at and listen to the anger. What's at the root of it? It's entirely possible that anger is trying to wake you up and call you to action.

Not until I got so angry at George the Second—who cheated on me, and cried and snotted like a baby when I said I was leaving, and who told me he would die without me—could I finally, finally escape his evil, manipulative grip. During my time with him I suffered some really devastating bouts of depression (upon which I poured much booze). I can't remember feeling much lower than I did when I was with him, which is saying something if you consider my stalking ex-husband. During my time with G2, someone told me that depression was anger turned inward. That resonated. Only when I turned the anger outward could I take the steps necessary to escape him.

When I finally got angry enough to get away from him, he accused me of being angry. *Duh.* What I think he meant was that he thought my anger was the root of the failed relationship. He couldn't see how his behavior was causing my anger. But my anger was the appropriate reaction. Was I supposed to dance the fucking dance of joy when he went off and had sex with another woman and then came back and discussed it with me? He also feared my anger—it was the one thing he couldn't control. When I was depressed, he could keep me down. When I was angry, he couldn't.

Some would argue that instead of getting angry, I should've walked away. Or, if I couldn't have avoided the anger, I should've still walked away and dealt with the anger on my own, instead of engaging in what became a bitter, ugly war. Well, you know, I should have. But I didn't. I stayed. I wrestled with the pig. I got dirty. And yes, George, I got angry. A perfectly acceptable response to my pain.

I failed by hanging on to the anger long after the relationship had ended. The key is to use the anger for what it's good for, then get rid of it. You wouldn't put a bloody tampon back in the box for future use, would you? This anger cannot be a permanent part of your emotional wardrobe. Use it. Be grateful for it. Then toss it.

Deal Effectively with Other People's Anger

Let me revisit the martial arts theme for a moment. There is one form of martial arts where, rather than exert yourself, you use your opponent's energy to do him in. If he throws a punch at you, for example, in theory you should be able to grab his arm and use the force he intended to destroy you with to propel him away from you. When someone is angry with you, if you can avoid responding with anger (which is a resistance), then you will keep the anger from spreading. Think of someone crossing the centerline on the highway, coming at you at eighty miles per hour. You can think, *You fucker! This is my side of the road! I'll teach you a lesson,* and plow into the other guy. Or you can think, *My life is something I value, so I am going to swerve out of the way to avoid this guy.*

I was in a large parking lot one day and I accidentally cut some guy off. It was entirely my fault. I felt bad. He apparently felt worse, because he chased me around the parking lot and I could see he was pissed. So I slowed down, rolled down my window, and said, "I'm really, really sorry. Gosh, I didn't even see you."

At first, because he assumed I was going to scream at him, the guy started screaming at me. He didn't even hear my apology, but his passenger did and she sort of scrunched up with embarrassment at his anger, trying to make herself invisible. I repeated my apology. He continued to yell. Then he looked puzzled. I hadn't given him a wall to bash his head against. His anger was going nowhere—it was ineffective.

I'm incredibly defensive, which I think goes back, in great part, to being raised by a hypercritical parent who made me feel that everything I ever did was wrong. I recognize my defensiveness, but I haven't been able to eradicate it. My defensiveness makes it nearly inevitable that I respond to anger with more anger. Anger gives the other guy a sense of being in control, and it gives me the same sense: *I will control you because I will flip out on you, and you will have no choice but to bow down to my domination.*

Times I am effective in not giving in to someone else's anger—or in not exhibiting anger myself—are times when I make myself stop and very consciously consider what's going on in front of me. Like Marty's mom, kindly addressing the wild stranger on the subway, I ask myself, "Why is this person freaking out?" Prone to passing judgment, I stop and I make myself recount my own bouts of anger. A mom yelling at her kids in Target? My first thought: *You bitch—you need to love those kids unconditionally.* Oh, but who was the one who had to take her kid to the ER because she'd induced a panic attack?

I think we all need to be easier on one another—and a lot of us need to be much easier on ourselves. Does that mean we must (or can) simply let go? Hell, no. I'm just saying, take time to contemplate your own anger and ways to deal with it when you're calm and alone and not near any anger. I practiced my high blocks and front kicks over and over in the dojang so that when it was time for a belt test (or if I needed to defend myself), those moves were all just in there—learned instinct, as I like to call it—and ready to apply to real-life situations.

Another technique I use involves showing my cards up front. If I had narcolepsy and was about to get behind the wheel of a car to drive a bunch of friends several hundred miles, I would feel duty-bound to inform them of my condition. Similarly, recognizing that I haven't completely gotten my temper to a place where I can turn the volume up or down at will, when I start feeling anxious around a person or in a situation, I speak up.

"I need you to know, I'm prone to anxiety," I say. Or, "You know, what you're saying is making me feel some anger." Then I might launch into a minispeech, laden with the sort of therapy-ese that drove me nuts when I was stuck in Colorado with Cranky. But there is a time and a place for everything. And I think the best thing we can say to someone with whom we're angry is, "You know, I'm really upset right now. I need a break. I'm just going to go walk for an hour, and then let's meet back here and discuss this." And, of course, you then need to meet back up and have that discussion.

When I was angry with Reggie for some of the things he'd said and done, I walked around with a hugely heavy heart. I was angry and sad and had nowhere to put these feelings except into angry letters. Some letters I wrote down, some I kept in my head. Some I sent, some I didn't. My anger affected my ability to sleep and eat. I was miserable. A zombie. Crying at night. Waking up in the morning feeling sick.

Finally, I asked Reggie if we could please talk our problems through. I was surprised when he responded that he'd been feeling pretty bad himself. We made an appointment. I brought a list, which I'd spent a week writing and revising. We talked. It didn't take long.

I felt much better. Neither of us yelled. My anger still wafts in at the way he handled some things. And I don't imagine we'll ever have the easy friendship we had when we first met. But because of that talk, Reggie and I have remained cordial and, as a result, I still get to hang out with his kids a lot, which brings me great joy. In the past, I would've cut him off, sent him packing, banished him to Grudgeland—and would have lost something greater in the process.

Learn How to Kneel

One of my favorite U2 lyrics is in the song "Mysterious Ways": *If you wanna kiss the sky/Better learn how to kneel.* U2 is a band that has never made its Catholic roots a secret, so I suppose these words are a specific reference to prayer. The way I interpret them in my life, though, is more secular: To really appreciate all we have, and to be less judging and more loving and more forgiving, we're going to have to get brought to our knees by the universe. You know, humbled with a capital *H*.

It's hard to say—or perhaps hard for people to believe me when I say—that I'm grateful for the piles of shit I've been through: the literally life-or-death crises that plagued me through my twenties and into my thirties, the emotional torment I subjected myself to with guys like my stalking ex-husband and my cheating ex-boyfriend. It would be easy to say I wish I'd never had a drinking problem, a malignant ovarian tumor, a mean father.

Look, I'm not going to play Enya in the background and harp on strange blessings here. I'm just saying, for every brush with pain and hardship I've had, I've had my eyes opened up that much wider to the hardships of others. This is absolutely the biggest thing that keeps me from voicing judgment, even when my initial desire is to condemn someone for a stupid action. I start to judge people in my head, for certain, but then I consciously try to stop myself, which is easy when I ask, *Who has been more stupid than me?* Hmm . . . let me get back to you on that one. It could take a while.

So my shit—the shit heaped upon me by the universe, as well as the shit I went out rooting for and rolled around in—has given birth to a compassion inside of me. I have been down on my knees, and my knees have bled. And these days, more often than not, I am just kissing that big blue sky.

You Cannot Simultaneously Prevent and Prepare for War

Einstein said that, and his words illustrate one of my biggest challenges. Getting back to the whole Northeast sarcasm phenomenon, I just won't ever, I don't think, stop thinking up smart-ass comebacks and funny but mean-spirited observations. I love sardonic wit, and that's that. But increasingly, I try to keep these comments to myself. I am not always successful.

I think it helps if you remember that preventing war (or creating a successful cease-fire) doesn't necessarily entail agreeing to dance joyously around the maypole with whomever has pissed you off. My sister Kit, who chased me down the beach, trying to convince me that Christianity would save me—was I pissed off at her? Hell yes. But I let my anger at her go much more quickly than I had in years past when she or other family members had pissed me off.

Here's how I did it. I told myself that, though I disagreed with her religious beliefs, and though I felt like she'd stabbed me when she suggested my friend might molest her daughter, she was entitled to her beliefs. I don't like her beliefs, but I can't change her, just as she sure as hell isn't going to change me. I am disappointed in her, and I don't, at this point, feel like I ever need to communicate with her again. But I don't wish her ill, and I don't walk around thinking evil things about her. What good would that do either of us?

(Time for a metacognitive aside: I realize that, in writing about her in a way that she certainly would find hurtful, I might seem hypocritical here. But I mean it: I don't harbor anger toward her. I just feel sorrow at what I view as her narrow-mindedness.)

Perhaps this isn't the ideal stance. Maybe if I were a better person, I'd never need to forgive others—I could operate from a place where I recognized that the hurt they inflicted on me wasn't so much about me as it was about something painful inside of them. I'm not there yet, though this is a road that might be worth exploring. For now, the best I can do, when someone pisses me off the way my sister did that day on the beach, is walk away and get the bad experience behind me as fast as I possibly can, rather than prepare for some next time when I can get even.

Find the Grilled Cheese

I cry at odd times. Sometimes parades overwhelm me—so many people gathered in one place, all that energy, and here comes a poodle in a tutu and I inexplicably start to weep.

That said, in all my years as a journalist, though I've heard a lot of intense stories, rarely have I cried during the interview process.

The most notable exception to this I-can-take-whatever-you-can-dish-out reporter persona of mine came when I interviewed a counselor in Dallas named Glenda. I can't even remember exactly what my article was about, but Glenda and I got to talking about a traumatized boy she'd been working with. In the little boy's therapy—he'd been abused and then abandoned by his mother—he was assigned one day to interact with one of those stand-on-the-floor punching bags that you bop and that bounces right back to you.

In the first part of the exercise, he had to state three things about his mother that made him angry. Each time he said something, he had to punch the bag. In the next part, he had to name three things he loved about his mother and then hug the bag.

The anger part went swiftly, Glenda said. The child had no hard time recalling things he hated about his mother. However, when it was time to say something nice, he couldn't think of anything. He stood there. Glenda coaxed him. Nothing. Then, finally, after a good stretch, he thought of something. "She made me a good grilled cheese sandwich," he recalled, and hugged the bag.

That story both breaks my heart and inspires the hell out of me. Was that the best his mom could do? Make him a grilled cheese sandwich? What kind of pain must she have been in that this was her greatest gift?

I remember being totally hooked on after-school specials when I was a kid, those melodramatic teledramas with big blaring built-in messages. I didn't care about the lessons. I just loved the way the stories unfolded. As I remember, in one show, a girl copes with the death of her sister, who has died after falling from a treehouse and breaking her neck. The whole story is presented in flashback, beginning with the broken neck, then going back and showing the dead girl predeath and how cheerful and happy she was.

And she was cheerful and happy. Her greatest trait was the ability to make people feel good about themselves. She visits one neighbor and exclaims that she is as beautiful as the (young) Elizabeth Taylor. The neighbor beams in response.

You get the sappy idea here. But look past the sap, because here's something that has saved my life emotionally: As pissed off as I have been at my father, I can always honestly say he gave me some things that I love dearly and that have always been not just parts of me, but indispensable parts of me. These would be the beach and music.

My father, in all his seething anger, loved the Atlantic Ocean. It is a love I have inherited. No place makes me feel deeper feelings than the ocean, even if my sister is trailing behind me with her crucifix and Bible. I find peace in the vast expanses of the salty water. I guess if my father and I had had the sort of relationship where we'd spoken to each other, I could've asked him to tell me what it was about the ocean that caused such a stirring in him. He probably wouldn't have been able to articulate it. I certainly can't.

The other thing my father gave me—my grilled cheese sandwich, if you will—is the gift of music. Much of his loud music playing revolved around his anger. He would go down to the basement, block us kids out, and crank up one pop record or another. You might think this would cause me to hate pop music the way Alex in *A Clockwork*

Orange reacted, post-aversion-therapy, to Beethoven's Ninth. But instead I embraced music, memorized piles of it, passed the passion on to my own son. The mutual love has served us well. Even times when we're angry with each other, one of us can put on a record we both love and something like calm starts to return to our space.

Even my ex-husband *(God help him if I ever run into him again)* introduced me to some books that I count among my favorites. I like to theorize—as one cynical friend suggested—that he simply plucked these books from some greatest-books-ever-written list, which he tracked down for purposes of wooing me. And for years after the divorce, when someone would ask me to recommend reading, I would hesitate before recommending a book I associated with a man who inflicted incredible pain on me. In order to proceed with the recommendation, I had to tell myself that he didn't write the books, he was just the conduit. Hey, at least I got something out of a union besides a permanent psychological condition that, among other things, causes me to scream and break into a sweat whenever a balloon pops.

I don't think that locating grilled cheese attributes in the people who have hurt you the most will necessarily guarantee that you find a way to forgive those people. But there's the chance that if you locate something salvageable, you can at least put down a tiny root of hope that one day, maybe far down the road, you can embrace the punching bag, if only for a moment.

Listen to My Mom

My mom loves to tell me, whenever I'm bellyaching, to think of the worse off. Thinking of the worse off is a lot like counting your blessings, but with the nice black twist I grew up with. Sort of like, *The glass is half empty, and what it contains is poison, but still, at least it only has a few chips around the top.*

Back when I was plagued by depression, sometimes my mother would counsel me in the usual manner and I would think, *Mom, if I start thinking about the worse off, it's only going to make my own despair that much worse and I'll wind up down at the bridge, chaining myself to the wheelchair of some double amputee Vietnam vet and hurling us both into the water.*

Okay, so that wasn't what she had in mind. But it used to irritate me that I couldn't even have my moments of being unhappy without some manifestation of my mother's advice appearing before me instantly. This has happened so many times that I simply laugh these days when reminded that my plight is not much of a plight.

Example: The day after my foot's condition was properly diagnosed (a condition that meant I had to stop my beloved long walks and acknowledge I'd never again have mobility in that foot), I was very unhappy. I also had that childlike urge to whip out my catharsis moves on a stranger. I wanted to announce to someone, anyone, that I was injured. Permanently. Woe was me.

I decided my victim would be the young woman working at the shoe store I visited to find shoes that could accommodate the prescription inserts the doctor had given me. I limped around the store, dropping hints that Something Was Amiss at the Bottom of My Right Leg. The clerk could not have been more disinterested if she'd lain down to take a nap on one of the benches. I persisted.

At last, with what I recall as an audible sigh of boredom, she took my bait, if only to shut me up. "What's wrong with your foot?" she asked, exasperated at having to play this game, like a mother tired after chasing a toddler for twelve hours straight.

As I opened my mouth to tell her, the door swung open and in strolled a confident woman in running clothes. She had precisely one leg. The other leg was not one of those nude-colored Barbie prosthetics, either. It was one of those carbon stick legs, something out of a *Terminator* movie. This woman had not a shred of self-pity. I looked at her. Then I looked at the clerk and, answering her question, mumbled, "Oh, nothing," and beat a hasty retreat.

Damn the one-legged woman for stealing my thunder! Damn my mother for telling me to watch out for the worse off. Couldn't I have five minutes of pity, from myself and from others? Apparently not.

(When I got home, the first friend I emailed with my story replied immediately with a laughing email, informing me that her mother only had one leg and *ha ha ha ha*. What were the odds I'd first unload my tale on the daughter of a woman with one leg? Well, in my case, the odds were about 100 percent.)

There's no way around it. There will always be people worse off. I like to joke that I am a lot of people's version of the worse off, and that filling this role is my purpose in life. But joking aside, pain isn't a competition—and if you're hurt (physically or mentally), you're hurt, and you need to get that fixed.

Not long ago, my friend Ben's lung collapsed. I went to visit him at the hospital the day after he was admitted. He was groggy from drugs, disheveled, unshaven, and, being Ben, utterly delightful to be around. As we sat and talked, a blissed-out look appeared on his face, and I was positive it wasn't just caused by the Vicodin. "I counted thirty-three people who helped me today. And that's just people in the hospital, not my friends," he said. Ben, who could've been pissed off, depressed, or freaked out, instead decided that this unforeseen trip to the hospital was all about reminding him how lucky he was in his life.

I'm not Ben, though the man has certainly inspired me. I'm much less able, in the moment, to see whatever bright light the universe might be trying to shine on me. But I'm trying. And I guess that's the best we can do to begin to let go of the idea that the world (and all its people) is out to get us.

Maybe that's the biggest source of anger—feeling singled out for abuse, and not knowing how to say *I won't take this anymore.*

This is a constant struggle, but one I am coming to understand a little better every day.

Acknowledgments

So, this is the third book, and the running joke continues about how, if I were to thank everyone who deserves thanks, the acknowledgments would add another couple hundred pages. I am blessed with more friends than I can count. I am not going to list everyone individually, but please, all y'all, you know who you are—thank you so much for all your ongoing love and support.

There are some people I do want to name. First, thanks to Marrit Ingman, who connected me with Seal Press—without Marrit, this book wouldn't have happened. And thanks to Brooke Warner and everyone at Seal who understood what I wanted to do and supported me while I did it. Thanks to Mike Tolleson, who always reads my contracts and pays me personal compliments that make me feel like a blushing fifth-grade girl. And while I'm at it, I must thank JoAnn Schatz and Max Tolleson, too, who, along with Mike, provide piles of support at every turn.

Much of this book was written on Elizabeth Street in Austin. I don't live on Elizabeth Street, but I used to, years ago. In fact, that's where I wrote my first book. So it was quite the sentimental journey to be back there again, and I must thank Jake and Fiona for giving me the occasion to revisit the place and the memories (and also for motivating me to get my ass out of bed at 6:00 AM to write).

Jake and Fiona are members of the indescribably generous Nudd clan. While I was writing the book, this family joined forces to restore my ability to walk without pain, limp, or cane, which I'd thought was an impossible dream. And so it is with the greatest love and deepest gratitude that I thank all of the Nudds, especially Chris Nudd, Beth and Martin Racine (and by extension their good friend and my genius surgeon, Yev Gray), and Terry Galloway for being such an incredible listener.

I thank all the women who shared their stories here—I know it wasn't easy but I appreciate it so much.

I must thank my canine assistants Satch and Tatum and, most especially, my late-in-life surprise puppy, Princess Bubbles.

I also want to thank Jill Parrish, Kenan Yaser, Everett McKinley, Kat and Richard Goldsmith, Amy Gottlieb, Paul Klemperer, Ross Harper, Southpaw Jones, Adam Wilson, Jim Hemphill, Sarah Barnes, Sue Neal, Kim Lane, Theresa May, Paula Judy, Norma Bradley Allen, Molly Ivins, Elena Eidelberg, Claudia Kolker and Mike Stravato, Luisa Kolker, The Polyphonic Spree, Dan Hardick, Michael McCarthy, Andy Cotton, Kristie Zamrazil, Venerable Thubten Chodron, Riki Dunn, Sue Reid, Erin Mayes, Steve Wilson, Jeff Tietz, Hank Stuever, Chris McDougall, George the Third and Brian and Cecil and Cooper, Makoto, Vadym and Sabine, Sarah Woelk, Matt Featherston, who makes me laugh and laugh, Ann and Hilary Johns, and everyone at BookPeople and BookWoman.

And with love and gratitude to Herman Bennett, for finally showing up and for filling my life with even more love and laughter than I dared hope for, even when I was hoping my biggest hopes. Thank you for taking my sad songs and making them so much better.

© E.J DURST

About the Author

Spike Gillespie has written for *The New York Times* and *The New York Times Magazine, Real Simple, Bust, Nerve, National Geographic Traveler, Smithsonian,* the *Washington Post, Elle, GQ, Playboy, Self, Cosmopolitan,* and many others. She has contributed to two Seal Press collections and numerous other anthologies, and is a former columnist for *The Dallas Morning News* and *Oxygen.* She is the author of *All the Wrong Men and One Perfect Boy: A Memoir* (Simon & Schuster, 1999) and the essay collection *Surrender (But Don't Give Yourself Away): Old Cars, Found Hope, and Other Cheap Tricks* (University of Texas Press, 2003). She is also a public speaker who teaches knitting, journaling for health, and anger contemplation at spas around the country. Her next book, *Quilty As Charged: Undercover in the Material World,* will be published in 2007. She lives in a little concrete house in Austin, Texas, with three dogs, two cats, a couple of chickens, a disabled parakeet, and her son, the Amazing Henry Mowgli Gillespie.

5

Selected Titles from Seal Press

For more than twenty-five years, Seal Press has published groundbreaking books. By women. For women. Visit our website at www.sealpress.com.

A Matter of Choice: 25 People Who Have Transformed Their Lives edited by Joan Chatfield-Taylor. $14.95. 1-58005-118-9. This inspiring collection of essays, by people who made profound changes in their work, personal life, location, or lifestyle, proves that it is indeed never too late to take the road less traveled.

Above Us Only Sky: A Woman Looks Back, Ahead, and Into the Mirror by Marion Winik. $14.95. 1-58005-144-8. NPR commentator Marion Winik delivers a witty and engaging book about facing midlife without getting tangled up in the past or hung up in the future.

Dirty Sugar Cookies: Culinary Observations, Questionable Taste by Ayun Halliday $14.95 1-58005-150-2. Ayun Halliday is back with comical and unpredictable essays about her disastrous track record in the kitchen and her culinary observations—though she's clearly no expert.

The F-Word: Feminism in Jeopardy by Kristin Rowe-Finkbeiner. $14.95. 1-58005-114-6. An astonishing look at the tenuous state of women's rights and issues in America, and a call to action for the young women who have the power to change their situation.

Reckless: The Outrageous Lives of Nine Kick-Ass Women by Gloria Mattioni. $14.95. 1-58005-148-0. From Lisa Distefano, who captains a pirate vessel on her quest to protect sea life, to Libby Riddles, the first woman to win the legendary Iditarod, this collection of profiles explores the lives of nine women who took unconventional life paths to achieve extraordinary results.

You Can Be Free: An Easy-to-Read Handbook for Abused Women by Ginny NiCarthy and Sue Davidson. $13.95. 1-58005-159-6. In this bestselling guide, the authors take practical and gentle guidance to help women work toward building relationships that are healthier and, most importantly, safer.